BERLITZ®

GERMAN
for travellers

D0717157

By the staff of Editions Berlitz

How best to use this phrase book

● We suggest that you start with the **Guide to pronunciation** (pp. 6–8), then go on to **Some basic expressions** (pp. 9–15). This gives you not only a minimum vocabulary, but also helps you get used to pronouncing the language. The phonetic transcription throughout the book enables you to pronounce every word correctly.

● Consult the **Contents** pages (3–5) for the section you need. In each chapter you'll find travel facts, hints and useful information. Simple phrases are followed by a list of words applicable to the situation.

● Separate, detailed contents lists are included at the beginning of the extensive **Eating out** and **Shopping guide** sections (Menus, p. 39, Shops and services, p. 97).

● If you want to find out how to say something in German, your fastest look-up is via the **Dictionary** section (pp. 164–189). This not only gives you the word, but is also cross-referenced to its use in a phrase on a specific page.

● If you wish to learn more about constructing sentences, check the **Basic grammar** (pp. 159–163).

● Note the **colour margins** are indexed in German and English to help both listener and speaker. And, in addition, there is also an **index in German** for the use of your listener.

● Throughout the book, this symbol ☞ suggests phrases your listener can use to answer you. If you still can't understand, hand this phrase book to the German-speaker to encourage pointing to an appropriate answer. The English translation for you is just alongside the German.

Second revised edition – 1st printing
Printed in Switzerland

Contents

4

Travelling around 65

Sightseeing 80

Relaxing 86

Making friends 92

Shopping guide 97

Acknowledgments
We are particularly grateful to Eva Bayer for her help in the preparation of this book, and to Dr.T.J.A.Bennett who devised the
phonetic transcription.

PRONUNCIATION

Aussprache

Guide to pronunciation

This and the following chapter are intended to make you familiar with the phonetic transcription we have devised and to help you get used to the sounds of German.

As a minimum vocabulary for your trip, we've selected a number of basic words and phrases under the title "Some Basic Expressions" (pages 9–15).

You'll find the pronunciation of the German letters and sounds explained below, as well as the symbols we use for them in the transcriptions.

The imitated pronunciation should be read as if it were English except for any special rules set out below. It is based on Standard British pronunciation, though we have tried to take into account General American pronunciation as well. Of course, the sounds of any two languages are never exactly the same; but if you follow carefully the indications supplied here, you'll have no difficulty in reading our transcriptions in such a way as to make yourself understood.

In the transcriptions, letters shown in bold print should be read with more stress (louder) than the others.

Consonants

Letter	Approximate pronunciation	Symbol	Example	
f, h, k, l, m, n, p, t, x	normally pronounced as in English			
b	1) at the end of a word or between a vowel and a consonant like **p** in up	p	**ab**	ahp
	2) elsewhere as in English	b	**bis**	biss
c	1) before **e, i, ö** and **ä**, like **ts** in hits	ts	**Celsius**	**tsehl**ziuss

	2) elsewhere like **c** in **c**at	k	**Café**	kah**fay**
ch	1) after back vowels (e.g. **ah**, **o**, **oo**) like **ch** in Scottish lo**ch**, otherwise more like **h** in **h**uge	kh	**doch**	dokh
	2) sometimes, especially before **s**, like **k** in **k**it	k	**Wachs**	vahks
d	1) at the end of a word or between a vowel and a consonant like **t** in ea**t**	t	**Rad**	raat
	2) elsewhere, like **d** in **d**o	d	**durstig**	**door**stikh
g	1) always hard as in **g**o but at the end of a word often more like **ck** in ta**ck**	g k	**gehen** **weg**	**gay**ern vehk
	2) when preceded by **i** at the end of a word like **ch** in Scottish lo**ch**	kh	**billig**	**bil**likh
j	like **y** in **y**es	y	**ja**	yaa
qu	like **k** followed by **v** in **v**at	kv	**Quark**	kvahrk
r	generally rolled in the back of the mouth	r	**warum**	vah**rum**
s	1) before or between vowels like **z** in **z**oo	z	**sie**	zee
	2) before **p** and **t** at the beginning of a syllable like **sh** in **sh**ut	sh	**spät**	shpait
	3) elsewhere, like **s** in **s**it	s/ss	**es ist**	ehss ist
ß	always like **s** in **s**it	s/ss	**heiß**	highss
sch	like **sh** in **sh**ut	sh	**schnell**	shnehl
tsch	like **ch** in **ch**ip	ch	**deutsch**	doych
tz	like **ts** in hi**ts**	ts	**Platz**	plahts
v	like **f** in **f**or	f	**vier**	feer
w	like **v** in **v**ice	v	**wie**	vee
z	like **ts** in hi**ts**	ts	**zeigen**	**tsigh**gern

Vowels

In German, vowels are generally long when followed by **h** or by one consonant and short when followed by two or more consonants.

a	1) short, like **u** in cut	ah	**lassen**	**lah**ssern
	2) long like **a** in car	aa	**Abend**	**aa**bernt
ä	1) short like **e** in let	eh	**Lärm**	**leh**rm
	2) long like **ai** in hair	ai	**spät**	**shpait**
e	1) short like **e** in let	eh	**sprechen**	**shpreh**khern
	2) long like **a** in late	ay	**geben**	**gay**bern
	3) in unstressed syllables it's generally pronounced like **er** in other	er*	**bitte**	**bitt**er
i	1) short like **i** in hit	i	**billig**	**billik**
	2) long like **ee** in meet	ee	**ihm**	**eem**
ie	like **ee** in bee	ee	**hier**	**heer**
o	1) short like **o** in got	o	**voll**	**fol**
	2) long like **o** in note	oa	**ohne**	**oa**ner
ö	like **ur** in fur (long or short)	ur*	**können**	**kur**nern
u	1) short like **oo** in foot	u	**Nuß**	**nuss**
	2) long like **oo** in moon	oo	**gut**	**goot**
ü	like French **u** in une; round your lips and try to say **ea** as in mean (long or short)	ew	**über**	**ew**ber
y	like German **ü**	ew	**typisch**	**tew**pish

Diphthongs

ai, ay, ei, ey	like **igh** in high	igh	**mein**	**mighn**
au	like **ow** in now	ow	**auf**	**owf**
äu, eu	like **oy** in boy	oy	**neu**	**noy**

---

* The **r** should not be pronounced when reading this transcription.

Some basic expressions

Yes.	**Ja.**	yaa
No.	**Nein.**	nighn
Please.	**Bitte.**	bitter
Thank you.	**Danke.**	dahnker
You're welcome.	**Bitte.**	bitter
Thank you very much.	**Vielen Dank.**	feelern dahnk
That's all right/ Don't mention it.	**Gern geschehen.**	gehrn gershayern

Greetings *Begrüßung*

Good morning.	**Guten Morgen.**	gootern morgern
Good afternoon.	**Guten Tag.**	gootern taag
Good evening.	**Guten Abend.**	gootern aabernt
Good night.	**Gute Nacht.**	gooter nahkht
Good-bye.	**Auf Wiedersehen.**	owf veederrzayern
See you later.	**Bis bald.**	biss bahlt
This is Mr./Mrs./ Miss ...	**Das ist Herr/Frau/ Fräulein ...**	dahss ist hehr/frow/ froylighn
How do you do? (Pleased to meet you.)	**Sehr erfreut.**	zayr ehrfroyt
How are you?	**Wie geht es Ihnen?**	vee gayt ehss eenern
Very well, thanks. And you?	**Sehr gut, danke. Und Ihnen?**	zayr goot, dahnker. unt eenern
How's life?	**Wie geht's?**	vee gayts
Fine.	**Gut.**	goot

I beg your pardon?	**Wie bitte?**	vee **bitter**
Excuse me. (May I get past?)	**Gestatten Sie?**	ger**shtah**tern zee
Sorry!	**Entschuldigung/ Verzeihung!**	ehnt**shul**diggung/ fehr**tsigh**ung

Questions *Fragen*

Where?	**Wo?**	voa
How?	**Wie?**	vee
When?	**Wann?**	vahn
What?	**Was?**	vahss
Why?	**Warum?**	vah**rum**
Who?	**Wer?**	vayr
Which?	**Welcher/Welche/ Welches?**	**vehl**kherr/**vehl**kher/ **vehl**kherss
Where is ...?	**Wo ist ...?**	voa ist
Where are ...?	**Wo sind ...?**	voa zint
Where can I find/ get ...?	**Wo finde/bekomme ich ...?**	voa **finder**/ber**kom**mer ikh
How far?	**Wie weit?**	vee vight
How long?	**Wie lange?**	vee **lahn**ger
How much?	**Wieviel?**	vee**feel**
How many?	**Wie viele?**	vee **feeler**
How much does this cost?	**Wieviel kostet das?**	vee**feel ko**stert dahss
When does ... open/ close?	**Wann öffnet/ schließt ...?**	vahn **urf**nert/shleest
What do you call this/that in German?	**Wie heißt dies/ das auf deutsch?**	vee highst deess/dahss owf doych
What does that mean?	**Was bedeutet das?**	vahss ber**doy**tert dahss
What does this word mean?	**Was bedeutet dieses Wort?**	vahss ber**doy**tert **dee**zerss vort

Do you speak ...? *Sprechen Sie ...?*

Do you speak English?	**Sprechen Sie Englisch?**	shprehkhern zee ehnglish
Is there anyone here who speaks English?	**Spricht hier jemand Englisch?**	shprikht heer yaymahnt ehnglish
I don't speak (much) German.	**Ich spreche kaum Deutsch.**	ikh shprehkher kowm doych
Could you speak more slowly?	**Könnten Sie bitte langsamer sprechen?**	kurntern zee bitter lahngzaamerr shprehkhern
Could you repeat that?	**Könnten Sie das bitte wiederholen?**	kurntern zee dahss bitter veederrhoalern
Could you spell it?	**Könnten Sie es bitte buchstabieren?**	kurntern zee ehss bitter bookhshtahbeerern
Please write it down.	**Schreiben Sie es bitte auf.**	shrighbern zee ehss bitter owf
Can you translate this for me/us?	**Könnten Sie mir/uns das übersetzen?**	kurntern zee meer/uns dahss ewberrzehtsern
Please point to the phrase/sentence in the book.	**Bitte zeigen Sie mir den Ausdruck/ den Satz im Buch.**	bitter tsighgern zee meer dayn owsdruk/ dayn zahts im bookh
Just a moment. I'll see if I can find it in this book.	**Einen Augenblick bitte, ich schaue mal im Buch nach, ob ich es finde.**	ighnern owgernblik bitter ikh shower maal im bookh naakh op ikh ehss finder
I understand.	**Ich verstehe.**	ikh fehrshtayer
I don't understand.	**Ich verstehe nicht.**	ikh fehrshtayer nikht
Do you understand?	**Verstehen Sie?**	fehrshtayern zee

Can/May ...? *Kann ...?*

Can I have ...?	**Kann ich ... haben?**	kahn ikh ... haabern
Can we have ...?	**Können wir ... haben?**	kurnern veer ... haabern
Can you show me ...?	**Können Sie mir ... zeigen?**	kurnern zee meer ... tsighgern
I can't.	**Leider nicht.**	lighderr nikht

Can you tell me ...?	**Können Sie mir sagen ...?**	kurnern zee meer **zaa**gern
Can you help me?	**Können Sie mir helfen?**	kurnern zee meer **hehl**fern
Can I help you?	**Kann ich Ihnen helfen?**	kahn ik **ee**nern **hehl**fern
Can you direct me to ...?	**Können Sie mir den Weg nach/ zu ... zeigen?**	kurnern zee meer dayn vayg naakh/ tsoo ... **tsigh**gern

What do you want? *Was wünschen Sie?*

I'd like ...	**Ich hätte gern/ Ich möchte ...**	ikh **heht**er gehrn/ ikh **murkh**ter
We'd like ...	**Wir hätten gern/ Wir möchten ...**	veer **heht**ern gehrn/ veer **murkh**tern
Give me ...	**Geben Sie mir ...**	**gay**bern zee meer
Give it to me.	**Geben Sie es mir.**	**gay**bern zee ehss meer
Bring me ...	**Bringen Sie mir ...**	**bring**ern zee meer
Bring it to me.	**Bringen Sie es mir.**	**bring**ern zee ehss meer
Show me ...	**Zeigen Sie mir ...**	**tsigh**gern zee meer
Show it to me.	**Zeigen Sie es mir.**	**tsigh**gern zee ehss meer
I'm looking for ...	**Ich suche ...**	ikh **zook**her
I'm hungry.	**Ich habe Hunger.**	ikh **haa**ber **hung**err
I'm thirsty.	**Ich habe Durst.**	ikh **haa**ber doorst
I'm tired.	**Ich bin müde.**	ikh bin **mew**der
I'm lost.	**Ich habe mich verirrt.**	ikh **haa**ber mikh fehr**eert**
It's important.	**Es ist wichtig.**	ehss ist **vikh**tikh
It's urgent.	**Es ist dringend.**	ehss ist **dring**ernt
Hurry up!	**Beeilen Sie sich!**	be**igh**lern zee zikh

It is/There is ... *Es ist/Es gibt ...*

It is ...	**Es ist ...**	ehss ist
Is it ...?	**Ist es ...?**	ist ehss

It isn't ...	**Es ist nicht ...**	ehss ist nikht
Here it is.	**Hier ist es.**	heer ist ehss
Here they are.	**Hier sind sie.**	heer zint zee
There it is.	**Dort ist es.**	dort ist ehss
There they are.	**Dort sind sie.**	dort zint zee
There is/are ...	**Es gibt ...**	ehss gipt
Is there/Are there ...?	**Gibt es ...?**	gipt ehss
There isn't (any) ...	**Es gibt keinen/Es gibt keine/Es gibt kein ...**	ehss gipt kighnern/ehss gipt kighner/ehss gipt kighn
There aren't (any) ...	**Es gibt keine ...**	ehss gipt kighner

Adjectives   *Eigenschaftswörter*

big/small	**groß/klein**	groass/klighn
quick/slow	**schnell/langsam**	shnehl/**lahng**zaam
cheap/expensive	**billig/teuer**	**bil**lik/**toy**err
hot/cold	**heiß/kalt**	highss/kahlt
full/empty	**voll/leer**	fol/layr
easy/difficult	**leicht/schwierig**	lighkht/**shwee**rikh
heavy/light	**schwer/leicht**	shvayr/lighkht
open/shut	**offen/geschlossen**	offern/ger**shlos**sern
right/wrong	**richtig/falsch**	**rikh**tikh/fahlsh
old/new	**alt/neu**	ahlt/noy
old/young	**alt/jung**	ahlt/yung
next/last	**nächste/letzte**	**naikh**ster/**lehts**ter
beautiful/ugly	**schön/häßlich**	shurn/**hehs**likh
free (vacant)/ occupied	**frei/besetzt**	frigh/ber**zehtst**
good/bad	**gut/schlecht**	goot/shlehkht
better/worse	**besser/schlechter**	**behs**serr/**shlehkh**terr
early/late	**früh/spät**	frew/shpait
near/far	**nah/weit**	naa/vight
left/right	**linke/rechte**	**lin**ker/**rehkh**ter

Quantities *Mengen*

a little	**ein wenig**	ighn **vay**nikh
a lot	**eine Menge**	**igh**ner **mehn**ger
few/a few	**wenige/einige**	**vay**nigger/**igh**nigger
much/many	**viel/viele**	feel/**feel**er
more (than)	**mehr (als)**	mayr (ahlss)
less (than)	**weniger (als)**	**vay**niggerr (ahlss)
enough/too (much)	**genug/zu (viel)**	ger**nook**/tsu (feel)
some/any (sing.)	**etwas**	**eht**vahss
some/any (pl.)	**einige**	**igh**nigger

A few more useful words *Weitere nützliche Wörter*

at	**an/bei**	ahn/bigh
on	**an/auf**	ahn/owf
in	**in**	in
to	**zu**	tsoo
after	**nach**	naakh
before	**vor**	foar
for	**für**	fewr
from	**von**	fon
with	**mit**	mit
without	**ohne**	**oan**er
through	**durch**	doorkh
towards	**gegen**	**gay**gern
until	**bis**	biss
during	**während**	**vair**ernt
next to	**neben**	**nay**bern
behind	**hinter**	**hin**terr
between	**zwischen**	**tsvi**shern
since	**seit**	zight
above	**oben**	**oa**bern
below	**unten**	**un**tern
over	**über**	**ew**berr
under	**unter**	**un**terr

inside	**drinnen**	drinnern
outside	**draußen**	drowssern
up	**hinauf**	hinnowf
down	**hinunter**	hinnunterr
here	**hier**	heer
there	**dort**	dort
and	**und**	unt
or	**oder**	oaderr
but	**aber**	aaberr
not	**nicht**	nikht
never	**nie**	nee
nothing	**nichts**	nikhts
none	**kein**	kighn
very	**sehr**	zayr
too (also)	**auch**	owkh
yet	**noch**	nokh
soon	**bald**	bahlt
now	**jetzt**	yehtst
only	**nur**	noor
then	**dann**	dahn
perhaps	**vielleicht**	feelighkht

Pronunciation of the German alphabet

A	aa	**H**	haa	**Ö**	ur	**V**	fow
Ä	ai	**I**	ee	**P**	pay	**W**	vay
B	bay	**J**	yot	**Q**	koo	**X**	eeks
C	tsay	**K**	kaa	**R**	ehr	**Y**	**ewp**sillon
D	day	**L**	ehl	**S**	ehss	**Z**	tseht
E	ay	**M**	ehm	**T**	tay		
F	ehf	**N**	ehn	**U**	oo		
G	gay	**O**	oa	**Ü**	ew		

In addition to these letters there is the **ß** sign, a combination of **s** and **z**. It is pronounced exactly like **ss**.

Arrival

<table>
<tr><td colspan="3">

PASSKONTROLLE
PASSPORT CONTROL

</td></tr>
</table>

Here's my passport.	**Hier ist mein Paß.**	heer is mighn pahss
I'll be staying ...	**Ich bleibe ...**	ikh **bligh**ber
a few days	**ein paar Tage**	ighn paar **taa**ger
a week	**eine Woche**	**igh**ner **vo**kher
a month	**einen Monat**	**igh**nern **moa**naht
I don't know yet.	**Ich weiß es noch nicht.**	ikh vighss ehss nokh nikht
I'm here on holiday.	**Ich bin auf Urlaub hier.**	ikh bin owf **oor**lowp heer
I'm here on business.	**Ich bin geschäftlich hier.**	ikh bin ger**shehft**likh heer
I'm just passing through.	**Ich bin nur auf der Durchreise.**	ikh bin noor owf derr **doork**righzer

If things become difficult:

I'm sorry, I don't understand.	**Es tut mir leid, ich verstehe nicht.**	ehss toot meer light ikh fehr**shtay**er nikht
Is there anyone here who speaks English?	**Spricht hier jemand Englisch?**	shprikht heer **yay**mahnt **ehng**lish

Customs *Zoll*

After collecting your baggage at the airport (*der Flughafen*— derr **floog**haafern) you have a choice: use the green exit if you have nothing to declare. Or leave via the red exit if you have items to declare (in excess of those allowed).

ANMELDEFREIE WAREN
NOTHING TO DECLARE
Zoll Customs

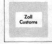

Zoll Customs
ANMELDEPFLICHTIGE WAREN
GOODS TO DECLARE

The chart below shows what you can bring in duty-free.

	Cigarettes		Cigars		Tobacco	Spirits (Liquor)	Wine
Germany 1)	200	or	50	or	250 g.	1 l. and	2 l.
2)	300	or	75	or	400 g.	1.5 l. and	5 l.
3)	400	or	100	or	500 g.	1 l. and	2 l.
Austria	200	or	50	or	250 g.	1 l. and	2 l.
Switzerland	200	or	50	or	250 g.	1 l. and	2 l.

1) Visitors arriving from EEC countries with tax-free items, and visitors from other European countries
2) Visitors arriving from EEC countries with non-tax-free items
3) Visitors arriving from countries outside Europe

I've nothing to declare.	Ich habe nichts zu verzollen.	ikh haaber nikhts tsoo fehrtsollern
I've ...	Ich habe ...	ikh haaber
a carton of cigarettes	eine Stange Zigaretten	ighner shtahnger tsiggahrehtern
a bottle of gin	eine Flasche Gin	ighner flahsher "gin"
It's for my personal use.	Es ist für meinen persönlichen Gebrauch.	ehss ist fewr mighnern pehrzurnlikhern gerbrowkh
This is a gift.	Das ist ein Geschenk.	dahss ist ighn gershenk

---

Ihren Paß, bitte.	Your passport, please.
Haben Sie etwas zu verzollen?	Do you have anything to declare?
Bitte öffnen Sie diese Tasche.	Please open this bag.
Dies ist zollpflichtig.	You'll have to pay duty on this.
Haben Sie noch mehr Gepäck?	Do you have any more luggage?

Baggage—Porters *Gepäck—Gepäckträger*

These days porters are only available at airports or the railway stations of large cities. Where no porters are available you'll find luggage trolleys for the use of the passengers.

Porter!	**Gepäckträger!**	gerpehktraigerr
Please take this luggage.	**Nehmen Sie bitte dieses Gepäck.**	naymern zee bitter deezerss gerpehk
That's mine.	**Das gehört mir.**	dahss gerhurrt meer
That's my suitcase/ (travelling) bag.	**Das ist mein Koffer/ meine (Reise)tasche.**	dahss ist mighn kofferr/ mighner (righzer)tahsher
There is one piece missing.	**Es fehlt ein Gepäck- stück.**	ehss faylt ighn gerpehk- shtewk
Please take this to the ...	**Bringen Sie das bitte ...**	bringern zee dahss bitter
bus/taxi	**zum Bus/Taxi**	tsum buss/tahksi
luggage lockers	**zu den Schließ- fächern**	tsoo dayn shleesfehkherrn
How much is that?	**Wieviel macht das?**	veefeel mahkht dahss
Where are the luggage trolleys (carts)?	**Wo sind die Koffer- kulis?**	voa zint dee kofferr- kooliss

Changing money *Geldwechsel*

Where's the nearest currency exchange?	**Wo ist die nächste Wechselstube?**	voa ist dee naikhster vehkserlshtoober
Can you change these traveller's cheques (checks)?	**Können Sie diese Reiseschecks einlösen?**	kurnern zee deezer righzershehks ighnlurzern
I want to change some ...	**Ich möchte ... wechseln.**	ikh murkhter ... vehkserln
dollars/pounds	**Dollar/Pfund**	dollahr/pfunt
Can you change this into ...?	**Können Sie das in ... umwechseln?**	kurnern zee dahss in ... umvehkserln
Austrian shillings	**Schilling**	shilling
German marks	**D-Mark**	day-mahrk
Swiss francs	**Schweizer Franken**	shvightserr frahnkern
What's the exchange rate?	**Wie ist der Wechselkurs?**	vee ist derr vehkserlkoors

BANK—CURRENCY, see page 129

Where is ...?   *Wo ist ...?*

Where is the ...?	**Wo ist ...?**	voa ist
booking office	**der Reservierungs-schalter**	derr rehzerr**vee**rungs-shahlterr
car hire	**der Autoverleih**	derr **ow**toffehrligh
duty-free shop	**der Duty-free-Shop**	derr "duty-free-shop"
newsstand	**der Zeitungsstand**	derr **tsight**ungsshtahnt
restaurant	**das Restaurant**	dahss rehstorr**rahng**
shopping gallery	**die Einkaufsgalerie**	dee **ighn**kowfsgahlehree
How do I get to Stuttgart?	**Wie komme ich nach Stuttgart?**	vee **kom**mer ikh nakh **shtut**gahrt
How do I get to the ... Hotel?	**Wie komme ich zum Hotel ...?**	vee **kom**mer ikh tsum hot**tehl**
Is there a bus into town?	**Fährt ein Bus ins Stadtzentrum?**	fairt ighn buss ins **shtahtt**sehntrum
Where can I get a taxi?	**Wo finde ich ein Taxi?**	voa **fin**der ikh ighn **tahk**si
Where can I hire (rent) a car?	**Wo kann ich ein Auto mieten?**	voa kahn ikh ighn **ow**to **mee**tern

Hotel reservation   *Hotelreservierung*

Do you have a hotel guide?	**Haben Sie ein Hotel-verzeichnis?**	**haa**bern zee ighn hot**tehl**-fehrtsighkhniss
Could you reserve a room for me at a hotel/boarding house?	**Können Sie mir bitte ein Hotel-/Pensions-zimmer reservieren?**	**kur**nern zee meer **bit**ter ighn hot**tehl**/pehnz**ioans**-tsimmerr rehzerr**vee**rern
in the centre	**im Zentrum**	im **tsehn**trum
near the railway station	**beim Bahnhof**	bighm **baan**hoaf
a single room	**ein Einzelzimmer**	ighn **ighnt**serltsimmerr
a double room	**ein Doppelzimmer**	ighn **dop**perltsimmerr
not too expensive	**nicht zu teuer**	nikht tsu **toy**err
Where is the hotel/boarding house?	**Wo liegt das Hotel/die Pension?**	voa leegt dahss hot**tehl**/dee pehnz**ioan**
Do you have a street map?	**Haben Sie einen Stadtplan?**	**haa**bern zee **igh**nern **shtahtt**plaan

HOTEL/ACCOMMODATION, see page 22

Car hire (rental) *Autoverleih*

To hire a car you must produce a valid driving licence (held for at least one year) and your passport. Some firms set a minimum age at 21, other 25. Holders of major credit cards are normally exempt from deposit payments, otherwise you must pay a substantial (refundable) deposit for a car. Third-party insurance is usually automatically included.

I'd like to hire (rent) a car.	**Ich möchte ein Auto mieten.**	ikh murkhter ighn owto meetern
small/medium-sized/ large automatic	**ein kleines/mittleres/ großes mit Automatik**	ighn klighnerss/mitlerrerss groasserss mit owtommaatik
I'd like it for a day/a week.	**Ich möchte es für einen Tag/eine Woche.**	ikh murkhter ehss fewr ighnern taag/ighner vokher
Are there any week-end arrangements?	**Gibt es Wochenend-pauschalen?**	gipt ehss vokhernehnt-powshaalern
Do you have any special rates?	**Haben Sie Sonder-tarife?**	haabern zee zonderr-tahreefer
How much does it cost per day/week?	**Wieviel kostet es pro Tag/Woche?**	veefeel kostert ehss proa taag/vokher
Is mileage included?	**Ist das Kilometer-geld inbegriffen?**	ist dahss killommayterr-gehlt inbergriffern
What's the charge per kilometer?	**Wieviel kostet es pro Kilometer?**	veefeel kostert ehss proa killommayterr
I want to hire the car here and leave it in ...	**Ich möchte den Wagen hier mieten und in ... zurück-geben.**	ikh murkhter dayn vaagern heer meetern unt in ... tsoorewkgaybern
I want full insurance.	**Ich möchte eine Vollkasko-versicherung.**	ikh murkhter ighner folkahskoffehrzikherrung
What's the deposit?	**Wieviel muß ich hinterlegen?**	veefeel muss ikh hinterrlaygern
I've a credit card.	**Ich habe eine Kreditkarte.**	ikh haaber ighner krehditkahrter
Here's my driving licence.	**Hier ist mein Führerschein.**	heer ist mighn fewrerrshighn

CAR, see page 75

Taxi *Taxi*

A taxi is usually caught at a rank (*der Taxistand*—der **tahk**si-shtahnt). You can also phone for a taxi wherever you are; numbers are listed on a separate page in front of the phone books. All taxis have meters.

Where can I get a taxi?	**Wo finde ich ein Taxi?**	voa **fin**der ikh ighn **tahk**si
Please get me a taxi.	**Besorgen Sie mir bitte ein Taxi.**	ber**zor**gern zee meer **bitt**er ighn **tahk**si
What's the fare to ...?	**Was kostet es bis ...?**	vahss **kos**tert ehss biss
How far is it to ...?	**Wie weit ist es bis ...?**	vee vight ist ehss biss
Take me to ...	**Bringen Sie mich ...**	**bring**ern zee mikh
this address	**zu dieser Adresse**	tsoo **dee**zerr ah**dreh**sser
the airport	**zum Flughafen**	tsum **floog**haafern
the railway station	**zum Bahnhof**	tsum **baan**hoaf
the town centre	**ins Stadtzentrum**	ins **shtaht**tsehntrum
the ... Hotel	**zum Hotel ...**	tsum **hot**tehl
Turn ... at the next corner.	**Biegen Sie an der nächsten Ecke ... ab.**	**bee**gern zee ahn derr **naikh**stern **ehk**er ... ahp
left/right	**links/rechts**	links/**rehkh**ts
Go straight ahead.	**Geradeaus.**	gerr**aa**derrowss
Please stop here.	**Halten Sie hier, bitte.**	**hahl**tern zee heer **bitt**er
I'm in a hurry.	**Ich habe es eilig.**	ikh **haa**ber ehss **igh**lik
Could you drive more slowly?	**Bitte fahren Sie langsamer.**	**bitt**er **faa**rern zee **lahng**zaamerr
Could you help me carry my luggage?	**Könnten Sie mir bitte beim Gepäcktragen helfen?**	**kurn**tern zee meer **bitt**er bighm ger**pehk**traagern **hehl**fern
Will you wait for me, please?	**Würden Sie bitte auf mich warten?**	**vewr**dern zee **bitt**er owf mikh **vahr**tern
I'll be back in 10 minutes.	**Ich bin in 10 Minuten zurück.**	ikh bin in 10 min**noo**tern tsoo**rewk**

TIPPING, see inside back-cover

Hotel—Other accommodation

Early reservation and confirmation are essential in most major tourist centres during the high season. Most towns and arrival points have a tourist information office (*Fremdenverkehrsbüro*—**frehm**dernfehrkayrsbewroa), and that's the place to go if you're stuck without a room.

Hotel
(hot**tehl**)

Hotel; simple or fancy, your room will be spotless. You'll probably sleep under a guilt filled with duck or goose down. *Hotel garni* means that only a room and breakfast are offered, no other meals.

Schloßhotel
(shlos**hottehl**)

Castle or palace converted into a hotel; often located in the countryside.

Rasthof
(**rahst**hoaf)

Wayside lodge, motel; most are located just off a motorway (expressway) or principal route.

Gasthaus/Gasthof
(**gahst**howss/**gahst**hoaf)

Inn

Pension/Fremdenheim
(pehn**zioan**/**frehm**dernhighm)

Boarding-house; offers full or half board. *Zimmer frei* will tell you there's a room to let, sometimes also in a private home.

Jugendherberge
(**yoo**gernthehrbehrger)

Youth hostel

Ferienwohnung
(**fay**riernvoanung)

Furnished flat (apartment) found in holiday resorts; you'll probably have to reserve it in advance. Otherwise, contact the local tourist office.

Can you recommend a hotel/pension?	**Können Sie mir ein Hotel/eine Pension empfehlen?**	kurnern zee meer ighn hottehl/ighner pehn**zioan** ehmp**fay**lern
Do you have a hotel guide?	**Haben Sie ein Hotel-verzeichnis?**	**haa**bern zee ighn hot**tehl**-fehrtsighkhniss
Are there any flats (apartments) vacant?	**Gibt es noch freie Ferienwohnungen?**	gipt ehss nokh **frigher fay**riernvoanungern

CAMPING, see page 32

Checking in — Reception *Empfang*

My name is ...	**Mein Name ist ...**	mighn **naa**mer ist
I've a reservation.	**Ich habe reservieren lassen.**	ikh **haa**ber rehzerr**vee**erern **lahss**ern
We've reserved two rooms, a single and a double.	**Wir haben zwei Zimmer reservieren lassen – ein Einzelzimmer und ein Doppelzimmer.**	veer **haa**bern tsvigh **tsimm**err rehzerr**vee**erern **lahss**ern – ighn **ighnt**serltsimmerr unt ighn **dopperl**tsimmerr
Here's the confirmation.	**Hier ist die Bestätigung.**	heer ist dee ber**shtait**tig-gung
Do you have any vacancies?	**Haben Sie noch freie Zimmer?**	**haa**bern zee nokh **frigh**er **tsimm**err
I'd like a...	**Ich hätte gern ein ...**	ikh **het**ter gehrn ighn
single room	**Einzelzimmer**	**ighnt**serltsimmerr
double room	**Doppelzimmer**	**dopperl**tsimmerr
A room ...	**Ein Zimmer ...**	ighn **tsimm**err
with twin beds	**mit zwei Einzelbetten**	mit tsvigh **ighnt**serlbehtern
with a double bed	**mit einem Doppelbett**	mit **ighn**erm **dopperl**beht
with a bath	**mit Bad**	mit baat
with a shower	**mit Dusche**	mit **dush**er
with a balcony	**mit Balkon**	mit bahl**koan**
with a view	**mit Aussicht**	mit **owss**ikht
facing the lake/ the mountains	**mit Blick auf den See/ auf die Berge**	mit blik owf dayn zay/ owf dee **behr**ger
in the front	**zur Straße**	tsoor **shtraa**sser
at the back	**zum Hof**	tsum hoaf
It must be quiet.	**Es muß ruhig sein.**	ehss muss **roo**ikh zighn
Is there ...?	**Gibt es ...?**	gipt ehss
air conditioning	**Klimaanlage**	**klee**mahnlaager
a radio/a television in the room	**Radio/Fernsehen im Zimmer**	**raa**dio/**fehrn**zayern im **tsimm**err
laundry service	**einen Wäschedienst**	**ighn**ern **vehsh**erdeenst
room service	**Zimmerbedienung**	**tsimm**errberdeenung
hot water	**warmes Wasser**	**vahr**merss **vahss**err
running water	**fließendes Wasser**	**fleess**enderss **vahss**err
a private toilet	**eine eigene Toilette**	**ighn**er **igh**gerner toah**leh**ter
Could you put an extra bed in the room?	**Könnten Sie ein zusätzliches Bett ins Zimmer stellen?**	**kurn**tern zee ighn tsoo**zehts**likhers beht ins **tsimm**err **shteh**lern

CHECKING OUT, see page 31

How much? *Wieviel?*

What's the price ...?	**Wieviel kostet es ...?**	veefeel kostert ehss
per night	**pro Nacht**	proa nahkht
per week	**pro Woche**	proa vokher
for bed and breakfast	**für Übernachtung mit Frühstück**	fewr ewbernahkhtung mit frewshtewk
excluding meals	**ohne Mahlzeiten**	oaner maaltsightern
for full board (A.P.)	**mit Vollpension**	mit folpehnzioan
for half board (M.A.P.)	**mit Halbpension**	mit hahlppehnzioan
Does that include ...?	**Ist ... inbegriffen?**	ist ... inbegriffern
breakfast	**Frühstück**	frewshtewk
service	**Bedienung**	berdeenung
Value-Added Tax (VAT)*	**Mehrwertsteuer**	mayrvayrtshtoyerr
Is there any reduction for children?	**Gibt es Ermäßigung für Kinder?**	gipt ehss ehrmaissiggung fewr kinderr
Do you charge for the baby?	**Berechnen Sie etwas für das Baby?**	berrehkhnern zee ehtvahss fewr dahss ''baby''
That's too expensive.	**Das ist zu teuer.**	dahss ist tsu toyerr
Haven't you anything cheaper?	**Haben Sie nichts Billigeres?**	haabern zee nikhts billiggerrerss

Decision *Entscheidung*

May I see the room?	**Kann ich das Zimmer sehen?**	kahn ikh dahss tsimmerr zayern
That's fine. I'll take it.	**Gut, ich nehme es.**	goot ikh naymer ehss
No, I don't like it.	**Nein, es gefällt mir nicht.**	nighn ehss gerfehlt meer nikht
It's too ...	**Es ist zu ...**	ehss ist tsu
cold/hot	**kalt/warm**	kahlt/vahrm
dark/small	**dunkel/klein**	dunkerl/klighn
noisy	**laut**	lowt
I asked for a room with a bath.	**Ich wollte ein Zimmer mit Bad.**	ikh volter ighn tsimmerr mit baat

---

* Americans note: a type of sales tax in Germany and Austria

NUMBERS, see page 147

Do you have anything ...?	**Haben Sie etwas ...?**	haabern zee ehtvahss
better/bigger cheaper/quieter higher up/lower down	**Besseres/Größeres Billigeres/Ruhigeres weiter oben/weiter unten**	behsserrerss/grursserrerss billiggerrerss/rooiggerrerss vighterr oabern/vighterr untern
Do you have a room with a better view?	**Haben Sie ein Zimmer mit einer besseren Aussicht?**	haabern zee ighn tsimmerr mit ighnerr behsserrern owssikht

Registration *Anmeldung*

Upon arrival at a hotel or boarding-house you may be asked to fill in a registration form. (*Anmeldeschein*—**ahn**mehl-dershighn).

Name/Vorname	Name/First name
Wohnort/Straße/Nr.	Home address/Street/Number
Nationalität/Beruf	Nationality/Profession
Geburtsdatum/Geburtsort	Date/Place of birth
Letzter Aufenthaltsort/ Reiseziel	Coming from/Going to
Paßnummer	Passport number
Kraftfahrzeugnummer	Car number
Ort/Datum	Place/Date
Unterschrift	Signature

What does this mean?	**Was bedeutet das?**	vahss berdoytert dahss

Kann ich Ihren Paß sehen?	May I see your passport?
Würden Sie bitte den Anmelde-schein ausfüllen?	Would you mind filling in the registration form?
Unterschreiben Sie hier, bitte.	Please sign here.
Wie lange bleiben Sie?	How long will you be staying?

We'll be staying ...	Wir bleiben ...	veer blighbern
overnight only	nur eine Nacht	noor ighner nahkht
a few days	einige Tage	ighnigger taager
a week (at least)	(mindestens) eine Woche	(mindersterns) ighner vokher
I don't know yet.	Ich weiß es noch nicht.	ikh vighss ehss nokh nikht

Hotel staff *Hotelpersonal*

hall porter	der Portier	derr portyayr
maid	das Zimmermädchen	dahss tsimmermaitkhern
manager	der Direktor	derr dirrehktor
page (bellboy)	der Page	derr paazher
porter	der Hausdiener	derr howsdeenerr
receptionist	der Empfangschef	derr empfahngsshehf
switchboard operator	die Telefonistin	dee taylayfoanistin
waiter	der Kellner	derr kehlnerr
waitress	die Kellnerin	dee kehlnerrin

If you want to address members of the staff, don't say *Herr, Frau* or *Fräulein,* but use an introductory phrase such as:

Excuse me. Could you please ...?	Entschuldigung. Könnten Sie bitte ...?	ehntshuldiggung. kurntern zee bitter

General requirements *Allgemeine Fragen*

What's my room number?	Welche Zimmernummer habe ich?	vehlkher tsimmerrnummerr haaber ikh
The key, please.	Den Schlüssel, bitte.	dayn shlewsserl bitter
Where can I park my car?	Wo kann ich meinen Wagen parken?	voa kahn ikh mighnern vaagern pahrkern
Does the hotel have a garage?	Gibt es eine Hotelgarage?	gipt ehss ighner hottehlgahraazher
Will you have our luggage sent up?	Bitte schicken Sie unser Gepäck hinauf.	bitter shikkern zee unzerr gerpehk hinnowf
I'd like to leave this in your safe.	Ich möchte dies in Ihrem Safe lassen.	ikh murkhter deess in eererm "safe" lahssern

TELLING THE TIME, see page 153

Is there a bath on this floor?	Gibt es ein Bad auf dieser Etage?	gipt ehss ighn baat owf deezerr aytaazher
What's the voltage here?	Welche Stromspannung haben Sie hier?	vehlkher shtroamshpahnung haabern zee heer
Where's the outlet for the shaver?	Wo ist die Steckdose für den Rasierapparat?	voa ist dee shtehkdoazer fewr dayn rahzeerahpahraat
Would you please wake me at ...?	Würden Sie mich bitte um ... Uhr wecken?	vewrdern zee mikh bitter um ... oor vehkern
Can we have breakfast in our room?	Können wir im Zimmer frühstücken?	kurnern veer im tsimmerr frewshtewkern
Can you find me a ...?	Können Sie mir ... besorgen?	kurnern zee meer ... berzorgern
babysitter	einen Babysitter	ighnern "babysitter"
secretary	eine Sekretärin	ighner zaykraytairin
typewriter	eine Schreibmaschine	ighner shrighpmahsheener
May I have a/an/some ...?	Kann ich ... haben?	kahn ikh ... haabern
ashtray	einen Aschenbecher	ighnern ahshernbehkherr
bath towel	ein Badetuch	ighn baadertookh
(extra) blanket	eine (extra) Decke	ighner (ekstraa) dehker
envelopes	Briefumschläge	breefumshlaiger
(more) hangers	(noch) einige Kleiderbügel	(nokh) ighnigger klighderrbewgerl
hot-water bottle	eine Wärmflasche	ighner vehrmflahsher
ice cubes	Eiswürfel	ighsvewrferl
needle and thread	eine Nadel und etwas Faden	ighner naaderl unt ehtvahss faadern
(extra) pillow	ein (extra) Kopfkissen	ighn(ekstraa) kopfkissern
reading-lamp	eine Leselampe	ighner layzerlahmper
soap	Seife	zighfer
writing-paper	Schreibpapier	shrighppahpeer
Where's the ...?	Wo ist ...?	voa ist
bathroom	das Bad	dahss baat
dining-room	der Speisesaal	derr shpighzerzaal
emergency exit	der Notausgang	derr noatowsgahng
hairdresser's	der Friseur	derr frizurr
lift (elevator)	der Fahrstuhl	derr faarshtool
television room	der Fernsehraum	derr fehrnzayrowm
toilet	die Toilette	dee toahlehter

Telephone—Mail *Telefon – Post*

Can you put me through to Vienna 1 2 3 4 5 6?	**Können Sie mich mit Wien 1 2 3 4 56 verbinden?**	**kur**nern zee mikh mit veen 1 2 3 4 56 fehr**bin**dern
Do you have stamps?	**Haben Sie Briefmarken?**	**haa**bern zee **breef**mahrkern
Would you please mail this for me?	**Würden Sie das bitte für mich aufgeben?**	**vewr**dern zee dahss **bit**ter fewr mikh **owf**gaybern
Is there any mail for me?	**Ist Post für mich da?**	ist post fewr mikh daa
Are there any messages for me?	**Hat jemand eine Nachricht für mich hinterlassen?**	haht **yay**mahnt **igh**ner **naakh**rikht fewr mikh hinter**lahss**ern
How much are my telephone charges?	**Wie hoch ist meine Telefonrechnung?**	vee hoakh ist **migh**ner taylay**foan**rehkhnung

Difficulties *Schwierigkeiten*

The ... doesn't work.	**... funktioniert nicht.**	... funktsion**neert** nikht
air conditioner	**die Klimaanlage**	dee **klee**mahahnlaager
fan	**der Ventilator**	derr vehntill**aa**tor
heating	**die Heizung**	dee **hight**sung
light	**das Licht**	dahss likht
radio	**das Radio**	dahss **raa**dio
television	**der Fernseher**	derr **fehrn**zayerr
The water tap is dripping.	**Der Wasserhahn tropft.**	derr **vahss**errhaan tropft
There's no hot water.	**Es gibt kein warmes Wasser.**	ehs gipt kighn **vahr**mers **vahss**err
The wash-basin is clogged.	**Das Waschbecken ist verstopft.**	dahss **vahsh**behkern ist fehr**shtopft**
The window/The door is jammed.	**Das Fenster/Die Tür klemmt.**	dahss **fehn**sterr/dee tewr klehmt
The curtain is stuck.	**Der Vorhang klemmt.**	derr **foar**hahng klehmt
The bulb is burned out.	**Die Birne ist kaputt.**	dee **beer**ner ist kah**put**
My room has not been made up.	**Mein Zimmer ist nicht gemacht.**	mighn **tsimm**err ist nikht ger**mahkht**

POST OFFICE AND TELEPHONE, see page 132

Hotel

The ... is broken.	... ist kaputt.	... ist kahput
blind	das Rollo	dahss rollo
lamp	die Lampe	dee lahmper
plug	der Stecker	derr shtehkerr
shutter	der Fensterladen	derr fehnsterrlaadern
switch	der Schalter	derr shahlterr
Can you get it repaired?	Können Sie es reparieren lassen?	kurnern zee ehss rehpahreerern lahssern

Laundry—Dry cleaner's *Wäscherei – Reinigung*

I want these clothes ...	Ich möchte diese Kleider ... lassen.	ikh murkhter deezer klighderr ... lahssern
cleaned	reinigen	righniggern
ironed	bügeln	bewgerln
pressed	dampfbügeln	dahmpfbewgerln
washed	waschen	vahshern
When will they be ready?	Wann sind sie fertig?	vahn zint zee fehrtikh
I need them ...	Ich brauche sie ...	ikh browkher zee
today	heute	hoyter
tonight	heute abend	hoyter aabernt
tomorrow	morgen	morgern
before Friday	vor Freitag	foar frightaag
Can you ... this?	Können Sie das ...?	kurnern zee dahss
mend	ausbessern	owsbehsserrn
patch	flicken	flikkern
stitch	nähen	naiern
Can you sew on this button?	Können Sie diesen Knopf annähen?	kurnern zee deezern knopf ahnnaiern
Can you get this stain out?	Können Sie diesen Fleck entfernen?	kurnern zee deezern flehk ehntfehrnern
Is my laundry ready?	Ist meine Wäsche fertig?	ist mighner vehsher fehrtikh
This isn't mine.	Das gehört nicht mir.	dahss gerhurrt nikht meer
There's one piece missing.	Es fehlt ein Stück.	ehss faylt ighn shtewk
There's a hole in this.	Da ist ein Loch drin.	daa ist ighn lokh drin

DAYS OF THE WEEK, see page 151

Hairdresser's—Barber's *Damen- und Herrenfriseur*

Is there a hairdresser/ beauty salon in the hotel?	Gibt es einen Friseur/ Kosmetiksalon im Hotel?	gipt ehss ** igh**nern fri**zurr**/ kosmay**tik**zahlong im hot**tehl**
Can I make an appointment for sometime on Thursday?	Kann ich mich für Donnerstag anmelden?	kahn ikh mikh fewr **donn**errstaag **ahn**mehldern
I'd like it cut and shaped.	Schneiden und Legen, bitte.	**shnigh**dern unt **lay**gern **bit**ter
The parting (part) left/right, please.	Den Scheitel links/ rechts, bitte.	dayn **shigh**terl links/ **rehkh**ts **bit**ter
I want a haircut, please.	Haare schneiden, bitte.	**haar**er **shnigh**dern **bit**ter
bleach	eine Aufhellung	**igh**ner **owf**hehllung
blow-dry	fönen	**fur**nern
colour rinse	eine Farbspülung	**igh**ner **fahrp**shpewlung
dye	färben	**fehr**bern
face-pack	eine Gesichtsmaske	**igh**ner ger**zikhts**mahsker
manicure	eine Maniküre	**igh**ner **mahni**kkewrer
permanent wave	eine Dauerwelle	**igh**ner **dow**errvehler
setting lotion	ein Haarfestiger	ighn **haar**fehstiggerr
shampoo and set	Waschen und Legen	**vah**shern unt **lay**gern
with a fringe (bangs)	mit Ponyfransen	mit **ponni**frahnzern
I'd like a shampoo for ... hair.	Ein Haarwaschmittel für ... Haar, bitte.	ighn **haar**vahshmitterl fewr ... haar **bit**ter
normal/dry/ greasy (oily)	normales/trockenes/ fettiges	**normaa**lerss/**trok**kernerss/ **feh**ttiggerss
Do you have a colour chart?	Haben Sie eine Farbtabelle?	**haa**bern zee **igh**ner **fahrp**tahbehler
Don't cut it too short.	Nicht zu kurz schneiden.	nikht tsu koorts **shnigh**dern
A little more off the ...	Bitte ... etwas kürzer.	**bit**ter ... **eht**vahss **kewrt**serr
back	hinten	**hin**tern
neck	im Nacken	im **nah**kern
sides	an den Seiten	ahn dayn **zigh**tern
top	oben	**oa**bern
I don't want any hairspray.	Kein Haarspray, bitte.	kighn **haar**shpray **bit**ter
I'd like a shave.	Rasieren, bitte.	rah**zee**rern **bit**ter

DAYS OF THE WEEK, see page 151

Would you please trim my ...?	**Stutzen Sie mir bitte ...**	shtutsern zee meer bitter
beard	**den Bart**	dayn baart
moustache	**den Schnurrbart**	dayn shnoorbaart
sideboards (sideburns)	**die Koteletten**	dee kotlehtern

Checking out *Abreise*

May I please have my bill?	**Kann ich bitte die Rechnung haben?**	kahn ikh bitter dee rehkhnung haabern
I'm leaving early tomorrow. Please have my bill ready.	**Ich reise morgen früh ab. Bereiten Sie bitte meine Rechnung vor.**	ikh righzer morgern frew ahp. berrightern zee bitter mighner rehkhnung foar
I must leave at once.	**Ich muß sofort abreisen.**	ikh muss zoafort ahprighzern
Is everything included?	**Ist alles inbegriffen?**	ist ahlerss inbergriffern
Can I pay by credit card?	**Kann ich mit Kreditkarte bezahlen?**	kahn ikh mit krehditkahrter bertsaalern
You've made a mistake in this bill, I think.	**Ich glaube, Sie haben sich verrechnet.**	ikh glowber zee haabern zikh fehrrehkhnert
Can you get us a taxi?	**Können Sie uns ein Taxi bestellen?**	kurnern zee uns ighn tahksi bershtehlern
Could you have our luggage brought down, please?	**Würden Sie bitte unser Gepäck herunterbringen lassen?**	vewrdern zee bitter unzerr gerpehk hehrunterrbringern lahssern
We're in a great hurry.	**Wir haben es sehr eilig.**	veer haabern ehss zayr ighlikh
Here's the forwarding address.	**Hier ist meine Nachsendeadresse.**	heer ist mighner naakhzehnderahdrehsser
You have my home address.	**Sie haben meine Wohnadresse.**	zee haabern mighner voanahdrehsser
It's been a very enjoyable stay.	**Es war ein sehr angenehmer Aufenthalt.**	ehss vaar ighn zayr ahngernaymerr owfehnthahlt

TIPPING, see inside back-cover

Camping

There are plenty of authorized camp sites in Germany, many with excellent facilities. Austria and Switzerland also have well-equipped camp sites, some of them high up in the mountains. For information apply to any Tourist Office.

Is there a camp site near here?	**Gibt es hier in der Nähe einen Campingplatz?**	gipt ehss heer in derr naier ighnern kehmpingplahts
Can we camp here?	**Können wir hier zelten?**	kurnern veer heer tsehltern
Have you room for a tent/caravan (trailer)?	**Haben Sie Platz für ein Zelt/einen Wohnwagen?**	haabern zee plahts fewr ighn tsehlt/ighnern voanvaagern
Is there/Are there (a) ...?	**Gibt es ...?**	gipt ehss
drinking water	**Trinkwasser**	trinkvahsserr
electricity	**Stromanschluß**	shtroamahnshluss
playground	**einen Spielplatz**	ighnern shpeelplahts
restaurant	**ein Restaurant**	ighn rehstorrahng
shopping facilities	**Einkaufs- möglichkeiten**	ighnkowfsmurglikhkightern
swimming pool	**ein Schwimmbad**	ighn shvimbaat
What's the charge ...?	**Wie hoch sind die Gebühren ...?**	vee hoakh zint dee gerbewrern
per day	**pro Tag**	proa taag
per person	**pro Person**	proa pehrzoan
for a car	**für ein Auto**	fewr ighn owto
for a caravan (trailer)	**für einen Wohn- wagen**	fewr ighnern voan- vaagern
for a tent	**für ein Zelt**	fewr ighn tsehlt
Is the tourist tax included?	**Ist die Kurtaxe inbegriffen?**	ist dee koortahkser inbergriffern
Where are the showers/toilets?	**Wo sind die Duschen/ die Toiletten?**	voa zint dee dushern/ dee toahlehtern
Where can I get butane gas?	**Wo kann ich Butan- gas bekommen?**	voa kahn ikh buttaangaass berkommern
Is there a youth hostel near here?	**Gibt es hier irgend- wo eine Jugend- herberge?**	gipt ehss heer eergerntvoa ighner yoogernthehrbehrger

CAMPING EQUIPMENT, see page 106

Eating out

There are many types of places where you can eat and drink in Germany, Austria and Switzerland.

Beisel
(bighzerl)

The Austrian equivalent to a *Gasthaus*.

Bierhalle
(beerhahler)

Beer hall; besides beer served from huge barrels, you'll also be able to order hot dishes, sausages, salads and pretzels. The best-known beer halls are those in Munich which has a giant beer festival *(Oktoberfest)* annually in late September.

Bierstube
(beershtoober)

The nearest equivalent to an English pub or an American tavern though the atmosphere may be very different; usually only serves a few "dishes of the day".

Café
(kahfay)

Coffee shop; besides coffee, you'll be able to get pastries, snacks and drinks. There's a small dance floor in a *Tanzcafé*.

Gasthaus/Gasthof
(gahsthowss/gahsthoaf)

Inn, usually in the country. It offers home-cooking and a folksy atmosphere.

Gaststätte
(gahststhtehter)

Another word for *Restaurant*.

Kaffeehaus
(kahfayhowss)

The Austrian equivalent to a *Café*.

Konditorei
(kondeetoarigh)

A pastry shop; will often have a salon for coffee and pastries.

Milchbar
(milkhbaar)

A bar serving mainly plain and flavoured milk drinks with pastries. Also called a *Milchstübl*.

Raststätte
(rahststhtehter)

Roadside restaurant; also called a *Rasthof* in Austria; it's usually found on a motorway (expressway). Lodging and service-station facilities are on the premises.

Ratskeller
(rahtskehlerr)

A restaurant in the cellar of the town-hall (often a very historic, old building); food is generally excellent.

Restaurant
(rehstorrahng)

These are generally found only in urban areas. Menus often cater to foreign visitors as well as offering numerous local specialities.

Schnellbuffet (shnehlbewfay)	A snack bar; often with counter service.
Schnellimbiß (shnehlimbiss)	Snack bar; the English term is also seen. The principal fare is beer and sausages. A sausage stand *(Würstchenstand)* is often quite similar.
Tea-room ("tea-room")	The Swiss equivalent to a *Café*.
Weinstube (vighnshtoober)	A cozy type of restaurant found in wine-producing districts where you can sample new wine with simple hot dishes and snacks. In Austria, it's called a *Heuriger* and is identified by a wreath hanging over the portal.

Meal times   *Essenszeiten*

Breakfast *(das Frühstück*—dahss **frew**shtewk) is served from 7 a.m. to 10 a.m. and is generally included in the hotel arrangement.

Lunch *(das Mittagessen*—dahss **mit**tahgehssern) is generally served from 11.30 a.m. until 2 p.m.

Dinner *(das Abendessen*—dahss **aa**berntehssern) is served from 6.30 to 8.30 p.m., in large restaurants to 10 or 11 p.m. After this it's usually a case of cold snacks or hot sausages only.

Eating habits   *Eßgewohnheiten*

Germans start the day early with a meal that is somewhat more substantial than the typical "continental" breakfast, and they like to eat their main meal in the middle of the day. Supper is generally a slightly more copious version of breakfast—cold meat and cheese, with the addition of a salad. Most restaurants will, however, serve a three course dinner in the evening.

On weekends Germans often eat an afternoon snack. It can be either coffee or tea with pastries, or cold meat and cheese.

Fellow diners usually wish each other *"Mahlzeit"* or *"Guten Appetit"*.

German cuisine *Die deutsche Küche*

German cuisine has undergone many changes in the postwar years. Non-fattening, healthy fare has become more popular, and the influence of French, Italian, Greek, Chinese and other cuisines is remarkable. However, rich hearty dishes, mostly with pork and potatoes, are still served. Each region has its own specialities, and almost each town its own beer (or wine), but everywhere you'll find an extraordinary range of sausages, smoked ham, soused fish and many kinds of good bread. Not to mention *Sauerkraut, Schnitzel, Spätzle, Frankfurter, Frikadellen, Rollmops* ... And if you like game, Germany is the place.

Möchten Sie etwas essen?	Would you like to eat something?
Was nehmen Sie?	What would you like?
Ich empfehle Ihnen ...	I recommend ...
Was trinken Sie?	What would you like to drink?
Möchten Sie ...?	Do you want ...?
... haben wir nicht.	We haven't got ...

Hungry? *Hungrig?*

I'm hungry/I'm thirsty.	**Ich habe Hunger/ Ich habe Durst.**	ikh **haa**ber **hun**ger/ikh **haa**ber doorst
Can you recommend a good restaurant?	**Können Sie mir ein gutes Restaurant empfehlen?**	**kur**nern zee meer ighn **goo**terss rehstor**rahng** ehmp**fay**lern
Is there an inexpensive restaurant around here?	**Gibt es in der Nähe ein preiswertes Restaurant?**	gibt ehss in derr **nai**er ighn **prighs**vehrterss rehstor**rahng**

If you want to be sure of getting a table in well-known restaurants, it may be better to telephone in advance.

I'd like to reserve a table for 4.	**Ich möchte einen Tisch für 4 Personen reservieren lassen.**	ikh **murkh**ter **igh**nern tish fewr 4 pehr**zo**anern reh**zehr**veeerern **lahss**ern
We'll come at 8.	**Wir kommen um 8 Uhr.**	veer **kom**mern um 8 oor
Could we have a table ...?	**Können wir einen Tisch ... haben?**	**kur**nern veer **igh**nern tish ... **haab**ern
in the corner	**in der Ecke**	in derr **ehk**er
by the window	**am Fenster**	ahm **fehn**sterr
outside	**im Freien**	im **frigh**ern
on the terrace	**auf der Terrasse**	owf derr teh**rah**sser
in a nonsmoking area	**in der Nichtraucher-ecke**	in derr **nikht**rowkherr-ehker

Asking and ordering *Fragen und Bestellen*

Waiter/Waitress!	**Herr Ober/Fräulein, bitte!**	hehr **oa**berr/**froy**lighn **bitt**er
I'd like something to eat/drink.	**Ich möchte gerne essen/etwas trinken.**	ikh **murkh**ter **gehr**ner **ehss**ern/**eht**vahss **trink**ern
May I have the menu, please?	**Kann ich bitte die Speisekarte haben?**	kahn ikh **bitt**er dee **shpigh**zerkahrter **haab**ern
Do you have a set menu/local dishes?	**Haben Sie ein Gedeck/ hiesige Gerichte?**	**haab**ern zee ighn ger**dehk**/ **hee**zigger ger**rikh**ter
What do you recommend?	**Was würden Sie mir empfehlen?**	vahss **vewr**dern zee meer ehm**pfay**lern
I'd like ...	**Ich hätte gern ...**	ikh **heht**er gehrn
Could we have a/ an ..., please?	**Könnten wir bitte ... haben?**	**kurn**tern veer **bitt**er ... **haab**ern
ashtray	**einen Aschenbecher**	**igh**nern **ah**shernbehkherr
cup	**eine Tasse**	**igh**ner **tahss**er
fork	**eine Gabel**	**igh**ner **gaab**erl
glass	**ein Glas**	ighn glaass
knife	**ein Messer**	ighn **mehss**err
napkin (serviette)	**eine Serviette**	**igh**ner **sehr**viehter
plate	**einen Teller**	**igh**nern **tehl**err
spoon	**einen Löffel**	**igh**nern **lurf**erl
May I have some ...?	**Könnte ich etwas ... haben?**	**kurn**ter ikh **eht**vahss ... **haab**ern
bread	**Brot**	broat
butter	**Butter**	**butt**err

lemon	**Zitrone**	tsitroaner
mustard	**Senf**	zehnf
pepper	**Pfeffer**	pfehferr
salt	**Salz**	zahlts
seasoning	**Würze**	vewrtser
sugar	**Zucker**	tsukkerr

Some useful expressions for dieters and special requirements:

I'm on a diet.	**Ich muß Diät leben.**	ikh muss deeait laybern
I don't drink alcohol.	**Ich trinke keinen Alkohol.**	ikh trinker kighnern ahlkohoal
I mustn't eat food containing ...	**Ich darf nichts essen, was ... enthält.**	ikh dahrf nikhts ehssern vahss ... ehnthehlt
flour/fat	**Mehl/Fett**	mayl/feht
salt/sugar	**Salz/Zucker**	zahlts/tsukkerr
Do you have ... for diabetics?	**Haben Sie ... für Diabetiker?**	haabern zee ... fewr deeahbaytikkerr
cakes	**Kuchen**	kookhern
fruit juice	**Fruchtsaft**	frukhtzahft
special menu	**ein Spezialmenü**	ighn shpehtsiahlmaynew
Do you have vegetarian dishes?	**Haben Sie vegetarische Gerichte?**	haabern zee vehgehtaarisher gerrikhter
Could I have cheese/ fruit instead of the dessert?	**Könnte ich statt der Süßspeise Käse/Obst haben?**	kurnter ikh shtaht derr zewsshpighzer kaizer/opst haabern
Can I have an artificial sweetener?	**Kann ich Süßstoff haben?**	kahn ikh zewsshtof haabern

And ...

I'd like some more.	**Ich möchte etwas mehr.**	ikh murkhter ehtvahss mayr
Can I have more ..., please.	**Kann ich noch ... haben, bitte?**	kahn ikh nokh ... haabern bitter
Just a small portion.	**Nur eine kleine Portion.**	noor ighner klighner portsioan
Nothing more, thanks.	**Nichts mehr, danke.**	nikhts mayr dahnker
Where are the toilets?	**Wo ist die Toilette?**	voa ist dee toahlehter

Breakfast *Frühstück*

A German breakfast is a rather substantial meal. You may be served cold meat, cheese, a variety of breads—*Schwarzbrot, Vollkornbrot, Roggenbrot, Weißbrot* (black, wholegrain, rye, white)—and rolls *(Brötchen* or *Semmeln)* or croissants *(Hörnchen)* with butter and jam, accompanied by coffee or tea.

I'd like breakfast, please.	Ich möchte frühstücken, bitte.	ikh murkhter frewshtewkern bitter
I'll have á/an/some ...	Ich hätte gern ...	ikh hehter gehrn
bacon and eggs	Spiegeleier mit Speck	shpeegerligherr mit shpehk
boiled egg	ein gekochtes Ei	ighn gerkokhterss igh
soft/hard	weich/hartgekocht	vighkh/hahrtgerkokht
cereal	Getreideflocken	gertrighderflokkern
cheese	Käse	kaizer
eggs	Eier	igherr
fried eggs	Spiegeleier	shpeegerligherr
scrambled eggs	Rühreier	rewrigherr
grapefruit juice	Grapefruitsaft	grehpfrootzahft
ham and eggs	Spiegeleier mit Schinken	shpeegerligherr mit shinkern
jam	Marmelade	mahrmehlaader
marmalade	Apfelsinenmarmelade	ahpferlzeenern- mahrmehlaader
orange juice	Orangensaft	orrahngzhernzahft
toast	Toast	toast
May I have some ...?	Kann ich ... haben?	kahn ikh ... haabern
bread	Brot	broat
butter	Butter	butterr
(hot) chocolate	(heiße) Schokolade	(highsser) shokkollaader
coffee	Kaffee	kahfay
caffein-free	koffeinfreien Kaffee	koffeheenfrighern kahfay
black	schwarzen Kaffee	shvahrtsern kahfay
with milk	Milchkaffee	milkhkahfay
honey	Honig	hoanikh
milk	Milch	milkh
hot/cold	heiße/kalte	highsser/kahlter
rolls	Brötchen	brurtkhern
tea	Tee	tay
with milk/lemon	mit Milch/Zitrone	mit milkh/tsitroaner
(hot) water	(heißes) Wasser	(highsserss) vahsserr

What's on the menu? *Was steht auf der Speisekarte?*

Most restaurants display a menu *(Speisekarte)* outside. Besides the à la carte menu, they'll usually offer one or more set menus *(Menü* or *Gedeck)*. Value-added tax—a type of sales tax *(Mehrwertsteuer* or *Mwst)*—and a service charge *(Bedienung)* are usually included.

Under the headings below you'll find alphabetical lists of dishes that might be offered on a German menu, with their English equivalent. You can simply show the book to the waiter. If you want some cheese, for instance, let *him* point to what's available on the appropriate list. Use pages 36 and 37 for ordering in general.

	page	
Starters (Appetizers)	41	**Vorspeisen**
Soups and stews	42	**Suppen und Eintopf-gerichte**
Fish and seafood	43	**Fisch und Meeresfrüchte**
Meat	45	**Fleisch**
Sausages	47	**Würste**
Game and poultry	48	**Wild und Geflügel**
Potatoes	48	**Kartoffeln**
Rice and noodles	49	**Reis und Nudeln**
Vegetables and salads	49	**Gemüse und Salate**
Cheese	52	**Käse**
Fruit and nuts	53	**Obst und Nüsse**
Dessert—Pastries	54	**Nachtisch – Gebäck**
Beer	56	**Bier**
Wine	57	**Wein**
Other alcoholic drinks	59	**Andere alkoholische Getränke**
Nonalcoholic drinks	61	**Alkoholfreie Getränke**
Hot beverages	61	**Warme Getränke**
Snacks—Picnic	63	**Imbiß – Picknick**

Reading the menu *Die Speisekarte entziffern*

Tagesgedeck	Set menu of the day
Tagesgericht	Dish of the day
Spezialität des Hauses	Speciality of the house
Unser Küchenchef empfiehlt ...	The chef recommends ...
Nach ... art	... style
Hausgemacht	Home-made
Dasselbe mit ...	The same served with ...
Nur auf Bestellung	Made to order
Alle Preise sind inklusive Bedienung und Mehrwertsteuer	Service charge and VAT (sales tax) included
... im Preis inbegriffen	... included in the price
Nach Wahl	At your choice
Extraaufschlag	Extra charge

Beilagen	bighlaagern	accompaniments
Eierspeisen	ighershpighzern	egg dishes
Eintopfgerichte	ighntopfgerrikhter	stews
Eis	ighss	ice-cream
Fischgerichte	fishgerrikhter	fish
Fleischgerichte	flighshgerrikhter	meat
Glace	glahsser	ice-cream
Gemüse	germewzer	vegetables
Geflügel	gerflewgerl	poultry
Getränke	gertrainker	drinks
Hauptgerichte	howptgerrikhter	main course
Käse	kaizer	cheese
Meeresfrüchte	mayrersfrewkhter	seafood
Nachspeisen/ Nachtisch	naakhshpighzern/ naakhtish	desserts
Obst	oapst	fruit
Reisgerichte	righsgerrikhter	rice
Salate	zahlaater	salads
Suppen	zuppern	soups
Süßspeisen	zewsshpighzern	desserts
Teigwaren	tighkvaarern	pasta
Vom Rost	fom roast	grilled (broiled)
Vorspeisen	foarshpighzern	first course
Wein	vighn	wine
Wild	vilt	game

Appetizers *Vorspeisen*

If you feel like something to whet your appetite, choose carefully, for the German appetizer can be filling. Starters may also be listed on the menu under *Kleine Gerichte* or *Kalte Platten*.

I'd like an appetizer.	Ich hätte gern eine Vorspeise.	ikh **hehter** gehrn **ighner foars**pigh**zer**
Aal (in Gelee)	aal in zher**lay**	(jellied) eel
Appetithäppchen	ahpeht**teet**hehpkhern	canapés
Artischocken	ahrti**shok**kern	artichoke
Austern	**ows**terrn	oysters
Bündnerfleisch	bewnd**nerr**flighsh	cured, dried beef served in thin slices
Bückling	**bewk**ling	bloater, kipper
Fleischpastete	**flighsh**pahs**tay**ter	meat loaf
Froschschenkel	**frosh**shehnkerl	frog's legs
Gänseleberpastete	**gehn**zerlayberr-pahs**tay**ter	pâté, goose liver purée
Hering	**hay**ring	herring
Hummer	**hummerr**	lobster
Hummerkrabben	**hummerr**krah**bern**	large prawns
Käsehäppchen	**kaizer**hehpkhern	cheese sticks
Krabben	**krah**bern	prawns, shrimps
Krebs	**krayps**	river crayfish
Lachs	**lahks**	salmon
Languste	lahng**gus**ter	spiny lobster
Makrele	mah**kray**ler	mackerel
Muscheln	**mush**erln	mussels
Pilze	**pilt**ser	mushrooms
Räucheraal	**roykh**erraal	smoked eel
Räucherhering	**roykh**err**hay**ring	smoked herring
Rollmops	**roll**mops	soused herring
Rohschinken	**roa**shinkern	cured ham
Russische Eier	**russ**isher **igh**err	hard-boiled eggs with mayonnaise
Sardellen	zahr**dehl**ern	anchovies
Sardinen	zahr**deen**ern	sardines
Schinken	**shin**kern	ham
Schnecken	**shneh**kern	snails
Spargelspitzen	**shpaar**gerlshpitsern	asparagus tips
Thunfisch	**toon**fish	tunny, tuna
Wurst	**voorst**	sausage
Wurstplatte	**voorst**plahter	assorted cold cuts

Bismarckhering (**bis**mahrkhayring)	soused herring with onions
Frisch geräucherte Gänsebrust auf Toast (frish gerroykherrter gehnzerbrust owf toast)	freshly smoked breast of goose on toast
Hoppel-Poppel (hopperl-popperl)	scrambled eggs with diced sausages or bacon
Königinpastete (kurnigginpahstayter)	puff-pastry shell filled with diced meat and mushrooms
Matjeshering (mahtyehshayring)	salted young herring
Matjesfilet nach Hausfrauenart (mahtyehsfillay nahkh howsfrowernahrt)	fillets of herring with apples and onions
Hausgemachte Rehpastete (howsgermakhkter raypahstayter)	home-made venison meatloaf
Schinkenröllchen mit Spargel (shinkernrurlkhern mit shpahrgerl)	rolled ham with asparagus filling
Strammer Max (shtrahmerr mahkss)	slice of bread with highly spiced minced pork served with fried eggs and onions

Soups and stews *Suppen und Eintopfgerichte*

German soup can be hearty fare and particularly welcome on a cold day. *Eintopf* is a stew and will usually be a meal in itself.

I'd like some soup.	**Ich möchte gern eine Suppe.**	ikh **murkh**ter gehrn **ighn**er **zupp**er
Aalsuppe	**aal**zupper	eel soup
Bauernsuppe	**bow**errnzupper	cabbage and frank-furter soup
Bohnensuppe	**boan**ernzupper	bean soup with bacon
Bouillon	bool**yong**	clear soup
Erbsensuppe	**ehrp**zernzupper	pea soup
Fischsuppe	**fish**zupper	fish soup
Fischbeuschelsuppe	**fish**boysherlzupper	fish roe and vegetable soup
Fridattensuppe	frid**dah**ternzupper	broth with pancake strips

Frühlingssuppe	frewlingszupper	spring vegetable soup
Grießnockerlsuppe	greesnokkerrlzupper	semolina-dumpling soup
Gulaschsuppe	goolahshzupper	spiced soup of stewed beef
Hühnerbrühe	hewnerrbrewer	chicken broth
Kartoffelsuppe	kahrtofferlzupper	potato soup
(Semmel-) Knödelsuppe	(zehmerl-) knurderlzupper	dumpling soup
Königinsuppe	kurnigginzupper	soup with beef, sour cream and almonds
Kraftbrühe	krahftbrewer	beef consommé
mit Ei	mit igh	with raw egg
mit Einlage	mit ighnlaager	with a garnish
Leberknödelsuppe	layberrknurderlzupper	liver-dumpling soup
Linsensuppe	linzernzupper	lentil soup
Nudelsuppe	nooderlzupper	noodle soup
Ochsenschwanz-suppe	oksernshvahntszupper	oxtail soup
Pichelsteiner Eintopf	pikherlshtighnerr ighntopf	meat and vegetable stew
Schildkrötensuppe	shiltkrurternzupper	turtle soup
Serbische Bohnensuppe	zehrbisher boanernzupper	spiced bean soup
Tomatensuppe	tommaaternzupper	tomato soup
Zwiebelsuppe	tsveeberlzupper	onion soup

Backerbsensuppe (bahkehrpsernzupper)	broth served with pea-sized balls of pasta
Basler Mehlsuppe (baaslerr maylzupper)	flour soup with grated cheese (Swiss)
Labskaus (laapskowss)	thick stew of minced and marinated meat with mashed potatoes

Fish and seafood *Fisch und Meeresfrüchte*

I'd like some fish.	**Ich hätte gern Fisch.**	ikh hehter gehrn fish
What kind of seafood do you have?	**Welche Meeresfrüchte haben Sie?**	vehlkher mayrersfrewkhter haabern zee
Aal	aal	eel
Austern	owsterrn	oysters
Barsch	bahrsh	freshwater perch
Brasse/Brachse	brahsser/brahkser	bream

Dorsch	dorsh	cod
Egli	ehglee	perch
Felchen	fehlkhern	kind of trout
Fischfrikadellen	fishfrikkahdehlern	fish croquettes
Forelle	forehler	trout
Flunder	flunderr	flounder
Garnelen	gahrnaylern	prawns/shrimps
Hecht	hehkht	pike
Heilbutt	highlbut	halibut
Hering	hayring	herring
Hummer	hummerr	lobster
Jakobsmuscheln	yaakopsmusherln	scallops
Kabeljau	kaaberlyow	cod
Kaisergranate	kighzerrgrahnahter	kind of scampi
Karpfen	kahrpfern	carp
Krebs	krayps	river crayfish
Lachs	lahks	salmon
Languste	lahnggooster	spiny lobster
Makrele	mahkrayler	mackerel
Muscheln	musherln	clams/mussels
Rotbarsch	roatbahrsh	red sea-bass
Salm	zahlm	salmon
Schellfisch	shehlfish	haddock
Scholle	sholler	plaice
Seebarsch	zaybahrsh	sea bass
Seebutt	zaybut	brill
Seezunge	zaytsunger	sole
Sprotten	shprottern	sprats
Steinbutt	shtighnbut	turbot
Stint	shtint	smelt
Stör	shturr	sturgeon
Zander	tsahnderr	(giant) pike-perch

baked	**gebacken**	gerbahkern
boiled in bouillon	**blau**	blow
breaded	**paniert**	pahneert
fried	**gebraten**	gerbraatern
deep-fried	**im schwimmenden**	im shvimmerndern
	Fett gebacken	feht gerbahkern
grilled	**gegrillt**	gergrilt
marinated	**mariniert**	mahrinneert
sautéed (in butter)	**(in Butter)**	(in butterr)
	geschwenkt	gershvehnkt
smoked	**geräuchert**	gerroykhert
steamed	**gedämpft**	gerdehmpft

Meat *Fleisch*

Bear in mind that the Germans most often write in one word
what would take us two or more. For example, *Rindszunge*
is *Rinds-* (beef) and *-zunge* (tongue) or *Kalbsbrust* is breast
of veal. So you may have to look under two entries in the
following lists to fully understand what's on the menu.

I'd like some ...	Ich hätte gern ...	ikh **heh**ter gehrn
beef	**Rindfleisch**	**rint**flighsh
lamb	**Lammfleisch**	**lahm**flighsh
mutton	**Hammelfleisch**	**hah**merlflighsh
pork	**Schweinefleisch**	**shvigh**nerflighsh
veal	**Kalbfleisch**	**kahlp**flighsh
Bauernomelett	bow**err**nomleht	diced bacon and onion omelet
(deutsches) Beefsteak	(doytsherss) beef-stayk	hamburger
Beuschel	**boy**sherl	veal offal with lemon sauce
-braten	-**braa**tern	joint, roast
-brust	-brust	breast
Eisbein	**ighs**bighn	pickled pig's knuckle
Faschiertes	fah**sheer**terss	minced meat
Filetsteak	fill**ay**stayk	beef steak
Fleischkäse	**flighsh**kaizer	type of bologna sausage
Frikadellen	frikkah**deh**lern	meat patties
Geschnetzeltes	ger**shneht**serlterss	chipped veal served in wine sauce
Geselchtes	ger**zehlkh**terss	smoked or salted meat usually pork
Gulasch	**goo**lahsh	gulash; chunks of beef stewed in a rich paprika gravy
Hackbraten	**hahk**braatern	meatloaf
-hachse/haxe	-**hahk**ser	shank
-herz	-**hehr**ts	heart
Kasseler Rippenspeer	**kahss**ehlerr **rip**pernshpayr	smoked pork chops
-klößchen	-**klurs**khern	meatballs
-kotelett	-**kot**leht	cutlet, chop
Krenfleisch	**krayn**flighsh	pork, usually brawn, served with shredded vegetables and horseradish

Kutteln	kutterln	tripe
Leber	layberr	liver
Leberkäse	layberrkaizer	type of meatloaf
Lenden-	lehndern	fillet of beef (tenderloin)
Nieren	neerern	kidneys
Nierenstück	neerernshtewk	loin
-plätzli	-plehtslee	escalope
Pökelfleisch	purkerlflighsh	marinated meat
Rippensteak	rippernshtayk	rib steak
Rostbraten	roastbraatern	rumpsteak
Rouladen	roolaadern	slices of beef or veal filled, rolled and braised (in brown gravy)
Sauerbraten	zowerrbraatern	marinated, brased beef
Schinken	shinkern	ham
Schlachtplatte	shlahkhtplahter	platter of various sausages and cold meats
Schnitzel	shnitserl	escalope
Spanferkel	shpaanfehrkerl	suck(l)ing pig
Speck	shpehk	bacon
-spießchen	-shpeeskhern	skewered meat
Sülze	zewltser	brawn (headcheese)
Wiener Schnitzel	veenerr shnitserl	breaded veal escalope
-zunge	-tsunger	tongue

Here are some hearty dishes you'll certainly want to try:

Bauernschmaus (bowerrnshmowss)	sauerkraut garnished with boiled bacon, smoked pork, sausages, dumplings, potatoes (Austrian)
Berner Platte (behrnerr plahter)	sauerkraut (or green beans) liberally garnished with pork chops, boiled bacon and beef, sausages, tongue and ham (Swiss)
Holsteiner Schnitzel (holshtighnerr shnitserl)	breaded veal escalope topped with fried egg, garnished with vegetables and usually accompanied by bread and butter, anchovies, mussels and smoked salmon
Kohlroulade (koalroolaader)	cabbage leaves stuffed with minced meat
Königsberger Klopse (kurnigsbehrgerr klopser)	Meatballs in white caper sauce

boiled	**gekocht**	gerkokht
braised	**geschmort**	gershmoart
fried	**(in der Pfanne)**	(in derr pfahner)
	gebraten	gerbraatern
grilled (broiled)	**gegrillt**	gergrilt
roasted	**(im Ofen)**	(im oafern)
	gebraten	gerbraatern
stewed	**gedämpft**	gerdehmpft
stuffed	**gefüllt**	gerfewlt
underdone (rare)	**blutig**	blootikh
medium	**mittel**	mitterl
well-done	**gut durchgebraten**	goot doorchgerbraatern

Sausages *Würste*

Sausages are produced in dozens of different varieties. Some with more garlic or spices than others. One of the mildest is the Frankfurter.

Bierwurst	beervoorst	smoked, pork and beef
Blutwurst	blootvoorst	black pudding (blood sausage)
Bockwurst	bokvoorst	large frankfurter
Bratwurst	braatvoorst	fried, pork
Jagdwurst	yaagtvoorst	smoked, with garlic and mustard
Leberwurst	layberrvoorst	liver sausage
Katenrauchwurst	kaaternrowkhvoorst	country-style, smoked
Nürnberger Bratwurst	newrnbehrgerr braatvoorst	fried, veal and pork
Regensburger	raygernsburgerr	highly spiced, smoked
Rotwurst	roatvoorst	black pudding (blood sausage)
Weißwurst	vighsvoorst	veal and bacon with parsley and onion
Wienerli	veenerrli	Vienna-style frankfurter
Zervelat(wurst)	zehrvehlaat(voorst)	seasoned, smoked, pork, beef and bacon
Zungenwurst	tsungernvoorst	blood sausage with pieces of tongue and diced fat
Zwiebelwurst	tsveeberlvoorst	liver and onion

Game and poultry *Wild und Geflügel*

German cuisine is often said to be unimaginative, but this certainly doesn't apply to game. The venison is usually carefully marinated till tender and served with sweet raisin or red currant sauce or a purée of chestnuts *(Maronenpüree)*.

If your meal is prepared *nach Jägerart* (in the hunter's style), it's likely sautéed with mushrooms and root vegetables and served in a wine gravy *(Weinsoße*—**vighn**zoasser).

Back-	bahk-	fried
Brat-	braat-	roast
-braten	-braatern	joint, roast
Ente	ehnter	duck
Fasan	fahzaan	pheasant
Gans	gahns	goose
Hähnchen	hainkhern	chicken
Hase	haazer	hare
-hendl	-hehndl	chicken
gespickter Hirsch	gershpikterr heersh	larded venison
Huhn	hoon	chicken
Kaninchen	kahneenkhern	rabbit
Kapaun	kahpown	capon
-keule	-koyler	haunch
Masthühnchen	mahsthewnkhern	pullet chicken
-pfeffer	-pfehferr	jugged game
Poulet	poolay	chicken
Rebhuhn	rehphoon	partridge
Reh	ray	venison
-rücken	-rewkern	saddle
Schnepfe	shnehpfer	woodcock
Taube	towber	pigeon, squab
Truthahn	troothaan	turkey
Wachtel	vahkhterl	quail
Wildschwein	viltshvighn	wild boar

Potatoes *Kartoffeln*

The Germans' favourite accompaniment *(Beilage)* is undoubtedly the potato which can be prepared in a seemingly endless variety of ways.

Bratkartoffeln	braatkahrtofferln	fried potatoes
Geröstete	gerrursterter	hashed-brown potatoes

Kartoffel(n)	kahrtofferl(n)	potato(es)
-bälle	-behler	balls
-brei	-brigh	mashed
-klöße	-klursser	dumplings
-mus	-mooss	mashed
-puffer	-pufferr	fritters
-stock	-shtok	mashed
-kroketten	-kroakehtern	croquettes
Kartoffelsalat	kahrtofferlzahlaat	potato salad
Pellkartoffeln	pehlkahrtofferln	potatoes boiled in their jackets
Petersilienkartoffeln	payterrzeeliern-kahrtofferln	parsley potatoes
Pommes frites	pom frit	chips (french fries)
Reibekuchen	righberkookhern	potato pancake
Rösti	rurshtee	hashed-brown potatoes
Röstkartoffeln	rurstkahrtofferln	fried potatoes
Salzkartoffeln	zahltskahrtofferln	boiled potatoes

Rice and noodles *Reis und Nudeln*

Butterreis	butterrighss	buttered rice
Curryreis	kurreerighss	curried rice
Knöpfli	knurpflee	kind of gnocchi
Mehlnockerln	maylnokkerrln	small dumplings
Nudeln	nooderln	noodles
Reis	righss	rice
Spätzle	shpehtsler	kind of gnocchi
Teigwaren	tighgvaarern	pasta

Vegetables and salads *Gemüse und Salate*

What vegetables do you recommend?	Welches Gemüse empfehlen Sie?	vehlkhers germewzer ehmpfaylern zee
I'd prefer some salad.	Ich nehme lieber Salat.	ikh naymer leeberr zahlaart

Auberginen	oaberrzheenern	aubergines (eggplant)
Blaukraut	blowkrowt	red cabbage
Blumenkohl	bloomernkoal	cauliflower
Bohnen	boanern	beans
grüne	grewner	French (green) beens
weiße	vighsser	haricot beans, white kidney beans
Brokkoli	brokkollee	broccoli

Champignons	shahmpinyong	button mushrooms
Chicorée	sheekorray	endive (Am. chicory)
Endivien	ehndeeviern	chicory (Am. endives)
Erbsen	ehrpsern	peas
Essiggurken	ehssikhgoorkern	gherkins (pickles)
Fenchel	fehnkherl	fennel
Fisolen	feezoalern	french (green) beans
Gemüse	germewzer	vegetables
gemischtes	germishterss	mixed vegetables
grüner Salat	grewnerr zahlaat	green salad
Grünkohl	grewnkoal	kale
Gurken	goorkern	cucumber
Häuptlsalat	hoyptlzahlaat	lettuce salad
Karfiol	kahrfioal	cauliflower
Karotten	kahrottern	carrots
Kohl	koal	cabbage
Kohlrabi	koalraabee	turnips
Kopfsalat	kopfzahlaat	lettuce salad
Krautstiel	krowtshteel	white beet
Kürbis	kewrbiss	pumpkin
Lattich	lahtikh	lettuce
Lauch	lowkh	leeks
Leipziger Allerlei	lighptseegerr ahlerrligh	peas, carrots, asparagus
Mais	mighss	sweet corn
Mohrrüben	moarrewbern	carrots
Paradeiser	pahrahdighzerr	tomatoes
Pfifferlinge	pfifferrlinger	chanterelle mushrooms
Pilze	piltser	mushrooms
Radieschen	rahdeeskhern	radishes
Rettich	rehtikh	black radish
Rosenkohl	roazernkoal	Brussels sprouts
rote Beete/Rüben	roater bayter/rewbern	beetroot
Rotkohl	roatkoal	red cabbage
Rüebli	rewblee	carrots
Salat	zahlaat	salad
Sauerkraut	zowerrkrowt	sauerkraut
Schwarzwurzeln	shvahrtsvoortserln	salsify
Sellerie	zehlerree	celery
Spargel	shpaargerl	asparagus
Spargelspitzen	shpaargerlshpitsern	asparagus tips
Spinat	shpeenaat	spinach
Tomaten	tommaatern	tomatoes
Weißkohl	vighskoal	cabbage
Zwiebeln	tsveeberln	onions
Zucchetti	tsuggehtee	courgette (zucchini)

Vegetables may be served ...

oven-browned	**überbacken**	ewberrbahkern
boiled	**gekocht**	gerkokht
creamed	**-püree**	-pewray
diced	**gehackt**	gerhahkt
stewed	**gedämpft**	gerdehmpft

As for the seasoning ...

Anis	ahnees	aniseed
Basilikum	bahzeelikkum	basil
Dill	dil	dill
Essig	ehssikh	vinegar
Estragon	ehstrahgon	tarragon
Gewürz	gervewrts	spice
Ingwer	ingverr	ginger
Kapern	kaaperrn	capers
Knoblauch	knoplowkh	garlic
Kräuter	kroyterr	mixture of herbs
Kren	krayn	horseradish
Kresse	krehsser	cress
Kümmel	kewmerl	caraway
Lorbeer	loarbayr	bay leaf
Majoran	mahyoraan	marjoram
Meerrettich	mayrrehtikh	horseradish
Muskatnuß	muskahtnuss	nutmeg
Nelke	nehlker	clove
Öl	url	oil
Petersilie	payterrzeelier	parsley
Pfeffer	pfehferr	pepper
Pfefferminz	pfehferrmints	mint
Rosmarin	rosmahreen	rosemary
Safran	zahfraan	saffron
Salbei	zahlbigh	sage
Salz	zahlts	salt
Schnittlauch	shnitlowkh	chives
Senf	zehnf	mustard
Süßstoff	zewsshtof	artificial sweetener
Thymian	tewmiaan	thyme
Tomatenketchup	tommaaternkehtshup	ketchup
Wacholder	vahkholderr	juniper
Würze	vewrtser	seasoning
Zimt	tsimt	cinnamon
Zucker	tsukkerr	sugar

Cheese *Käse*

Most of the cheese produced in Germany, Austria and Switzerland is mild. You may see *Käseteller* (**kai**zertehlerr) on the menu. This means you'll get a plate of three or four varieties of cheese, doubtless including the renowned *Emmentaler* (**eh**merntaalerr), which we call simply Swiss cheese. If you are looking for curd cheese, ask for *Frischkäse*.

| What sort of cheese do you have? | Welche Käsesorten haben Sie? | vehlkher **kai**zerzoartern **haa**bern zee |
| A piece of that one, please. | Ein Stück von dem da, bitte. | ighn shtewk fon daym daa bitter |

mild	Allgäuer Bergkäse (like Swiss cheese), Allgäuer Rahmkäse, Altenburger (made of goat's milk), Appenzeller, Greyerzer, Kümmelkäse (made with caraway seeds), Quark, Räucherkäse (smoked cheese), Schichtkäse, Sahnekäse, Tilsiter, Topfen, Weißkäse.	
sharp	Handkäse, Harzer Käse, Schabzieger.	
curd	**frisch**	frish
hard	**hart**	hahrt
mild	**mild**	millt
ripe	**reif**	righf
sharp	**scharf**	shahrf
soft	**weich**	vighkh

The following dish in Switzerland makes a meal in itself:

fondue (**fong**dew)	a hot, bubbly mixture of melted cheese, white wine, a drop of kirsch and a hint of garlic; each guest dips a bite-size piece of bread on a fork into the pot of cheese.

And for a cheesy snack try one of the following specialities:

Käsewähe (**kai**zervaier)	a hot cheese tart
Käseschnitte (**kai**zershnitter)	an open-faced melted cheese sandwich

Fruit and nuts *Obst und Nüsse*

Do you have (fresh) fruit?	**Haben Sie (frisches) Obst?**	haabern zee (frisherss) oapst
I'd like a fruit cocktail.	**Ich hätte gern einen Obstsalat.**	ikh hehter gehrn ighnern oapstzahlaat
Ananas	ahnahnahss	pineapple
Apfel	ahpferl	apple
Apfelsine	ahpferlzeener	orange
Aprikosen	ahprekkoazern	apricots
Backpflaumen	bahkpflowmern	prunes
Banane	bahnaaner	banana
Birne	beerner	pear
Blaubeeren	blowbayrern	blueberries
Brombeeren	brombayrern	blackberries
Datteln	dahterln	dates
Erdbeeren	ehrtbayrern	strawberries
Erdnüsse	ehrdnewsser	peanuts
Feigen	fighgern	figs
Haselnüsse	haazerlnewsser	hazelnuts
Heidelbeeren	highderlbayrern	blueberries
Himbeeren	himbayrern	raspberries
Johannisbeeren	yohhahnisbayrern	currants
rote/schwarze	roater/shvahrtser	red/black
Kirschen	keershern	cherries
Kokosnuß	kokkosnuss	coconut
Mandarine	mahndahreener	tangerine
Mandeln	mahnderln	almonds
Marillen	mahrillern	apricots
Melone	mayloaner	melon (cantaloupe)
Mirabellen	meerahbehlern	a variety of plums
Nüsse	newsser	nuts
Pampelmuse	pahmperlmoozer	grapefruit
Pfirsich	pfeerzikh	peach
Pflaumen	pflowmern	plums
Preiselbeeren	prighzerlbayrern	cranberries
Quitte	kvitter	quince
Rhabarber	rahbahrberr	rhubarb
Ribisel	reebeezl	currants
Rosinen	rozeenern	raisins
Stachelbeeren	stahkherlbayrern	gooseberries
Walnüsse	vahlnewsser	walnuts
Wassermelone	vahsserrmayloaner	watermelon
Weintrauben	vighntrowbern	grapes
Zitrone	tsitroaner	lemon
Zwetsch(g)en	tsvehtsh(g)ern	plums

Dessert–Pastries *Nachtisch–Gebäck*

Desserts may also be listed on the menu under *Nachspeisen* or *Süßspeisen*. If you want an ice-cream, look under *Eis* in Germany and Austria and under *Glace* in Switzerland. The German waiter may ask you if you want your dessert served with *Schlagsahne*, the Austrian will say *Schlagobers* or simply *Schlag* and the Swiss *Schlagrahm*. Wherever you are it means whipped cream.

I'd like a dessert, please.	**Ich hätte gern eine Nachspeise.**	ikh **heh**ter gehrn **ighn**er naakhshp**igh**zer
Something light, please.	**Etwas Leichtes, bitte.**	ehtvahss **ligkh**terss bitter
Just a small portion.	**Nur eine kleine Portion.**	noor **ighn**er **kligh**ner portsioan
Nothing more, thanks.	**Nein danke, nichts mehr.**	nighn **dahn**ker nikhts mayr
Götterspeise	gurt**errshpigh**zer	fruit jelly (Jell-O)
Kaltschale	**kahlt**shaaler	chilled fruit soup
Obstsalat	**oap**stzahlaat	fruit cocktail

Here are some basic words you'll need to know if you want to order a dessert. Remember that Germans often write in one word what would take us two. The words below may be combined with a fruit or a flavour, e.g. *Apfelauflauf, Erdbeereis*, etc.

-auflauf	-**owf**lowf	soufflé
-creme	-**kraym**	pudding
-eis, -glace	-**ighss** -**glahss**er	ice-cream
-kompott	-**kompot**	compote
-kuchen	-**kook**hern	cake
-pudding	-**pudding**	pudding
-torte	-**torter**	layer cake

These flavours of ice-cream are very popular:

Erdbeer-	**ehrt**bayr-	strawberry
Karamel-	kahrah**mehl**-	caramel
Mokka-	**mokk**ah-	coffee
Schokoladen-	shokkoll**aad**ern-	chocolate
Vanille-	vah**nill**er-	vanilla
Zitronen-	tsit**roan**ern-	lemon

If you'd like to try something more filling with your coffee, we'd recommend ...

Apfelstrudel
(ahpferlshtrooderl)
paper-thin layers of pastry filled with apple slices, nuts, raisins and jam

Berliner
(behrleenerr)
jam doughnut

Bienenstich
(beenernshtikh)
honey-almond cake

Cremeschnitte
(kraymshnitter)
millefeuille (napoleon)

Gugelhupf
(googerlhupf)
a moulded cake with a hole in the centre, usually filled with raisins and almonds

Hefekranz
(hayferkrahnts)
ring-shaped cake of yeast dough, with almonds and sometimes candied fruit

Kaiserschmarren
(kighzerrshmahrern)
shredded pancake with raisins served with syrup (Austrian)

Mohrenkopf
(moarernkopf)
chocolate meringue with whipped-cream filling

Palatschinken
(pahlahtshinkern)
when listed under desserts, pancakes with a jam or white cheese filling, otherwise they are a savoury dish

Schillerlocke
(shillerlokker)
pastry cornet with vanilla cream filling

Schwarzwälder Kirschtorte
(shvahrtsvehlderr keershtorter)
chocolate layer cake filled with cream and cherries, flavoured with cherry brandy

Topfenstrudel
(topfernshtrooderl)
flaky pastry filled with creamed, vanilla-flavoured white cheese, rolled and baked

Windbeutel
(vintboyterl)
cream puff

Here are the names of some favourite biscuits (cookies):

Honigkuchen	hoanikhkookhern	honey biscuits
Leckerli	lehkerrli	ginger biscuits
Makronen	mahkroanern	macaroons
Printen	printern	honey biscuits
Spekulatius	shpehkoolaatsiuss	almond biscuits

Beer *Bier*

Needless to say, beer is the Germans' favourite drink. Almost every town with a sizable population has at least one brewery. You'll want to try some of the local brews. However, Dortmund and Bavarian beer are found throughout the country. *Bier vom Faß* (draught or draft beer) is considered to have a better taste and is less expensive, too, than bottled beer.

I'd like a beer.	**Ich hätte gern ein Bier.**	ikh **heh**ter gehrn ighn beer
a dark beer	**ein Dunkles**	ighn **dunk**lerss
a light beer	**ein Helles**	ighn **heh**lerss
I'd like a ... of beer.	**Ich hätte gern ... Bier.**	ikh **heh**ter gehrn ... beer
bottle	**eine Flasche**	**igh**ner **flah**sher
glass	**ein Glas**	ighn glaass
a small one	**ein kleines**	ighn **kligh**nerss
a large one	**ein großes**	ighn **groass**ers
mug (a quart)	**eine Maß**	**igh**ner maass
Waiter! Another beer, please!	**Herr Ober, noch ein Bier, bitte!**	hehr **oab**err nokh ighn beer **bit**ter

Altbier (**ahlt**beer)	a bitter beer with a high hops content
Bockbier, Doppel-bock, Märzen, Starkbier (**bok**beer, **dopperl**bok, **mehrt**sern, **shtahrk**beer)	these are beers with a high alcoholic and malt content
Malzbier (**mahlts**beer)	a dark, sweetish beer with a low alcoholic content but high in calories
Pilsener (**pilz**ernerr)	has a particularly strong aroma of hops
Radlermaß (**raadler**rmaass)	a light beer to which a bit of lemonade is added; in north Germany it's called *Alsterwasser* (**ahl**sterrvahsserr)
Weißbier (**vighs**beer)	a light beer brewed from wheat grain; Berliners love a *Berliner Weiße mit Schuß—Weißbier* with a shot of raspberry juice.

Wine

The best wine-producing regions of Germany are those round the Rhine and Moselle rivers—the northernmost wine-producing areas of Europe.

More so than French vintners to the west, German wine producers are at the mercy of the vagaries of the country's climatic conditions. One type of wine can have a quite different character from one year to the next depending upon the weather. For this reason, you'll have to learn to recognize a few basic terms on German labels which will tell you something about how you can likely expect a certain wine to taste.

In good years wine may be labeled *naturrein* or *Naturwein* which just means it's been produced under ordinary methods. In a bad year, sugar is sometimes added to increase the alcoholic content. If this is done, *verbessert* (improved) is euphemistically printed on the label.

There are four other words commonly found on German wine labels which you should know. They indicate the ripeness of the grapes when they were picked—or the degree of dryness or sweetness of the wine.

Spätlese (spaitlayzer)	gathered late after the normal harvesting; dry wine
Auslese (owslayzer)	selected gathering of particularly ripe bunches of grapes; slightly dry wine
Beerenauslese (bayrernowslayzer)	selected overripe grapes, slightly sweet wine
Trockenbeerenauslese (trokkernbayrern-owslayzer)	selected dried or raisin-like grapes; one drop of nectar can be squeezed out of each grape; a sweet or dessert wine is produced.

In neighbouring German-speaking Switzerland, mostly red wine is produced. Austria's Wachau region along the fabled Danube riverbanks produces white wine while Burgenland to the east of Vienna has red wine.

Type of wine	Examples	Accompanies
sweet white wine	Rheinpfalz is noted for wine in this category; bottles labeled *Trockenbeerenauslese* also fall into this section.	desserts, especially puddings and cake
dry white wine	The Rheingau region produces extraordinary white wine in good vintage years; Moselle wine can usually be counted on to be very dry; wine labelled *Spätlese* or *Auslese* can go into this category as well as those with the term *naturrein* or *Naturwein*.	cold meat or shellfish, fish, boiled meat, egg dishes, first courses, fowl, veal, dishes served with sauerkraut, sausages
rosé	Sometimes referred to as *Schillerwein*	goes with almost anything but especially cold dishes, eggs, pork, lamb
light-bodied red wine	Most local red wine fits into this category, particularly the wine of Austria's Burgenland, German-speaking Switzerland, the Ahr region (look for the names *Ahrweiler*, *Neuenahr* and *Walporzheim* on the label) and Baden-Württemberg.	roast chicken, turkey, veal, lamb, beef steak, ham, liver, quail, pheasant, stews, dishes served with gravy
full-bodied red wine	A difficult wine to find but a *Spätburgunder* from the Ahr Valley is a good example.	duck, goose, kidneys, most game, goulash, in short, any strong-flavoured preparations
sparkling wine	German *Sekt* comes into this category; some of it rivals French champagne in quality.	if it's dry, it goes with anything; may be drunk as an aperitif or as the climax to the dinner; goes well with shellfish, nuts and dried fruit; if it's sweet, it'll go nicely with dessert and pastry like *Strudel*

May I please have the wine list?	**Die Weinkarte, bitte.**	dee **vighn**kahrter **bitter**
I want a bottle of white wine/red wine/sparkling wine.	**Ich möchte eine Flasche Weißwein/Rotwein/Schaumwein.**	ikh **murkhter ighner flahsher vighs**vighn/**roat**vighn/**showm**vighn
I'd like a glass/carafe of ...	**Ich hätte gern ein Glas/eine Karaffe ...**	ikh **hetter** gehrn ighn **glaass/ighner** kah**rahfer**
Please bring me another ...	**Bitte bringen Sie mir noch ...**	**bitter bringern** zee mir nokh
Where does this wine come from?	**Woher kommt dieser Wein?**	voa**hayr** kom **deezerr vighn**

red/white/rosé	**rot/weiß/rosé**	roat/**vighss/rozay**
(very) dry/sweet	**(sehr) trocken/süß**	(zayr) **trokkern/zewss**
light	**leicht**	**lighkht**
full-bodied	**vollmundig**	**vol**mundig

A refreshing highball for the ladies is sparkling wine and orange juice, *Damengedeck* (**daa**merngerdehk) or for the men, *Herrengedeck* (**heh**rerngerdehk), which is sparkling wine and beer. The German champagne (*Sekt*—sehkt) is also worth trying.

Other alcoholic drinks   *Andere alkoholische Getränke*

I'd like a/an/some ...	**Ich hätte gern ...**	ikh **hehter** gehrn
aperitif	**einen Aperitif**	**ighnern** ahpayrit**teef**
brandy	**einen Weinbrand**	**ighnern vighn**brahnt
cider	**Apfelwein**	**ahpferl**vighn
cognac	**einen Kognak**	**ighnern kon**yahk
liqueur	**einen Likör**	**ighnern** lik**kurr**
mulled wine	**Glühwein**	**glew**vighn
port	**Portwein**	**port**vighn
rum	**einen Rum**	**ighnern** rum
vermouth	**einen Wermut**	**ighnern vayr**moot
vodka	**einen Wodka**	**ighnern vot**kah
whisky	**einen Whisky**	**ighnern** "whisky"
neat (straight)	**pur**	poor
on the rocks	**mit Eis**	mit **ighss**

You'll certainly want to take the occasion to sip a liqueur or brandy after your meal. The names of some well-known wine-distilled brandies are *Asbach-Uralt, Chantré* and *Dujardin*. Here are some other after-dinner drinks:

Are there any local specialities?	**Haben Sie hiesige Spezialitäten?**	haabern zee heezigger shpehtsiahlitaitern
I'd like to try a glass of ..., please.	**Ich möchte ein Glas ... probieren.**	ikh murkhter ighn glaass ... proabeerern
Apfelschnaps	ahpferlshnahps	apple brandy
Aprikosenlikör	ahprikkoazernlikkurr	apricot liqueur
Birnenschnaps	beernernshnahps	pear brandy
Bommerlunder	bommerrlunderr	caraway-flavoured brandy
Doornkaat	dornkaat	German gin, juniper-berry brandy
Eierlikör	igherrlikkurr	eggflip, eggnog
Heidelbeergeist	highderlbayrgighst	blueberry brandy
Himbeergeist	himbayrgighst	raspberry brandy
Himbeerlikör	himbayrlikkurr	raspberry liqueur
Kirschlikör	kirshlikkurr	cherry liqueur
Kirschwasser	kirshvahsserr	cherry brandy
(Doppel)Korn	(dopperl)korn	grain-distilled liquor, akin to whisky
Kümmel	kewmerl	caraway-flavoured liquor
Obstler	oapstlerr	fruit brandy
Pflümli(wasser)	pflewmli(vahsserr)	plum brandy
Steinhäger	shtighnhaigerr	juniperberry brandy, akin to gin
Träsch	traish	pear and apple brandy
Weizenkorn	vightsernkorn	wheat-distilled liquor, akin to whisky
Zwetschgenwasser	tsvehtshgernvahsserr	plum brandy

> **ZUM WOHL / PROST!**
> (tsum voal / proast)
> YOUR HEALTH / CHEERS!

Nonalcoholic drinks *Alkoholfreie Getränke*

I'd like a/an ...	Ich hätte gern ...	ikh hehter gehrn
apple juice	einen Apfelsaft	ighnern ahpferlzahft
currant juice (red or black)	einen Johannisbeer- saft	ighnern yohhahnisbayrzaft
fruit juice	einen Fruchtsaft	ighnern frukhtzahft
grape juice	einen Traubensaft	ighnern trowbernzahft
herb tea	einen Kräutertee	ighnern kroyterrtay
iced tea	einen Eistee	ighnern ighstay
lemonade	eine Limonade	ighner limmonnaader
(glass of) milk	(ein Glas) Milch	(ighn glaass) milkh
milkshake	ein Milchmixgetränk	ighn milkhmiksgertrehnk
mineral water	ein Mineralwasser	ighn minnerraalvahsserr
fizzy (carbonated)	mit Kohlensäure	mit koalernzoyrer
still	ohne Kohlensäure	oaner koalernzoyrer
orange juice	einen Orangensaft	ighnern orrahngzhernzahft
orangeade	eine Orangeade	ighner orahngzhaader
tomato juice	einen Tomatensaft	ighnern tommaaternzahft
tonic water	ein Tonic	ighn tonnik

Hot beverages *Warme Getränke*

Perhaps you'd like a coffee after dinner. In Austria, you can't ask for just "a cup of coffee"; the varieties are endless. There, you can ask for anything from a *Nußschwarzer* (**nus**shvahrtserr) or *Neger* (**nay**gerr)—strong black coffee— to an *Einspänner* (**ighn**shpehnerr)—topped with whipped cream—or a *Melange* (may**lahng**zher)—coffee and hot milk.

I'd like a/an ...	Ich hätte gern ...	ikh hehter gehrn
(hot) chocolate	eine (heiße) Schokolade	ighner (highsser) shokkollaader
coffee	einen Kaffee	ighnern kahfay
with cream	mit Sahne	mit zaaner
with milk	einen Milchkaffee	ighnern milkhkahfay
black/caffeine- free coffee	einen schwarzen/ koffeinfreien Kaffee	ighnern shvahrtsern/ koffeheenfrighern kahfay
espresso coffee	einen Expresso	ighnern ehksprehsoa
mokka	einen Mokka	ighnern mokkah
tea	einen Tee	ighnern tay
cup of tea	eine Tasse Tee	ighner tahsser tay
with milk/lemon	mit Milch/Zitrone	mit milkh/tsitroaner

Complaints *Reklamationen*

There is a plate/glass missing.	Es fehlt ein Teller/ein Glas.	ehss faylt ighn tehlerr/ighn glaass
I have no knife/fork/spoon.	Ich habe kein Messer/keine Gabel/keinen Löffel.	ikh haaber kighn mehsserr/kighner gaaberl/kighnern lurferl
That's not what I ordered.	Das habe ich nicht bestellt.	dahss haaber ikh nikht berstehlt
I asked for ...	Ich wollte ...	ikh volter
There must be some mistake.	Es muß ein Irrtum sein.	ehss muss ighn irtoom zighn
May I change this?	Können Sie mir dafür etwas anderes bringen?	kurnern zee meer daafewr ehtvahss ahnderrerss bringern
I asked for a small portion (for the child).	Ich wollte eine kleine Portion (für das Kind).	ikh volter ighner klighner portsioan (fewr dahss kint)
The meat is ...	Das Fleisch ist ...	dahss flighsh ist
overdone	zu stark gebraten	tsu shtahrk gerbraatern
underdone (too rare)	zu roh	tsu roa
too tough	zu zäh	tsu tsai
This is too ...	Das ist zu ...	dahss ist tsu
bitter/sour	bitter/sauer	bitter/zowerr
salty/sweet	salzig/süß	zahltsikh/zewss
I don't like this.	Das schmeckt mir nicht.	dahs shmehkt meer nikht
The food is cold.	Das Essen ist kalt.	dahss ehssern ist kahlt
This isn't fresh.	Das ist nicht frisch.	dahss ist nikht frish
What's taking you so long?	Weshalb dauert es so lange?	vehshahlp dowerrt ehss zoa lahnger
Have you forgotten our drinks?	Haben Sie unsere Getränke vergessen?	haabern zee unzerrer gertrehnker fehrgehssern
The wine is corked.	Der Wein schmeckt nach Korken.	derr vighn shmehkt naakh koarkern
This isn't clean.	Das ist nicht sauber.	dahss ist nikht zowberr
Would you ask the head waiter to come over?	Würden Sie bitte den Oberkellner rufen?	vewrdern zee bitter dayn oaberrkehlnerr roofern

The bill (check) *Die Rechnung*

A service charge is generally included automatically in restaurant bills. Anything extra for the waiter is optional. Credit cards may be used in an increasing number of restaurants.

I'd like to pay.	**Ich möchte zahlen.**	ikh **murkh**ter **tsaa**lern
We'd like to pay separately.	**Wir möchten getrennt bezahlen.**	veer **murkh**tern geh**trehnt** bert**saa**lern
I think you made a mistake in this bill.	**Ich glaube, Sie haben sich verrechnet.**	ikh **glow**ber zee **haa**bern zikh fehr**rehkh**nert
What is this amount for?	**Wofür ist dieser Betrag?**	voa**fewr** ist **dee**zerr ber**traakh**
Is service included?	**Ist die Bedienung inbegriffen?**	ist dee ber**dee**nung **in**bergriffern
Do you accept traveller's cheques?	**Nehmen Sie Reise-schecks?**	**nay**mern zee **righ**zer-shehks
Can I pay with this credit card?	**Kann ich mit dieser Kreditkarte bezahlen?**	kahn ikh mit **dee**zerr kray**dit**kahrter bert**saa**lern
That was a very good meal.	**Das Essen war sehr gut.**	dahss **eh**ssern vaar zayr goot

> **BEDIENUNG INBEGRIFFEN**
> SERVICE INCLUDED

Snacks—Picnic *Imbiß – Picknick*

A *Café* (in Austria *Kaffeehaus*) will serve anything from simple pastries to luscious, monumental sweet delicacies and often snacks. For a fast meal the German *Schnellimbiß* (snack bar) is the place. Ordering is easy since most of the snacks are on display. And if you are in a hurry have a sausage at a *Würstchenstand*.

Give me two of these and one of those.	**Geben Sie mir davon zwei und davon eins.**	**gay**bern zee meer **daa**fon tsvigh unt **daa**fon ighns
to the left/right above/below	**links/rechts darüber/darunter**	links/**rehkh**ts da**rew**berr/da**run**terr
It's to take away.	**Es ist zum Mitnehmen.**	ehss ist tsum **mit**naymern

TIPPING, see inside back-cover

I'd like a piece of cake.	Ich hätte gern ein Stück Kuchen.	ikh **heh**ter gehrn ighn shtewk **koo**khern
fried sausage	eine Bratwurst	**igh**ner **braat**voorst
omelet	ein Omelett	ighn om**leht**
open sandwich	ein belegtes Brot	ighn ber**layg**terss broat
with ham	mit Schinken	mit **shin**kern
with cheese	mit Käse	mit **kai**zer
potato salad	Kartoffelsalat	kahr**tof**ferlzahlaat
sandwich	ein Sandwich	ighn **sehnd**vitsh

Here's a basic list of food and drink that might come in useful when shopping for a picnic.

I'd like a/an/ some ...	Ich hätte gern ...	ikh **heh**ter gehrn
apples	Äpfel	**ehp**ferl
bananas	Bananen	bah**naa**nern
biscuits (Br.)	Kekse	**kayk**ser
beer	Bier	beer
bread	ein Brot	ighn broat
butter	Butter	**butt**err
cheese	Käse	**kai**zer
chips (Am.)	Kartoffelchips	kahr**tof**ferlcheeps
chocolate bar	eine Tafel Schoko-lade	**igh**ner **taa**ferl shokkol-**laa**der
coffee	Kaffee	**kah**fay
cold cuts	Aufschnitt	**owf**shnit
cookies	Kekse	**kayk**ser
crisps	Kartoffelchips	kahr**tof**ferlcheeps
eggs	Eier	**igh**err
gherkins (pickles)	Essiggurken	**ehss**ikhgoorkern
grapes	Trauben	**trow**bern
ice-cream	ein Eis	ighn ighss
milk	Milch	milkh
mustard	Senf	zehnf
oranges	Orangen	or**rahng**zhern
pepper	Pfeffer	**pfeh**ferr
rolls	Brötchen	**brurt**khern
salt	Salz	zahlts
sausage	eine Wurst	**igh**ner voorst
soft drink	ein alkoholfreies Getränk	ighn **ahl**kohoalfrigherss ger**trehnk**
sugar	Zucker	**tsuk**kerr
tea	Tee	tay
yoghurt	Joghurt	**yoa**goort

Travelling around

Plane *Flugzeug*

Is there a flight to Vienna?	**Gibt es einen Flug nach Wien?**	gipt ehss **igh**nern floog naakh veen
Is it a direct flight?	**Ist es ein Direktflug?**	ist ehss ighn dir**rehkt**floog
When's the next flight to Hamburg?	**Wann ist der nächste Flug nach Hamburg?**	vahn ist derr **naikh**ster floog nahkh **hahm**boorg
Do I have to change planes?	**Muß ich umsteigen?**	muss ikh **um**shtighgern
Can I make a connection to Cologne?	**Habe ich Anschluß nach Köln?**	**haa**berr ikh **ahn**shluss nahkh kurln
I'd like a ticket to Zurich.	**Bitte ein Flugticket nach Zürich.**	bitter ighn **floog**tikkert naakh **tsew**rikh
single (one-way) return (roundtrip)	**Hinflug Hin- und Rückflug**	**hin**floog hin unt **rewk**floog
What time does the plane take off?	**Wann ist der Abflug?**	vahn ist derr **ahp**floog
What time do I have to check in?	**Wann muß ich einchecken?**	vahn muss ikh **ighn**shehkern
Is there an airport-bus?	**Gibt es einen Flughafenbus?**	gipt ehss **igh**nern **floog**haafernbuss
What's the flight number?	**Welche Flugnummer ist es?**	**vehl**kher **floog**nummerr ist ehss
What time do we arrive?	**Wann landen wir?**	vahn **lahn**dern veer
I'd like to ... my reservation.	**Ich möchte meine Reservierung ...**	ikh **murkh**ter **migh**ner rehzer**vee**rung
cancel change confirm	**annullieren umbuchen bestätigen**	ahn**ullee**rern **um**bookhern ber**shtai**tiggern

ANKUNFT ARRIVAL	**ABFLUG** DEPARTURE

Train *Eisenbahn*

Travel on the main railway lines is generally fast, and the trains run on time. First-class coaches are comfortable; second-class, more than adequate.

TEE (tay-ay-ay)	Trans-Europ-Express: a luxury international service for which you pay a surcharge; reservation compulsory
Intercity ("intercity")	Long distance inter-city trains; some only first, others with first and second class, with surcharge; in Switzerland the equivalent of the Austrian *Städteschnellzug*
City-D-Zug ("city"-**day**-tsoog)	Short-distance inter-city trains, with few stops at major points only; first and second class with surcharge on trips of less than 50 kilometres (Germany)
D-Zug (**day**-tsoog)	Intermediate- to long-distance trains (Germany)
Schnellzug (shneh**l**tsoog)	Fast trains, stop at big and medium towns (Austria, Switzerland)
Städteschnellzug (shteh**t**ershnehltsoog)	Fast trains, connecting the biggest towns (Austria)
Expreßzug (ayks**prehs**tsoog)	Fast trains, stop at big and medium towns (Austria)
Eilzug (**ighl**tsoog)	Medium-distance trains, not stopping at small stations (Germany, Austria)
Nahverkehrszug (**naa**fehrkayrstsoog)	Local trains, stopping at all stations; in Austria called *Personenzug* and in Switzerland *Regionalzug*
Triebwagen (**treep**vaagern)	Small diesel coach used for short runs (Austria, Germany); in Germany sometimes *Schienenbus*

Here are a few more useful terms:

Speisewagen (**shpigh**zervaagern)	Dining-car
Schlafwagen (**shlaaf**vaagern)	Sleeping-car, compartments with wash basins and 1, 2 or 3 berths
Liegewagen (**lee**gervaagern)	Coach containing berths with sheets, blankets and pillows

To the railway station *Unterwegs zum Bahnhof*

Where's the railway station?	**Wo ist der Bahnhof?**	voa ist derr **baan**hoaf
Taxi, please!	**Taxi bitte!**	**tahk**si **bitter**
Take me to the ...	**Fahren Sie mich ...**	**faa**rern zee mikh
main railway station	**zum Hauptbahnhof**	tsum **howpt**baanhoaf
railway station	**zum Bahnhof**	tsum **baan**hoaf
What's the fare?	**Was macht das?**	vahss mahkht dahss

EINGANG	ENTRANCE
AUSGANG	EXIT
ZU DEN BAHNSTEIGEN	TO THE PLATFORMS
AUSKUNFT	INFORMATION

Where's the ...? *Wo ist ...?*

Where is/are the ...?	**Wo ist/sind ...?**	voa ist/zint
booking office	**die Platz-reservierung**	dee **plahts**rehzerrveerung
currency-exchange	**die Wechselstube**	dee **wehk**zerlshtoober
left-luggage office (baggage check)	**die Gepäckauf-bewahrung**	dee ger**pehk**owfbervaarung
lost property (lost-and-found) office	**das Fundbüro**	dahss **funt**bewroa
luggage lockers	**die Schließfächer**	dee **shlees**fehkherr
newsstand	**der Zeitungsstand**	derr **tsight**ungsshtahnt
platform 3	**Bahnsteig 3**	**baan**shtighg 3
reservations office	**die Platz-reservierung**	dee **plahts**rehzerrveerung
restaurant	**das Restaurant**	dahss rehstor**rahng**
snack bar	**der Schnellimbiß**	derr **shneh**limbiss
ticket office	**der Fahrkarten-schalter**	derr **faar**kahrternshahlterr
track 7	**Gleis 7**	**glighss** 7
waiting room	**der Wartesaal**	derr **vahrter**zaal
Where are the toilets?	**Wo sind die Toiletten?**	voa zint dee toah**leh**tern

TAXI, see page 21

Inquiries *Auskunft*

When is the ... train to Kiel?	**Wann fährt der ... Zug nach Kiel?**	vahn fairt derr ... tsoog naakh keel
first/last/next	**erste/letzte/nächste**	ehrster/lehtster/naikhster
What's the fare to Basle?	**Was kostet die Fahrt nach Basel?**	vahss kostert dee faart naakh baazerl
Is it a through train?	**Ist es ein durchgehender Zug?**	ist ehss ighn doorkhgayernderr tsoog
Must I pay a surcharge?	**Muß ich einen Zuschlag bezahlen?**	muss ikh ighnern tsushlaag bertsahlern
Is there a connection to ...?	**Gibt es einen Anschluß nach ...?**	gipt ehss ighnern ahnshluss naakh
Do I have to change trains?	**Muß ich umsteigen?**	muss ikh umshtighgern
Is there sufficient time to change?	**Reicht die Zeit zum Umsteigen?**	righkht dee tsight tsum umshtighgern
Will the train leave on time?	**Fährt der Zug pünktlich ab?**	fairt derr tsoog pewnktlikh ahp
What time does the train arrive at Münster?	**Wann kommt der Zug in Münster an?**	vahn komt derr tsoog in mewnsterr ahn
Is there a dining-car/sleeping-car on the train?	**Führt der Zug einen Speisewagen/Schlafwagen?**	fewrt derr tsoog ighnern shpighzervaagern/shlaafvaagern
Does the train stop at Ingolstadt?	**Hält der Zug in Ingolstadt?**	hehlt derr tsoog in ingolshtaht
What platform does the train for Bonn leave from?	**Auf welchem Bahnsteig fährt der Zug nach Bonn ab?**	owf vehlkherm baanshtighg fairt derr tsoog naakh bon ahp
What track does the train from Hamburg arrive at?	**Auf welchem Gleis kommt der Zug aus Hamburg an?**	owf vehlkherm glighss komt derr tsoog owss hahmboorg ahn
I'd like a time-table.	**Ich hätte gern einen Fahrplan.**	ikh hehter gehrn ighnern faarplaan

| **ANKUNFT** ARRIVAL | **ABFAHRT** DEPARTURE |

Es ist ein durchgehender Zug.	It's a through train.
Sie müssen in ... umsteigen.	You have to change at ...
Steigen Sie in Heidelberg in einen Nahverkehrszug um.	Change at Heidelberg and get a local train.
Bahnsteig 7 ist ...	Platform 7 is ...
dort drüben/oben/unten links/rechts	over there/upstairs/downstairs on the left/on the right
Es gibt einen Zug nach Bonn um ...	There's a train to Bonn at ...
Ihr Zug fährt auf Gleis ... ab.	Your train will leave from track ...
Der Zug hat ... Minuten Verspätung.	There'll be a delay of ... minutes.
Erste Klasse an der Spitze/in der Mitte/ am Ende des Zuges.	First class at the front/ in the middle/at the end.

Tickets *Fahrkarten*

I want a ticket to ...	Ich möchte eine Fahrkarte nach ...	ikh **murkh**ter **ig**hner **faar**kahrter naakh
single (one-way)	einfach	**ig**hnfahkh
return (roundtrip)	hin und zurück	hin unt **stoo**rewk
first class	erste Klasse	**ehr**ster **klah**sser
second class	zweite Klasse	**tsvigh**ter **klah**sser
half price	zum halben Preis	tsum **hah**lbern **prigh**ss

Reservation *Reservierung*

I want to book a ...	Ich möchte ... reservieren lassen.	ikh **murkh**ter ... **reh**zerr-**vee**rern **lah**ssern
seat (by the window)	einen (Fenster)platz	**ig**hnern (**fehn**sterr)plahts
berth	einen Platz im Liegewagen	**ig**hnern plahts im **lee**gervaagern
upper	oben	**oa**bern
middle	in der Mitte	in derr **mit**ter
lower	unten	**un**tern
berth in the sleeping car	einen Platz im Schlafwagen	**ig**hnern plahts im **shlaaf**vaagern

NUMBERS, see page 147

All aboard *Einsteigen bitte*

Is this the right platform for the train to Vienna?	**Ist das der richtige Bahnsteig für den Zug nach Wien?**	ist dahss derr **rikh**tigger **baan**shtighg fewr dayn tsoog naakh veen
Is this the right train to Graz?	**Ist das der Zug nach Graz?**	ist dahss derr tsoog naakh graats
Excuse me. May I get by?	**Verzeihung. Kann ich vorbei?**	**fehrtsigh**ung. kahn ikh for**bigh**
Is this seat taken?	**Ist dieser Platz besetzt?**	ist **dee**zerr plahts ber**zehtst**

RAUCHER SMOKER	**NICHTRAUCHER** NONSMOKER

I think that's my seat.	**Ich glaube, das ist mein Platz.**	ikh **glow**ber dahss ist mighn plahts
Would you let me know before we get to Bamberg?	**Sagen Sie mir bitte, wenn wir in Bamberg ankommen?**	**zaa**gern zee mir **bit**ter vehn veer in **bahm**behrg **ahn**kommern
What station is this?	**Wie heißt dieser Ort?**	vee highst **dee**zerr ort
How long does the train stop here?	**Wie lange hält der Zug hier?**	vee **lahn**ger hehlt derr tsoog heer
When do we get to Cologne?	**Wann kommen wir in Köln an?**	vahn **kom**mern veer in kurln ahn

Sleeping *Im Schlafwagen*

Are there any free compartments in the sleeping-car?	**Sind im Schlafwagen noch Abteile frei?**	zint im **shlaaf**vaagern nokh **ahp**tighler frigh
Where's the sleeping-car?	**Wo ist der Schlafwagen?**	voa ist derr **shlaaf**vaagern
Where's my berth?	**Wo ist mein Schlafplatz?**	voa ist mighn **shlaaf**plahts
I'd like a lower berth.	**Ich möchte unten schlafen.**	ikh **murkh**ter **un**tern **shlaa**fern

Would you make up our berths?	**Würden Sie unsere Schlafplätze machen?**	vewrdern zee unzerrer shlaafplehtser mahkhern
Would you call me at 7 o'clock?	**Würden Sie mich um 7 Uhr wecken?**	vewrdern zee mikh um 7 oor vehkern
Would you bring me coffee in the morning?	**Würden Sie mir bitte morgen früh Kaffee bringen?**	vewrdern zee meer bitter morgern frew kahfay bringern

Eating *Im Speisewagen*

You can get snacks and drinks in the buffet-car and in the dining-car when it isn't being used for main meals. On some trains an attendant comes around with a cart with snacks, tea, coffee and soft drinks.

| Where's the dining-car? | **Wo ist der Speisewagen?** | voa ist derr shpighzer-vaagern |

Baggage—Porters *Gepäck – Gepäckträger*

Porter!	**Gepäckträger!**	gerpehktraiger
Can you help me with my luggage?	**Können Sie mir mit meinem Gepäck helfen?**	kurnern zee mir mit mighnerm gerpehk hehlfern
Where are the luggage trolleys (carts)?	**Wo sind die Koffer-kulis?**	voa zint dee kofferr-kooliss
Where are the luggage lockers?	**Wo sind die Schließfächer?**	voa zint dee shleesfehkherr
Where's the left-luggage office (baggage check)?	**Wo ist die Gepäck-aufbewahrung?**	voa ist dee gerpehk-owfbervaarung
I'd like to leave my luggage, please.	**Ich möchte mein Gepäck einstellen.**	ikh murkhter mighn gerpehk ighnshtehlern
I'd like to register (check) my luggage.	**Ich möchte mein Gepäck aufgeben.**	ikh murkhter mighn gerpehk owfgaybern

---

GEPÄCKAUFGABE
REGISTERING (CHECKING) BAGGAGE

PORTERS, see also page 18

Coach (long-distance bus) *Überlandbus*

To reach out-of-the-way places, you'll find frequent bus services available including the *Kraftpost* or *Postauto*. You'll find information on destinations and timetables at the coach terminals, usually situated near railway stations.

When's the next coach to ...?	**Wann fährt der nächste Bus nach ...?**	vahn fairt derr **naikh**ster buss naakh
Does the coach stop at ...?	**Hält der Bus in ...?**	hehlt derr buss in
How long does the journey (trip) take?	**Wie lange dauert die Fahrt?**	vee **lahng**er **dow**errt dee faart

Note: Most of the phrases on the previous pages can be used or adapted for travelling on local transport.

Bus—Tram (streetcar) *Bus – Straßenbahn*

In most cities you'll find automatic ticket dispensers at each stop enabling you to buy your ticket in advance. In major cities it may be worthwhile to get a pass or a booklet of tickets.

I'd like a pass/booklet of tickets.	**Ich möchte eine Mehrfahrkarte/ein Fahrscheinheft.**	ikh **murkh**ter **ighn**er **mayr**faarkahrter/ighn **faars**highnhehft
Which tram (streetcar) goes to the centre of town?	**Welche Straßenbahn fährt ins Stadtzentrum?**	**vehl**kher shtraassernbaan fairt ins **shtaht**tsehntrum
Where can I get a bus into town?	**Wo hält der Bus, der ins Stadtzentrum fährt?**	voa hehlt derr buss derr ins **shtaht**tsehntrum fairt
What bus do I take for ...?	**Welchen Bus muß ich nach ... nehmen?**	**vehl**khern buss muss ikh naakh ... **nay**mern
Where's the ...?	**Wo ist ...?**	voa ist
bus stop terminus	**die Bushaltestelle die Endstation**	dee **buss**hahltershtehler dee **ehnt**shtahtsioan
When is the ... bus to ...?	**Wann fährt der ... Bus nach ...?**	vahn fairt derr ... buss naakh
first/last/next	**erste/letzte/nächste**	**ehr**ster/**lehts**ter/**naikh**ster

How often do the buses to the airport run?	**Wie oft fahren die Busse zum Flughafen?**	vee oft **faa**rern dee **bus**ser tsum **floog**haafern
How much is the fare to ...?	**Was kostet es nach ...?**	vahss **kos**tert ehss naakh
Do I have to change buses?	**Muß ich umsteigen?**	muss ikh **um**shtighgern
How many bus stops are there to ...?	**Wie viele Haltestellen sind es bis ...?**	vee **fee**ler **hahl**tershtehlern zint ehss biss
Will you tell me when to get off?	**Können Sie mir bitte sagen, wann ich aussteigen muß?**	**kur**nern zee meer **bit**ter **zaa**gern vahn ikh **owss**shtighgern muss
I want to get off at the next stop.	**Ich möchte an der nächsten Haltestelle aussteigen.**	ikh **murkh**ter ahn derr **naikh**stern **hahl**tershtehler **owss**shtighgern

| **BUSHALTESTELLE** | REGULAR BUS STOP |
| **BEDARFSHALTESTELLE** | STOPS ON REQUEST |

Underground (subway) *U-Bahn*

The *U-Bahn* (**oo**-baan) in Berlin, Bonn, Düsseldorf, Cologne, Frankfurt, Hamburg and Munich corresponds to the London underground or the New York subway. A map showing the various lines and stations is displayed outside every station.

Where's the nearest underground station?	**Wo ist die nächste U-Bahnstation?**	voa ist dee **naikh**ster **oo**-baanshtahtsioan
Does this train go to ...?	**Fährt dieser Zug nach ...?**	fairt **dee**zerr tsoog naakh
Where do I change for ...?	**Wo muß ich nach ... umsteigen?**	voa muss ikh naakh ... **um**shtighgern
Is the next station ...?	**Ist die nächste Station ...?**	ist dee **naikh**ster shtahtsioan
Which line should I take for ...?	**Welche Linie fährt nach ...?**	**vehl**kher **lee**nier fairt naakh

Boat service *Auf dem Schiff*

When does a boat for ... leave?	**Wann fährt ein Schiff nach ...?**	vahn fairt ighn shif naakh
Where's the embarkation point?	**Wo ist der Anlege-platz?**	voa ist derr **ahn**layger-plahts
When do we call at Cologne?	**Wann legen wir in Köln an?**	vahn **lay**gern veer in kurln ahn
I'd like to take a harbour roundtour.	**Ich möchte eine Hafenrundfahrt machen.**	ikh **murkh**ter **ighn**er haa-fern**runt**aart **mah**khern
boat	**das Schiff/das Boot**	dahss shif/dahss boat
cabin	**die Kabine**	dee kah**bee**ner
single	**Einzelkabine**	**ighnt**serlkah**bee**ner
double	**Zweierkabine**	**tsvigh**errkah**bee**ner
cruise	**die Kreuzfahrt**	dee **kroyts**faart
crossing	**die Überfahrt**	dee **ew**berrfaart
deck	**das Deck**	dahss dehk
ferry	**die Fähre**	dee **fai**rer
hydrofoil	**das Tragflächenboot**	dahss **traag**flehkhernboat
life belt	**der Rettungsring**	derr **reh**tungsring
life boat	**das Rettungsboot**	dahss **reh**tungsboat
port	**der Hafen**	derr **haa**fern
river cruise	**die Flußfahrt**	dee **flus**faart
ship	**das Schiff**	dahss shif
steamer	**das Dampfschiff**	dahss **dahmpf**shif

Bicycle hire *Fahrradverleih*

Many railway stations provide a bicycle-hire service.

| I'd like to hire a bicycle. | **Ich möchte ein Fahrrad mieten.** | ikh **murkh**ter ighn **faar**raat **mee**tern |

Other means of transport *Weitere Transportmittel*

cable car	**die Seilbahn**	dee **zighl**baan
helicopter	**der Hubschrauber**	derr **hoop**shrowberr
moped	**das Moped**	dahss **moa**peht
motorbike	**das Motorrad**	dahss **moa**torraat
scooter	**der Motorroller**	derr **moa**torrollerr

Or perhaps you prefer:

to hike	**wandern**	**vahn**derrn
to hitchhike	**trampen**	**trehm**pern
to walk	**zu Fuß gehen**	tsoo fuss **gay**ern

Car *Das Auto*

In general roads are good in Germany, Austria and Switzerland. Motorways (expressways) are free in Germany. In Austria some Alpine roads and tunnels charge tolls *(die Maut)*. If you use the motorways in Switzerland you must purchase a sticker *(die Vignette)* to be displayed on the windscreen.

A red reflector warning triangle must be carried for use in case of a breakdown, and seat-belts *(der Sicherheitsgurt)* are obligatory. In winter snow tyres or chains are compulsory on Alpine passes.

Where's the nearest filling station?	**Wo ist die nächste Tankstelle?**	voa ist dee **naikh**ster **tahnk**shtehler
Full tank, please.	**Volltanken, bitte.**	**volt**ahnkern **bitter**
Give me ... litres of petrol (gasoline).	**Geben Sie mir ... Liter Benzin.**	**gay**bern zee mir ... **lee**terr behn**tseen**
super (premium)/ regular/lead-free/ diesel	**Super/Normal/ bleifreies Benzin/ Diesel**	**zoo**perr/nor**maal**/ **bligh**frigherss behn**tseen**/ **dee**zerl
Please check the ...	**Kontrollieren Sie bitte ...**	kontro**lee**rern zee **bitter**
battery	**die Batterie**	dee bahteh**ree**
brake fluid	**die Bremsflüssigkeit**	dee **brehms**flewssikh**kight**
oil	**das Öl**	dahss url
water	**das Wasser**	dahss **vahs**serr
Would you check the tyre pressure?	**Würden Sie bitte den Reifendruck prüfen?**	**vew**rdern zee **bitter** dayn **righ**ferndruk **prewf**ern
1.6 front, 1.8 rear.	**Vorne 1,6, hinten 1,8.**	**for**ner ighns zehks **hint**ern ighns ahkht
Please check the spare tyre, too.	**Prüfen Sie auch den Ersatzreifen, bitte.**	**prewf**ern zee owkh dayn ehr**zahts**righern **bitter**
Can you mend this puncture (fix this flat)?	**Können Sie diesen Reifen flicken?**	**kurn**ern zee **dee**zern **righ**fern **flik**kern
Would you please change the ...?	**Würden Sie bitte ... wechseln?**	**vew**rdern zee **bitter** ... **vehk**serln
bulb	**die Glühbirne**	dee **glew**birner
fan belt	**den Keilriemen**	dayn **kighl**reemern

CAR HIRE, see page 20

spark(ing) plugs	die Zündkerzen	dee tsewntkehrtsern
tyre	den Reifen	dayn righfern
wipers	die Scheibenwischer	dee shighbernvisherr
Would you clean the windscreen (windshield)?	Würden Sie bitte die Windschutzscheibe reinigen?	vewrdern zee bitter dee vintshutsshighber righniggern

Asking the way—Street directions *Nach dem Weg fragen*

Can you tell me the way to ...?	Können Sie mir sagen, wie ich nach ... komme?	kurnern zee meer zaagern vee ikh naakh ... kommer
How do I get to ...?	Wie komme ich nach ...?	vee kommer ikh naakh ...
Are we on the right road for ...?	Sind wir auf der richtigen Straße nach ...?	zint veer owf derr rikhtiggern shtraasser naakh
How far is the next village?	Wie weit ist es bis zum nächsten Dorf?	vee vight ist ehss biss tsum nehkhstern dorf
How far is it to ... from here?	Wie weit ist es von hier nach ...?	vee vight ist ehss fon heer naakh
Is there a motorway (expressway)?	Gibt es eine Autobahn?	gipt ehss ighner owtobbaan
Is there a road with little traffic?	Gibt es eine wenig befahrene Straße?	gipt ehss ighner vaynikh berfaarerner shtraasser
How long does it take by car/on foot?	Wie lange dauert es mit dem Auto/ zu Fuß?	vee lahnger dowerrt ehss mit daym owto/tsoo fuss
Can I drive to the centre of town?	Kann ich bis ins Stadtzentrum fahren?	kahn ikh biss ins shtahttsehntrum faarern
Can you tell me, where ... is?	Können Sie mir sagen, wo ... ist?	kurnern zee meer zaagern voa ... ist
Where can I find this address/place?	Wie komme ich zu dieser Adresse/ diesem Ort?	vee kommer ikh tsoo deezerr ahdrehsser/ deezerm ort
Where's this?	Wo ist das?	voa ist dahss
Can you show me on the map where I am?	Können Sie mir auf der Karte zeigen, wo ich bin?	kurnern zee meer owf derr kahrter tsighgern voa ikh bin

Sie sind auf der falschen Straße.	You're on the wrong road.
Fahren Sie geradeaus.	Go straight ahead.
Es ist dort vorne ...	It's down there on the ...
links/rechts	left/right
gegenüber/hinter ...	opposite/behind ...
neben/nach ...	next to/after ...
Nord/Süd/Ost/West	north/south/east/west
Fahren Sie bis zur ersten/ zweiten Kreuzung.	Go to the first/second crossroad (intersection).
Biegen Sie bei der Ampel links ab.	Turn left at the traffic lights.
Biegen Sie bei der nächsten Ecke rechts ab.	Turn right at the next corner.
Nehmen Sie die Straße nach ...	Take the road for ...
Sie müssen zurück nach ...	You have to go back to ...

Parking *Parken*

In town centres there are blue zones for which you need a parking disk (*eine Parkscheibe*—**igh**nerr **pahrk**shighber). You set it to show when you arrived and when you must leave. The disk can be obtained from tourist offices, petrol stations and hotels.

Where can I park?	**Wo kann ich parken?**	voa kahn ikh **pahr**kern
Is there a car park nearby?	**Gibt es einen Park- platz hier in der Nähe?**	gipt ehss **igh**nern pahrk- plahts heer in derr **nai**er
May I park here?	**Darf ich hier parken?**	dahrf ikh heer **pahr**kern
How long can I park here?	**Wie lange kann ich hier parken?**	vee **lah**nger kahn ikh heer **pahr**kern
What's the charge per hour?	**Wieviel kostet es pro Stunde?**	vee**feel kos**tert ehss proa **shtun**der
Do you have some change for the parking meter?	**Haben Sie Kleingeld für die Parkuhr?**	**haa**bern zee **klighn**gehlt fewr dee **pahr**koor

Breakdown—Road assistance   *Panne – Pannendienst*

Where's the nearest garage?	**Wo ist die nächste Reparaturwerkstatt?**	voa ist dee **naikh**ster raypahrah**toor**vehrkshtaht
Excuse me. My car has broken down.	**Entschuldigung, mein Wagen hat eine Panne.**	ehnt**shul**diggung mighn **vaa**gern haht **igh**ner **pah**ner
I've had a breakdown.	**Ich habe eine Panne.**	ikh **haa**ber **igh**ner **pah**ner
Can you send a mechanic?	**Können Sie einen Mechaniker schicken?**	**kur**nern zee **igh**nern meh**khah**nikkerr **shik**kern
My car won't start.	**Mein Auto springt nicht an.**	mighn **ow**to shpringt nikht ahn
The battery is dead.	**Die Batterie ist leer.**	dee bahteh**ree** ist layr
I've run out of petrol (gasoline).	**Ich habe eine Benzinpanne.**	ikh **haa**ber **igh**ner behnt**seen**pahner
I have a flat tyre.	**Ich habe einen Platten.**	ikh **haa**ber **igh**nern **plah**tern
The engine is overheating.	**Der Motor läuft heiß.**	derr **moa**tor loyft highss
There is something wrong with ...	**... ist/sind nicht in Ordnung.**	... ist/zint nikht in **ort**nung
brakes	**die Bremsen**	dee **brehm**zern
carburettor	**der Vergaser**	derr **fehr**gaazerr
exhaust pipe	**der Auspuff**	derr **ows**puf
radiator	**der Kühler**	derr **kew**lerr
a wheel	**ein Rad**	ighn roat
Can you send a breakdown van (tow truck)?	**Können Sie einen Abschleppwagen schicken?**	**kur**nern zee **igh**nern **ahp**shlehpvaagern **shik**kern
How long will you be?	**Wie lange dauert es?**	vee **lahn**ger **dow**errt ehss

Accident—Police   *Verkehrsunfall – Polizei*

Please call the police.	**Rufen Sie bitte die Polizei.**	**roo**fern zee **bit**ter dee polli**tsigh**
There's been an accident. It's about 2 km. from ...	**Es ist ein Unfall passiert, ungefähr 2 Kilometer von ...**	ehss ist ighn **un**fahl pahss**eert un**gerfair 2 killoam**may**terr fon

Where's the nearest telephone?	Wo ist das nächste Telefon?	voa ist dahss **naikh**ster taylay**foan**
Call a doctor/an ambulance, quickly.	Rufen Sie schnell einen Arzt/einen Krankenwagen.	**roo**fern zee shnehl **igh**nern ahr**tst**/**igh**nern **krahn**kernvaagern
There are people injured.	Es hat Verletzte gegeben.	ehss haht fehr**leht**ster ger**gay**bern
Here's my driving licence.	Hier ist mein Führerschein.	heer ist mighn **few**rershighn
What's your name and address?	Ihr Name und Ihre Anschrift, bitte?	eer **naa**mer unt **ee**rer **ahn**shrift **bit**ter
What's your insurance company?	Ihre Versicherungsgesellschaft, bitte?	**ee**rer fehr**zee**kherrungsger**zehl**shahft **bit**ter

Road signs *Verkehrszeichen*

AUSFAHRT	Exit (motorway)
DURCHGANGSVERKEHR	Through traffic
EINBAHNSTRASSE	One-way street
EINORDNEN	Get in lane
FROSTSCHÄDEN	Ice damage
FUSSGÄNGER	Pedestrians
GEFÄHRLICHES GEFÄLLE	Steep descent
GLATTEIS	Icy road
HALT, POLIZEI	Stop, police
HUPEN VERBOTEN	No honking
KURZPARKZONE	Limited parking zone
LANGSAM FAHREN	Slow down
LAWINENGEFAHR	Avalanche area
LKW	Heavy vehicles
NUR FÜR ANLIEGER	Access to residents only
PARKEN VERBOTEN	No parking
RECHTS FAHREN	Keep right
SCHLECHTE FAHRBAHN	Bad road surface
SCHULE	School
STAU	Traffic jam
STEINSCHLAG	Falling rocks
STRASSENARBEITEN	Road works ahead (men working)
UMLEITUNG	Diversion (detour)
... VERBOTEN	No ...
VORFAHRT GEWÄHREN	Give way (yield)
VORSICHT	Caution

Sightseeing

Where's the tourist office?	Wo ist das Fremdenverkehrsbüro?	voa ist dahss **frehm**dern-fehrkayrsbewroa
What are the main points of interest?	Was sind die Hauptsehenswürdigkeiten?	vahss zint dee **howpt**-zayernsvewrdikhkightern
We're here for ...	Wir sind für ... hier.	veer zint fewr ... heer
a few hours	ein paar Stunden	ighn paar **shtun**dern
a day	einen Tag	**igh**nern taag
a week	eine Woche	**igh**ner vokher
Can you recommend a sightseeing tour/an excursion?	Können Sie eine Stadtrundfahrt/einen Ausflug empfehlen?	kurnen zee **igh**ner **shtaht**-runtfaart/**igh**nern **ows**floog ehmpfaylern
What's the point of departure?	Von wo fahren wir ab?	fon voa **fah**rern veer ahp
Will the bus pick us up at the hotel?	Holt uns der Bus vorm Hotel ab?	hoalt uns derr buss foarm **hot**tehl ahp
How much does the tour cost?	Was kostet die Rundfahrt?	vahss **kos**tert dee **runt**faart
What time does the tour start?	Wann beginnt die Rundfahrt?	vahn ber**gint** dee **runt**faart
Is lunch included?	Ist das Mittagessen inbegriffen?	ist dahss **mit**taagehssern **in**bergriffern
What time do we get back?	Wann werden wir zurück sein?	vahn **vayr**dern veer tsoo**rewk** zighn
Do we have free time in ...?	Haben wir in ... Zeit zu freier Verfügung?	**haa**bern veer in ... tsight tsoo **frigh**err fehr**few**gung
Is there an English-speaking guide?	Gibt es einen englischsprechenden Fremdenführer?	gipt ehss **igh**nern **ehng**lishshprehkherndern **frehm**dernfewrerr
I'd like to hire a private guide for ...	Ich möchte einen Fremdenführer für ...	ikh **murch**ter **igh**nern **frehm**dernfewrerr fewr
half a day	einen halben Tag	**igh**nern **hahl**bern taag
a full day	einen Tag	**igh**nern taag

Where is/Where are the ...?	Wo ist/Wo sind ...?	voa ist/voa zint
abbey	die Abtei	dee ahptigh
alley	die Gasse	dee gahsser
amusement park	der Vergnügungspark	derr fehrgnewgungspahrk
art gallery	die Kunstgalerie	dee kunstgahlehree
botanical gardens	der Botanische Garten	derr bottaanisher gahrtern
building	das Gebäude	dahss gerboyder
business district	das Geschäftsviertel	dahss gershehftsfeerterl
cathedral	die Kathedrale/der Dom	dee kahtehdraaler/derr doam
cave	die Höhle	dee hurler
cemetery	der Friedhof	derr freethoaf
chapel	die Kapelle	dee kahpehler
church	die Kirche	dee keerkher
city walls	die Stadtmauern	dee shtahtmowerrn
concert hall	die Konzerthalle	dee kontsehrthahler
convent	das Kloster	dahss kloasterr
convention hall	die Kongreßhalle	dee kongrehshahler
court house	das Gericht	dahss gerrikht
downtown area	die Innenstadt	dee innernshtaht
exhibition	die Ausstellung	dee owsshtehlung
factory	die Fabrik	dee fahbrik
fair	die Messe	dee mehsser
flea market	der Flohmarkt	derr floamahrkt
fortress	die Festung	dee fehstung
fountain	der Brunnen/Springbrunnen	derr brunnern/shpringbrunnern
gardens	die Grünanlagen	dee grewnahnlaagern
harbour	der Hafen	derr haafern
lake	der See	derr zay
library	die Bibliothek	dee bibliotayk
market	der Markt	derr mahrkt
memorial	das Denkmal	dahss dehnkmaal
monastery	das Kloster	dahss kloasterr
monument	das Denkmal	dahss dehnkmaal
museum	das Museum	dahss muzayum
old town	die Altstadt	dee ahltshtaht
opera house	das Opernhaus	dahss oaperrnhowss
palace	der Palast/das Schloß	derr pahlahst/dahss shloss
park	der Park	derr pahrk
parliament building	das Parlamentsgebäude	dahss pahrlahmehntsgerboyder
ruins	die Ruinen	dee rueenern
shopping area	das Geschäftsviertel	dahss gershehftsfeerterl

square	der Platz	derr plahts
stadium	das Stadion	dahss shtaadion
statue	die Statue	dee shtaatuer
stock exchange	die Börse	dee burrzer
street	die Straße	dee shtrahsser
theatre	das Theater	dahss tayaaterr
tomb	das Grab	dahss graap
tower	der Turm	derr toorm
town hall	das Rathaus	dahss raathowss
university	die Universität	dee unnivehrzitait
wall	die Mauer	dee mowerr
zoo	der Zoo	derr tsoa

Admission *Eintritt*

Is ... open on Sundays?	Ist ... sonntags geöffnet?	ist ... zontaags gerurfnert
What are the opening hours?	Welches sind die Öffnungszeiten?	vehlkherss zint dee urfnungstsightern
When does it close?	Wann schließt es?	vahn shleest ehss
How much is the entrance fee?	Was kostet der Eintritt?	vahss kostert derr ighntrit
Is there any reduction for ...?	Gibt es Ermäßigung für ...?	gipt ehss ehrmaissigung fewr
children	Kinder	kinderr
disabled	Behinderte	berhinderrter
groups	Gruppen	gruppern
pensioners	Rentner	rehntnerr
students	Studenten	shtuddehntern
Have you a guide book (in English)?	Haben Sie einen Reiseführer (in Englisch)?	haabern zee ighnern righzerfewrerr (in ehnglish)
Can I buy a catalogue?	Kann ich einen Katalog kaufen?	kahn ikh ighnern kahtahloag kowfern
Is it all right to take pictures?	Darf man fotografieren?	dahrf mahn fotto-grahfeerern

EINTRITT FREI	ADMISSION FREE
FOTOGRAFIEREN VERBOTEN	NO CAMERAS ALLOWED

Who—What—When? *Wer – Was – Wann?*

What's that building?	**Was für ein Gebäude ist das?**	vahss fewr ighn gerboyder ist dahss
Who was the ...?	**Wer war der ...?**	vayr vaar derr
architect	**Architekt**	ahrkhittehkt
artist	**Künstler**	kewnstlerr
painter	**Maler**	maalerr
sculptor	**Bildhauer**	bilthowerr
Who built it?	**Wer hat es gebaut?**	vayr haht ehss gerbowt
Who painted that picture?	**Wer hat das Bild gemalt?**	vayr haht dahss bilt germaalt
When did he live?	**Wann hat er gelebt?**	vahn haht ehr gerlaybt
When was it built?	**Wann wurde es erbaut?**	vahn voorder ehss ehrbowt
Where's the house where ... lived?	**Wo ist das Haus, in dem ... wohnte?**	voa ist dahss howss in daym ... voanter
We're interested in ...	**Wir interessieren uns für ...**	veer intehrehsseerern uns fewr
antiques	**Antiquitäten**	ahntikvittaitern
archaeology	**Archäologie**	ahrkhehollogee
art	**Kunst**	kunst
botany	**Botanik**	bottaanik
ceramics	**Keramik**	kehrraamik
coins	**Münzen**	mewntsern
fine arts	**bildende Künste**	bildernder kewnster
furniture	**Möbel**	murberl
geology	**Geologie**	gayollogee
handicrafts	**Kunsthandwerk**	kunsthahntvehrk
history	**Geschichte**	gershikhter
medicine	**Medizin**	mehditseen
music	**Musik**	muzeek
natural history	**Naturkunde**	nahtoorkunder
ornithology	**Vogelkunde**	foagerlkunder
painting	**Malerei**	maalehrigh
pottery	**Töpferei**	turpfehrigh
religion	**Religion**	rayliggioan
sculpture	**Bildhauerei**	bilthowerrigh
zoology	**Zoologie**	tsoaollogee
Where's the ... department?	**Wo ist die ...-Abteilung?**	voa ist dee ... ahptighlung

It's ...	Es ist ...	ehss ist
amazing	erstaunlich	ehrshtownlikh
awful	scheußlich	shoysslikh
beautiful	schön	shurn
gloomy	düster	dewsterr
impressive	eindrucksvoll	ighndruksfol
interesting	interessant	intehrehssahnt
lovely	wunderschön	voonderrshurn
magnificent	großartig	groassahrtikh
overwhelming	überwältigend	ewberrvehltiggernt
pretty	hübsch	hewpsh
romantic	romantisch	rommahntish
sinister	unheimlich	unhighmlikh
strange	seltsam	zehltzaam
superb	prächtig	prehkhtikh
terrible	schrecklich	shrehklikh
tremendous	außerordentlich	owsserrorderntlikh
ugly	häßlich	hehsslikh

Churches—Religious services   *Kirchen – Gottesdienste*

Most churches and cathedrals are open to the public except, of course, when a service is being conducted.

Services are conducted in English in many towns. Ask the local tourist office for further details.

Is there a ... near here?	Gibt es eine ... in der Nähe?	gipt ehss ighner ... in derr naier
Catholic church	katholische Kirche	kahtoalisher keerkher
Protestant church	evangelische/pro- testantische Kirche	ehvahngaylisher/protteh- shtahntisher keerkher
synagogue	Synagoge	zewnahgoager
mosque	Moschee	moshay
At what time is ...?	Wann beginnt ...?	vahn bergint
mass	die Messe	dee mehsser
the service	der Gottesdienst	derr gottersdeenst
Where can I find a ... who speaks English?	Wo finde ich einen ..., der Englisch spricht?	voa finder ikh ighnern ... derr ehnglish shprikht
priest/minister rabbi	Priester/Pfarrer Rabbiner	preesterr/pfahrerr/ rahbeenerr
I'd like to visit the church.	Ich möchte die Kirche besichtigen.	ikh murkhter dee kirkherr berzikhtiggern

In the countryside *Auf dem Lande*

Is there a scenic route to …?	**Gibt es eine landschaftlich schöne Straße nach …?**	gipt ehss **ighner** lahntshahftlikh **shurner** shtraasser naakh
How far is it to …?	**Wie weit ist es bis …?**	vee vight ist ehss biss
Can we walk?	**Können wir zu Fuß gehen?**	kurnern veer tsoo fooss gayern
How high is that mountain?	**Wie hoch ist dieser Berg?**	vee hoakh ist **deezerr** behrg
What kind of … is that?	**Was für … ist das?**	vahss fewr … ist dahss
animal/bird	**ein Tier/ein Vogel**	ighn teer/ighn **foagerl**
flower/tree	**eine Blume/ein Baum**	**ighner bloomer**/ighn bowm

Landmarks *Zur Orientierung*

bridge	**die Brücke**	dee **brewker**
castle	**das Schloß/die Burg**	dahss shloss/dee boorg
farm	**der Bauernhof**	derr **bowernhoaf**
field	**das Feld**	dahss fehlt
footpath	**der Fußweg**	derr **foosvayg**
forest	**der Wald**	derr vahlt
garden	**der Garten**	derr **gahrtern**
hill	**der Hügel**	derr **hewgerl**
house	**das Haus**	dahss howss
lake	**der See**	derr zay
meadow	**die Wiese**	dee **veezer**
path	**der Weg**	derr vayg
mountain pass	**der Paß**	derr pahss
peak	**die Bergspitze**	dee **behrgshpitser**
pond	**der Teich**	derr tighkh
river	**der Fluß/der Strom**	derr fluss/derr shtroam
rock	**der Felsen**	derr **fehlzern**
road	**die Straße**	dee **shtraasser**
sea	**die See/das Meer**	dee zay/dahss mayr
spring	**die Quelle**	dee **kvehler**
valley	**das Tal**	dahss taal
village	**das Dorf**	dahss dorf
vineyard	**der Weinberg**	derr **vighnbehrg**
waterfall	**der Wasserfall**	derr **vahsserfahl**
well	**der Brunnen**	derr **brunnern**
wood	**der Wald**	derr vahlt

ASKING THE WAY, see page 76

Relaxing

Cinema (movies) — Theatre *Kino – Theater*

Foreign films are usually dubbed into German, though some cinemas also screen them in the original, with German subtitles, at certain times on certain days. Since cinema showings are seldom continuous you can buy your tickets in advance. Theatre curtain time is about 8 p.m. Advance booking is advisable.

You can find out what's playing from newspapers and billboards. In most large towns you can buy a publication of the type "This Week in ...".

What's showing at the cinema tonight?	**Was gibt es heute abend im Kino zu sehen?**	vahss gipt ehss hoyter aabernt im keeno tsoo zayern
What's playing at the ... theatre?	**Was wird im ...theater gegeben?**	vahss veert im ... tayaaterr gergaybern
What sort of play is it?	**Was für ein Stück ist es?**	vahss fewr ighn shtewk ist ehss
Who's it by?	**Von wem ist es?**	fon vaym ist ehss
Can you recommend a ...?	**Können Sie mir ... empfehlen?**	kurnern zee meer ... ehmpfaylern
good film	**einen guten Film**	ighnern gootern film
comedy	**eine Komödie**	ighner kommurdier
musical	**ein Musical**	ighn "musical"
Where's that new film by ... being shown?	**Wo läuft der neue Film von ...?**	voa loyft derr noyer film fon
Who's in it?	**Mit welchen Schauspielern?**	mit vehlkhern show-shpeelerrn
Who's playing the lead?	**Wer spielt die Hauptrolle?**	vayr shpeelt dee howptroller
Who's the director?	**Wer ist der Regisseur?**	vayr ist derr rehzhissurr
At what theatre is that new play by ... being performed?	**In welchem Theater wird das neue Stück von ... gespielt?**	in vehlkherm tayaaterr veert dahss noyer shtewk fon ... gershpeelt

What time does the show begin?	**Wann beginnt die Vorstellung?**	vahn bergint dee foarshtehlung
What time does the performance end?	**Wann ist die Vorstellung zu Ende?**	vahn ist dee foarshtehlung tsoo ehnder
Are there any tickets for tonight?	**Gibt es noch Karten für heute abend?**	gipt ehss nokh kahrtern fewr hoyter aabernt
How much are the tickets?	**Wie teuer sind die Karten?**	vee toyerr zint dee kahrtern
I want to reserve 2 tickets for the show on Friday evening.	**Ich möchte 2 Karten für Freitag abend vorbestellen.**	ikh murkhter 2 kahrtern fewr frightaag aabernt foarbershtehlern
Can I have a ticket for the matinée on …?	**Kann ich eine Karte für die Nachmittagsvorstellung am … bekommen?**	kahn ikh ighner kahrter fewr dee nahkhmittaags-foarshtehlung ahm … berkommern
I want a seat in the stalls (orchestra).	**Ich hätte gern einen Platz im Parkett.**	ikh hehter gehrn ighnern plahts im pahrkeht
Not too far back.	**Nicht zu weit hinten.**	nikht tsu vight hintern
Somewhere in the middle.	**Irgendwo in der Mitte.**	eergerntvoa in derr mitter
How much are the seats in the circle (mezzanine)?	**Wie teuer sind die Plätze im Rang?**	vee toyer zint dee plehtser im rahng
May I please have a programme?	**Kann ich bitte ein Programm haben?**	kahn ikh bitter ighn prograhm haabern
Where's the cloakroom?	**Wo ist die Garderobe?**	voa ist dee gahrderroaber

---

Bedaure, es ist alles ausverkauft.	I'm sorry, we're sold out.
Es gibt nur noch ein paar Plätze im Rang.	There are only a few seats left in the circle (mezzanine).
Darf ich Ihre Eintrittskarte sehen?	May I see your ticket?
Hier ist Ihr Platz.	This is your seat.

Unterhaltung

DAYS OF THE WEEK, see page 151

Opera—Ballet—Concert *Oper – Ballett – Konzert*

Can you recommend a ...?	**Können Sie mir ... empfehlen?**	kurnern zee meer ehmpfaylern
ballet	**ein Ballett**	ighn bahleht
concert	**ein Konzert**	ighn kontsehrt
opera	**eine Oper**	ighner oaperr
operetta	**eine Operette**	ighner oppehrehter
Where's the opera house/the concert hall?	**Wo ist das Opernhaus/die Konzerthalle?**	voa ist dahss oaperrnhowss/ dee kontsehrthahler
What's on at the opera tonight?	**Was wird heute abend in der Oper gegeben?**	vahss veert hoyter aabernt in derr oaperr gergaybern
Who's singing/ dancing?	**Wer singt/tanzt?**	vayr zingt/tahntst
What orchestra is playing?	**Welches Orchester spielt?**	vehlkhers orkehsterr shpeelt
What are they playing?	**Was wird gespielt?**	vahss veert gershpeelt
Who's the conductor/ soloist?	**Wer ist der Dirigent/ der Solist?**	vayr ist derr dirriggehnt/ derr sollist

Nightclubs *Nachtlokale*

Can you recommend a good nightclub?	**Können Sie mir ein gutes Nachtlokal empfehlen?**	kurnern zee meer ighn gooterss nahkhtlokkaal ehmpfaylern
Is there a floor show?	**Gibt es Attraktionen?**	gipt ehss ahtrahktsioanern
Is evening dress necessary?	**Wird Abendgarderobe verlangt?**	veert aaberntgahrdehroaber fehrlahngt

Discos *Diskotheken*

Where can we go dancing?	**Wo können wir tanzen gehen?**	voa kurnern veer tahntsern gayern
Is there a discotheque in town?	**Gibt es hier eine Diskothek?**	gipt ehss heer ighner diskottayk
Would you like to dance?	**Möchten Sie tanzen?**	murkhtern zee tahntsern

Sports *Sport*

You name the sport, and you'll doubtless be able to find it in Germany, Austria and Switzerland. The most popular spectator sport is by far football (soccer).

Is there a football (soccer) game anywhere this Saturday?	**Findet diesen Samstag irgendwo ein Fußballspiel statt?**	findert deezern zahmstaag irgerntvoa ighn foosbahlshpeel shtaht
Which teams are playing?	**Welche Mannschaften spielen?**	vehlker mahnshahftern shpeelern
Can you get me a ticket?	**Können Sie mir eine Karte besorgen?**	kurnern zee meer ighner kahrter berzorgern

basketball	**Basketball**	baaskertbahl
boxing	**Boxen**	boksern
car racing	**Autorennen**	owtorrehnern
cycling	**Radfahren**	raatfaarern
football (soccer)	**Fußball**	foosbahl
horse racing	**Pferderennen**	pfayrderrehnern
horseback riding	**Reiten**	rightern
mountaineering	**Bergsteigen**	behrgshtighgern
skiing	**Skifahren**	sheefaarern
swimming	**Schwimmen**	shvimmern
tennis	**Tennis**	tehniss
volleyball	**Volleyball**	vollibbahl

I'd like to see a boxing match.	**Ich möchte gern einen Boxkampf sehen.**	ikh murkhter gehrn ighnern bokskahmpf zayern
What's the admission charge?	**Was kostet der Eintritt?**	vahss kostert derr ighntrit
Where's the nearest golf course?	**Wo ist der nächste Golfplatz?**	voa ist derr naikhster golfplahts
Where are the tennis courts?	**Wo sind die Tennisplätze?**	voa zint dee tehnisplehtser
Can I hire (rent) rackets?	**Kann ich Tennisschläger mieten?**	kahn ikh tehnisshlaigerr meetern
What's the charge per ...?	**Wieviel kostet es pro ...**	veefeel kostert ehss proa
day/round/hour	**Tag/Spiel/Stunde**	taag/shpeel/shtunder

DAYS OF THE WEEK, see page 151

Where's the nearest race course (track)?	**Wo ist die nächste Pferderennbahn?**	voa ist dee **naikh**ster **pfehr**derrehnbaan
Is there any good fishing around here?	**Kann man hier in der Nähe angeln?**	kahn mahn heer in derr **naier ahng**erln
Do I need a permit?	**Brauche ich einen Angelschein?**	**brow**kher ikh **igh**nern **ahng**erlshighn
Where can I get one?	**Wo bekomme ich einen?**	voa ber**kom**mer ikh **igh**nern
Can one swim in the lake/river?	**Kann man im See/Fluß baden?**	kahn mahn im zay/ fluss **baa**dern
Is there a swimming pool here?	**Gibt es hier ein Schwimmbad?**	gipt ehss heer ighn **shvim**baat
Is it open-air or indoors?	**Ist es ein Freibad oder ein Hallenbad?**	ist ehss ighn **frigh**baat oaderr ighn **hah**lernbaat
Is it heated?	**Ist es geheizt?**	ist ehss ger**hights**t
What's the temperature of the water?	**Welche Temperatur hat das Wasser?**	**vehl**kher tehmperrah**toor** haht dahss **vahs**ser
Is there a sand beach?	**Gibt es einen Sandstrand?**	gipt ehss **igh**nern **zahnt**shtrahnt

On the beach *Am Strand*

The sea is very calm.	**Das Meer ist sehr ruhig.**	dahss mayr ist zayr **roo**ikh
There are some big waves.	**Das Meer hat hohen Wellengang.**	dahss mayr haht **hoa**ern **vehl**erngahng
Is it safe for swimming?	**Kann man hier gefahrlos schwimmen?**	kahn mahn heer ger**faar**loass **shvim**mern
Is there a lifeguard?	**Gibt es einen Rettungsdienst?**	gipt ehss **igh**nern **reh**tungsdeenst
Is it safe for children?	**Ist es für Kinder ungefährlich?**	ist ehss fewr **kin**derr **un**gerfairlikh
Are there any dangerous currents?	**Gibt es gefährliche Strömungen?**	gipt ehss ger**fair**likher **shtrur**mungern
What time is high tide/low tide?	**Wann ist Flut/Ebbe?**	vahn ist floot/**ehb**er

I want to hire (rent) a/an/some ...	**Ich möchte ... mieten.**	ikh **murkh**ter ... **mee**tern
bathing hut (cabana)	**eine Badekabine**	**igh**ner baa**der**kahbeener
deck-chair	**einen Liegestuhl**	**igh**nern **lee**gershtool
motorboat	**ein Motorboot**	ighn **moa**torboat
rowing-boat	**ein Ruderboot**	ighn **roo**derrboat
sailboard	**einen Windsurfer**	**igh**nern **vint**surrferr
sailing-boat	**ein Segelboot**	ighn **zay**gerlboat
skin-diving equipment	**eine Taucher- ausrüstung**	**igh**ner **tow**kherr- owsrewstung
sunshade (umbrella)	**einen Sonnenschirm**	**igh**nern **zon**nernsheerm
surfboard	**ein Surfbrett**	ighn **surf**breht
water-skis	**Wasserski**	**vahs**sershee

PRIVATSTRAND	PRIVATE BEACH
BADEN VERBOTEN	NO SWIMMING

Winter sports *Wintersport*

Is there a skating-rink near here?	**Gibt es hier in der Nähe eine Eisbahn?**	gipt ehss heer in derr **nai**er **igh**ner **ighs**baan
I'd like to ski.	**Ich möchte skifahren.**	ikh **murkh**ter **shee**faarern
downhill/cross-country skiing	**Abfahrtslauf/ Langlauf**	**ahp**fahrtslowf/ **lahng**lowf
Are there any ski runs for ...?	**Gibt es Skipisten für ...?**	gipt ehss **shee**pistern fewr
beginners	**Anfänger**	**ahn**faingerr
good skiers	**Fortgeschrittene**	**fort**gershritterner
Can I take skiing lessons?	**Kann ich Ski- unterricht nehmen?**	kahn ikh **shee**unterrrikht **nay**mern
Are there ski lifts?	**Gibt es Skilifte?**	gipt ehss **shee**lifter
I want to hire a/some ...	**Ich möchte ... mieten.**	ikh **murkh**ter ... **mee**tern
poles	**Skistöcke**	**shee**shturker
skates	**Schlittschuhe**	**shlit**shooer
ski boots	**Skischuhe**	**shee**shooer
skiing equipment	**eine Skiausrüstung**	**igh**ner **shee**owsrewstung
skis	**Skier**	**shee**err

Making friends

Introductions *Vorstellen*

May I introduce ...?	**Darf ich ... vorstellen?**	dahrf ikh ... foarshtehlern
John, this is ...	**John, das ist ...**	John dahss ist
My name is ...	**Ich heiße ...**	ikh highsser
Glad to know you.	**Sehr erfreut.**	zayr ehrfroyt
What's your name?	**Wie heißen Sie?**	vee highssern zee
How are you?	**Wie geht es Ihnen?**	vee gayt ehss eenern
Fine, thanks. And you?	**Danke, gut. Und Ihnen?**	dahnker goot. unt eenern

Follow-up *Näheres Kennenlernen*

How long have you been here?	**Wie lange sind Sie schon hier?**	vee lahnger zint zee shoan heer
We've been here a week.	**Wir sind seit einer Woche hier.**	veer zint zight ighnerr vokher heer
Is this your first visit?	**Sind Sie zum ersten Mal hier?**	zint zee tsum ehrstern maal heer
No, we came here last year.	**Nein, wir waren schon letztes Jahr hier.**	nighn veer vaarern shoan lehtsterss yaar heer
Are you enjoying your stay?	**Gefällt es Ihnen hier?**	gerfehlt ehss eenern heer
Yes, I like it very much.	**Ja, mir gefällt es sehr gut.**	yaa meer gerfehlt ehss zayr goot
I like the landscape a lot.	**Die Landschaft gefällt mir sehr.**	dee lahntshahft gerfehlt meer zayr
What do you think of the country/ the city?	**Wie gefällt Ihnen das Land/die Stadt?**	vee gerfehlt eenern dahss lahnt/dee shtaht
Where do you come from?	**Woher kommen Sie?**	voahayr kommern zee
I'm from ...	**Ich bin aus ...**	ikh bin owss

COUNTRIES, see page 146

I'm ...	Ich bin ...	ikh bin
American	Amerikaner(in)	ahmehrikkaanerr(in)
British	Brite (Britin)	britter (brittin)
Canadian	Kanadier(in)	kahnaadierr(rin)
English	Engländer(in)	ehnglehnderr(in)
Irish	Ire (Irin)	eerer (eerin)

Where are you staying?	Wo wohnen Sie?	voa voanern zee
Are you on your own?	Sind Sie allein hier?	zint zee ahlighn heer
I'm with my ...	Ich bin mit ... hier.	ikh bin mit ... heer
wife	meiner Frau	mighnerr frow
husband	meinem Mann	mighnerm mahn
family	meiner Familie	mighnerr fahmeelier
parents	meinen Eltern	mighnern ehlterrn
boyfriend	meinem Freund	mighnerm froynt
girlfriend	meiner Freundin	mighnerr froyndin

father/mother	der Vater/die Mutter	derr faaterr/dee mutterr
son/daughter	der Sohn/die Tochter	derr zoan/dee tokhterr
brother/sister	der Bruder/die Schwester	derr brooderr/dee shvehsterr
uncle/aunt	der Onkel/die Tante	derr onkerl/dee tahnter
nephew/niece	der Neffe/die Nichte	derr nehfer/dee neekhter
cousin	der Cousin/die Cousine	derr kuzehng/dee kuzeener

Are you married/ single?	Sind Sie verheiratet/ ledig?	zint zee fehrhighraatert/ laydikh
Do you have children?	Haben Sie Kinder?	haarbern zee kinderr
What's your occupation?	Was machen Sie beruflich?	vahss mahkhern zee berrooflikh
I'm a student.	Ich bin Student(in).	ikh bin shtuddehnt(in)
What are you studying?	Was studieren Sie?	vahss shtuddeerern zee
I'm here on a business trip.	Ich bin auf einer Geschäftsreise hier.	ikh bin owf ighnerr gershehftsrighzer heer
Do you travel a lot?	Reisen Sie viel?	righzern zee feel
Do you play cards/ chess?	Spielen Sie Karten/ Schach?	shpeelern zee kahrtern/ shahkh

The weather *Das Wetter*

What a lovely day!	**Was für ein herrlicher Tag!**	vahss fewr ighn hehrlikherr taag
What awful weather!	**Was für ein scheußliches Wetter!**	vahss fewr ighn shoysslikherss vehterr
Isn't it cold/hot today?	**Welche Kälte/Hitze heute!**	vehlkher kehlter/hitser hoyter
Is it usually as warm as this?	**Ist es immer so warm?**	ist ehss immerr zoa vahrm
Do you think it's going to ... tomorrow?	**Glauben Sie, es wird morgen ...?**	glowbern zee ehss veert morgern
be a nice day	**schön sein**	shurn zighn
rain	**regnen**	raygnern
snow	**schneien**	shnighern
What is the weather forecast?	**Was sagt der Wetterbericht?**	vahss zahgt derr vehterrberrikht

cloud	**die Wolke**	dee volker
fog	**der Nebel**	derr nayberl
frost	**der Frost**	derr frost
ice	**das Eis**	dahss ighss
lightning	**der Blitz**	derr blits
moon	**der Mond**	derr moant
rain	**der Regen**	derr raygern
sky	**der Himmel**	derr himmerl
snow	**der Schnee**	derr shnay
star	**der Stern**	derr shtehrn
sun	**die Sonne**	dee zonner
thunder	**der Donner**	derr donnerr
thunderstorm	**das Gewitter**	dahss gervitterr
wind	**der Wind**	derr vint

Invitations *Einladungen*

| Would you like to have dinner with us on ...? | **Möchten Sie am ... mit uns zu Abend essen?** | murkhtern zee ahm ... mit uns tsoo aabernt ehssern |
| May I invite you for lunch? | **Darf ich Sie zum Mittagessen einladen?** | dahrf ikh zee tsum mittaagehssern ighnlaadern |

DAYS OF THE WEEK, see page 151

Can you come over for a drink this evening?	Kommen Sie heute abend auf ein Gläschen zu uns?	kommern zee hoyter aabernt owf ighn glaiskhern tsoo uns
There's a party. Are you coming?	Es gibt eine Party. Kommen Sie auch?	ehss gipt ighner paartee. kommern zee owkh
That's very kind of you.	Das ist sehr nett von Ihnen.	dahss ist zayr neht fon eenern
Great. I'd love to come.	Prima, ich komme sehr gerne.	preemaa ikh kommer zayr gehrner
What time shall we come?	Wann sollen wir da sein?	vahn zollern veer daa zighn
May I bring a friend/ a girlfriend?	Kann ich einen Freund/eine Freundin mitbringen?	kahn ikh ighnern froynt/ighnerr froyndin mitbringen
I'm afraid we've got to leave now.	Leider müssen wir jetzt gehen.	lighderr mewssern veer yehtst gayern
Next time you must come to visit us.	Nächstes Mal müssen Sie uns besuchen.	naikhsterss maal mewssern zee uns berzookhern
Thanks for the evening. It was great.	Vielen Dank für den schönen Abend.	feelern dahnk fewr dayn shurnern aabernt

Dating *Verabredung*

Do you mind if I smoke?	Stört es Sie, wenn ich rauche?	shturt ehss zee vehn ikh rowkher
Would you like a cigarette?	Möchten Sie eine Zigarette?	murkhtern zee ighner tsiggahrehter
Do you have a light, please?	Können Sie mir bitte Feuer geben?	kurnern zee meer bitter foyerr gaybern
Why are you laughing?	Warum lachen Sie?	vahroom lahkhern zee
Is my German that bad?	Ist mein Deutsch so schlecht?	ist mighn doych zoa shlehkht
Can I get you a drink?	Möchten Sie etwas trinken?	murkhtern zee ehtvahss trinkern
Are you waiting for someone?	Warten Sie auf jemanden?	vahrtern zee owf yaymahndern
Are you free this evening?	Sind Sie heute abend frei?	zint zee hoyter aabernt frigh

Would you like to go out with me tonight?	**Möchten Sie heute abend mit mir ausgehen?**	murkhtern zee hoyter aabernt mit meer owsgayern
Would you like to go dancing?	**Möchten Sie gern tanzen gehen?**	murkhtern zee gehrn tahntsern gayern
I know a good discotheque.	**Ich kenne eine gute Diskothek.**	ikh kehner ighner gooter diskottayk
Shall we go to the cinema (movies)?	**Wollen wir ins Kino gehen?**	vollern veer ins keeno gayern
Would you like to go for a drive?	**Wollen wir ein bißchen durch die Gegend fahren?**	vollern veer ighn bisskhern doorkh dee gaygernt faarern
Where shall we meet?	**Wo treffen wir uns?**	voa trehfern veer uns
I'll pick you up at your hotel.	**Ich hole Sie in Ihrem Hotel ab.**	ikh hoaler zee in eererm hottehl ahp
I'll call for you at 8.	**Ich hole Sie um 8 Uhr ab.**	ikh hoaler zee um 8 oor ahp
May I take you home?	**Darf ich Sie nach Hause bringen?**	dahrf ikh zee naakh howzer bringern
Can I see you again tomorrow?	**Kann ich Sie morgen wiedersehen?**	kahn ikh zee morgern veederrzayern
What's your telephone number?	**Wie ist Ihre Telefonnummer?**	vee ist eerer taylayfoan-nummerr

... and you might answer:

I'd love to, thank you.	**Danke, sehr gern.**	dahnker zayr gehrn
Thank you, but I'm busy.	**Vielen Dank, aber ich habe keine Zeit.**	feelern dahnk aaberr ikh haaber kighner tsight
No, I'm not interested, thank you.	**Nein, das interessiert mich nicht.**	nighn dahss intehrehsseert mikh nikht
Leave me alone, please.	**Lassen Sie mich bitte in Ruhe!**	lahssern zee mikh bitter in rooer
Thank you. It's been a wonderful evening.	**Danke, es war ein wunderbarer Abend.**	dahnker ehss vaar ighn voonderrbaarerr aabernt
I've enjoyed myself.	**Ich habe mich gut unterhalten.**	ikh haaber mikh goot unterrhahltern

Shopping guide

This shopping guide is designed to help you find what you want with ease, accuracy and speed. It features:

1. a list of all major shops, stores and services (p. 98)
2. some general expressions required when shopping to allow you to be specific and selective (p. 100)
3. full details of the shops and services most likely to concern you. Here you'll find advice, alphabetical lists of items and conversion charts listed under the headings below.

LAUNDRY, see page 29/HAIRDRESSER'S, see page 30

Einkaufsführer

Shops, stores and services   *Geschäfte, Läden usw.*

Shops in Germany, Austria and Switzerland usually open
around 8 or 9 a.m. and close at 6 or 6.30 p.m. Some close for
an hour or two at noon—but never department stores. On
Saturdays shops in Germany and Austria remain open until
noon or 2 p.m. (the first Saturday of the month German
shops are open until 6 p.m.). In Switzerland most shops
remain open until 4 or 5 p.m. on Saturdays, usually taking
Monday morning off.

Where's the nearest ...?	**Wo ist der/die/das nächste ...?**	voa ist derr/dee/dahss naikhster
antique shop	**das Antiquitäten- geschäft**	dahss ahntikvitt**ay**tern- gershehft
art gallery	**die Kunstgalerie**	dee **kunst**gahlehree
baker's	**die Bäckerei**	dee beh**ker**righ
bank	**die Bank**	dee bahnk
barber's	**der Friseur**	derr friz**urr**
beauty salon	**der Kosmetiksalon**	derr kos**may**tikzahlong
bookshop	**die Buchhandlung**	dee **bukh**hahndlung
butcher's	**die Fleischerei/ Metzgerei**	dee **fligh**sher**righ**/ mehtsger**righ**
cake shop	**die Konditorei**	dee kondit**or**righ
camera shop	**das Fotogeschäft**	dahss **fo**atogershehft
chemist's	**die Apotheke**	dee ahpott**ay**ker
dairy	**die Milchhandlung**	dee **milkh**hahndlung
delicatessen	**das Delikatessen- geschäft**	dahss dehlikkah**teh**ssern- gershehft
dentist	**der Zahnarzt**	derr **tsaa**nahrtst
department store	**das Warenhaus**	dahss **vaa**rernhowss
doctor	**der Arzt**	derr ahrtst
dress shop	**das Modengeschäft**	dahss **mo**aderngershehft
drugstore	**die Apotheke**	dee ahpott**ay**ker
dry cleaner's	**die chemische Reinigung**	dee **khay**misher **righ**nig- gung
electrician	**der Elektriker**	derr ay**lehk**trikkerr
fishmonger's	**die Fischhandlung**	dee **fish**hahndlung
flea market	**der Flohmarkt**	derr **floa**mahrkt
florist's	**das Blumengeschäft**	dahss **bloo**merngershehft
furrier's	**das Pelzgeschäft**	dahss **pehlts**gershehft
greengrocer's	**die Gemüsehandlung**	dee ger**mew**zerhahndlung
grocery	**das Lebensmittel- geschäft**	dahss **lay**bernsmitterl- gershehft

hairdresser's (ladies/men)	der Damenfriseur/ Herrenfriseur	derr **daa**mernfrizurr/ **heh**rernfrizurr
hardware store	die Eisenwaren- handlung	dee **igh**zernvaarern- hahndlung
health food shop	das Reformhaus	dahss reh**form**howss
hospital	das Krankenhaus	dahss **krahn**kernhowss
ironmonger's	die Eisenwaren- handlung	dee **igh**zernvaarern- hahndlung
jeweller's	der Juwelier	derr yuvveh**leer**
launderette	der Waschsalon	derr **vahsh**zahlong
laundry	die Wäscherei	dee vehsher**righ**
library	die Bibliothek	dee bibliott**ayk**
market	der Markt	derr mahrkt
newsagent's	der Zeitungshändler	derr **tsight**ungshehndlerr
newsstand	der Zeitungsstand	derr **tsight**ungsshtahnt
optician	der Optiker	derr **opt**ikkerr
pastry shop	die Konditorei	dee kondittor**righ**
photographer	der Fotograf	derr foato**graaf**
police station	die Polizeiwache	dee pollit**sigh**vahkher
post office	das Postamt	dahss **post**ahmt
second-hand shop	der Gebrauchtwaren- laden	derr ger**browkht**vaarern- laadern
shoemaker's (repairs)	der Schuhmacher	derr **shoo**mahkherr
shoe shop	das Schuhgeschäft	dahss **shoo**gershehft
shopping centre	das Einkaufszentrum	dahss **ighn**kowfstsehntrum
souvenir shop	der Andenkenladen	derr ahn**dehn**kernlaadern
sporting goods shop	das Sportgeschäft	dahss **shport**gershehft
stationer's	das Schreibwaren- geschäft	dahss **shrighp**vaarern- gershehft
supermarket	der Supermarkt	derr **zoo**perrmahrkt
tailor's	der Schneider	derr **shnigh**derr
telegraph office	das Telegrafenamt	dahss taylay**graa**fernahmt
tobacconist's	der Tabakladen	derr tah**bahk**laadern
toy shop	das Spielwaren- geschäft	dahss **shpeel**vaarern- gerhehft
travel agency	das Reisebüro	dahss **righ**zerbewroa
vegetable store	die Gemüsehandlung	dee ger**mew**zerhahndlung
veterinarian	der Tierarzt	derr **teer**ahrtst
watchmaker's	der Uhrmacher	derr **oor**mahkherr
wine merchant's	die Weinhandlung	dee **vighn**hahndlung

	EINGANG	ENTRANCE
	AUSGANG	EXIT
	NOTAUSGANG	EMERGENCY EXIT

General expressions *Allgemeine Redewendungen*

Where? *Wo?*

Where's there a good ...?	**Wo gibt es einen guten/eine gute/ ein gutes ...?**	voa gipt ehss **igh**nern **goo**tern/**igh**ner **goo**ter/ ighn **goo**terss
Where can I find ...?	**Wo finde ich ...?**	voa **fin**der ikh
Where's the main shopping area?	**Wo ist das Geschäftsviertel?**	voa ist dahss ger**shehfts**feerterl
Is it far from here?	**Ist es weit von hier?**	ist ehss vight fon heer
How do I get there?	**Wie komme ich dorthin?**	vee **kom**mer ikh dort**hin**

Service *Bedienung*

Can you help me?	**Können Sie mir helfen?**	**kur**nern zee meer **hehl**fern
I'm just looking.	**Ich sehe mich nur um.**	ikh **zay**er mikh noor um
I want ...	**Ich möchte ...**	ikh **murkh**ter
Can you show me some ...?	**Können Sie mir einige ... zeigen?**	**kur**nern zee meer **igh**nigger ... **tsigh**gern
Do you sell ...?	**Verkaufen Sie ...?**	fehr**kow**fern zee
I'd like to buy ...	**Ich möchte ... kaufen.**	ikh **murkh**ter ... **kow**fern
Do you have any ...?	**Haben Sie ...?**	**haa**bern zee
Where's the ... department?	**Wo ist die ... -Abteilung?**	voa ist dee ... **ahp**tighlung
Where is the lift (elevator)/escalator?	**Wo ist der Fahrstuhl/ die Rolltreppe?**	voa ist derr **faar**shtool/ dee **rol**trehper

That one *Das da*

Can you show me ...?	**Können Sie mir ... zeigen?**	**kur**nern zee meer ... **tsigh**gern
that/those	**das da/die dort**	dahss daa/dee dort
the one in the window/in the display case	**das im Schaufenster/ in der Vitrine**	dahss im **show**fehnsterr/ in derr vi**tree**ner

Defining the article   *Beschreibung des Artikels*

It must be ...	**Es muß ... sein.**	ehss muss ... zighn
big	**groß**	groass
cheap	**billig**	billikh
dark	**dunkel**	dunkerl
good	**gut**	goot
heavy	**schwer**	shvayr
large	**groß**	groass
light (weight)	**leicht**	lighkht
light (colour)	**hell**	hehl
oval	**oval**	oavaal
rectangular	**rechteckig**	rehkhtehkikh
round	**rund**	runt
small	**klein**	klighn
square	**viereckig**	feerehkikh
sturdy	**robust**	robbust
I don't want any-thing too expensive.	**Ich möchte nichts allzu Teures.**	ikh murkhter nikhts ahlltsu toyrerss

Preference   *Ich hätte lieber ...*

Can you show me some more?	**Können Sie mir noch andere zeigen?**	kurnern zee meer nokh ahnderrer tsighgern
Haven't you anything ...?	**Haben Sie nichts ...?**	haabern zee nikhts
cheaper/better	**Billigeres/Besseres**	billiggerrerss/behsserrerss
larger/smaller	**Größeres/Kleineres**	grurserrerss/klighnerrerss

How much?   *Wieviel?*

How much is this?	**Wieviel kostet das?**	veefeel kostert dahss
I don't understand.	**Ich verstehe nicht.**	ikh fehrshtayer nikht
Please write it down.	**Schreiben Sie es bitte auf.**	shrighbern zee ehss bitter owf
I don't want to spend more than ... marks.	**Ich möchte nicht mehr als ... Mark ausgeben.**	ikh murkhter nikht mayr ahlss ... mahrk owsgaybern

---

AUSVERKAUF   SALE

COLOURS, see page 113

Decision *Entscheidung*

It's not quite what I want.	**Es ist nicht ganz das, was ich möchte.**	ehss ist nikht gahnts dahss vahss ikh **murkh**ter
No, I don't like it.	**Nein, das gefällt mir nicht.**	nighn dahss ger**fehlt** meer nikht
I'll take it.	**Ich nehme es.**	ikh **nay**mer ehss

Ordering *Bestellen*

| Can you order it for me? | **Können Sie es mir bestellen?** | **kur**nern zee ehss meer ber**shteh**lern |
| How long will it take? | **Wie lange dauert es?** | vee **lahng**er **dow**errt ehss |

Delivery *Lieferung*

I'll take it with me.	**Ich nehme es mit.**	ikh **nay**mer ehss mit
Deliver it to the ... Hotel.	**Liefern Sie es bitte ins Hotel ...**	**lee**ferrn zee ehss **bit**ter ins hot**tehl**
Please send it to this address.	**Senden Sie es bitte an diese Anschrift.**	**zehn**dern zee ehss **bit**ter ahn **dee**zer **ahn**shrift
Will I have any difficulty with the customs?	**Werde ich Schwierigkeiten mit dem Zoll haben?**	**vayr**der ikh **shvee**rikh-kightern mit daym tsol **haa**bern

Paying *Bezahlen*

Where do I pay?	**Wo ist die Kasse?**	voa ist dee **kah**sser
How much is it?	**Wieviel kostet es?**	vee**feel** **kos**tert ehss
Can I pay with this credit card?	**Kann ich mit dieser Kreditkarte bezahlen?**	kahn ikh mit **dee**zerr kray**dit**kahrter ber**tsaa**lern
Do you accept ...?	**Nehmen Sie ...?**	**nay**mern zee
dollars	**Dollar**	**dol**lahr
pounds	**Pfund**	pfunt
traveller's cheques	**Reiseschecks**	**righ**zershehks
Do I have to pay the VAT (sales tax)?	**Muß ich die Mehrwertsteuer bezahlen?**	muss ikh dee **mayr**vayrt-shtoyerr ber**tsaa**lern
Haven't you made a mistake in the bill?	**Haben Sie sich nicht verrechnet?**	**haa**bern zee zikh nikht fehr**rehkh**nert

Anything else? *Sonst noch etwas?*

No, thanks, that's all.	**Nein danke, das ist alles.**	nighn **dahn**ker dahss ist **ah**lerss
Yes. I want ...	**Ja, ich möchte ...**	yaa ikh **murkh**ter
Show me ...	**Zeigen Sie mir ...**	**tsigh**gern zee meer
May I have a bag, please?	**Kann ich bitte eine Tragetasche haben?**	kahn ikh **bit**ter **igh**ner **traa**gertahsher **haa**bern

Dissatisfied *Unzufrieden*

Can you please exchange this?	**Können Sie das bitte umtauschen?**	**kur**nern zee dahss **bit**ter **um**towshern
I want to return this.	**Ich möchte das zurückgeben.**	ikh **murkh**ter dahss tsoo**rewk**gaybern
I'd like a refund. Here's the receipt.	**Ich möchte das Geld zurückerstattet haben. Hier ist die Quittung.**	ikh **murkh**ter dahss gehlt tsoo**rewk**ehrshtahtert **haa**bern. heer ist dee **kvit**tung

🖝	🖚
Kann ich Ihnen helfen?	Can I help you?
Was wünschen Sie?	What would you like?
Welche ... möchten Sie?	What ... would you like?
Farbe/Form Qualität/Menge	colour/shape quality/quantity
Es tut mir leid, das haben wir nicht.	I'm sorry, we haven't any.
Das haben wir nicht vorrätig.	We're out of stock.
Sollen wir es für Sie bestellen?	Shall we order it for you?
Nehmen Sie es mit oder sollen wir es Ihnen senden?	Will you take it with you or shall we send it?
Sonst noch etwas?	Anything else?
Das macht ... Mark, bitte.	That's ... marks, please.
Die Kasse ist dort drüben.	The cash desk is over there.

Bookshop *Buchhandlung*

In Germany, bookshops and stationers' are usually separate shops, though the latter will often sell paperbacks. Newspapers and magazines are sold at newsstands.

Where's the nearest ...?	**Wo ist der/die/ das nächste ...?**	voa ist derr/dee/dahss **naikh**ster
bookshop	**die Buchhandlung**	dee **bukh**hahndlung
stationer's	**das Schreibwaren- geschäft**	dahss **shrighp**vaaarern- gershehft
newsstand	**der Zeitungsstand**	derr **tsight**ungsshtahnt
Where can I buy an English-language newspaper?	**Wo kann ich eine englische Zeitung kaufen?**	voa kahn ikh **igh**ner **ehng**lisher **tsight**ung **kow**fern
Where's the guide- book section?	**Wo stehen die Reiseführer?**	voa **shtay**ern dee **righ**zerfewrerr
Where do you keep the English books?	**Wo stehen die englischen Bücher?**	voa **shtay**ern dee **ehng**lishern **bew**kherr
Have you any of ... 's books in English?	**Haben Sie ein Buch von ... in Englisch?**	**haa**bern zee ighn bookh fon ... in **ehng**lish
Do you have second- hand books?	**Haben Sie auch anti- quarische Bücher?**	**haa**ben zee owkh ahnti- **kvaa**risher **bew**kherr
I want a/an/ some ...	**Ich möchte ...**	ikh **murkh**ter
address book	**ein Adressen- büchlein**	ighn ah**dreh**ssern- **bew**khlighn
ball-point pen	**einen Kugelschreiber**	**igh**nern **koo**gerlshrighberr
book	**ein Buch**	ighn bukh
calendar	**einen Kalender**	**igh**nern kah**leh**nderr
carbon paper	**Durchschlagpapier**	**doorkh**shlaagpahpeer
cellophane tape	**Klebstreifen**	**klayp**shtrighfern
crayons	**Buntstifte**	**bunt**shtifter
dictionary	**ein Wörterbuch**	ighn **vurr**terrbookh
German-English	**deutsch-englisch**	doych-**ehng**lish
pocket dictionary	**ein Taschen- wörterbuch**	ighn **tah**shernvurrterr- bookh
drawing paper	**Zeichenpapier**	**tsigh**khernpahpeer
drawing pins	**Reißzwecken**	**righs**tsvehkern
envelopes	**Briefumschläge**	**bree**fumshlaiger
eraser	**einen Radiergummi**	**igh**nern rah**dee**rgummi
exercise book	**ein Schreibheft**	ighn **shrighp**hehft

felt-tip pen	**einen Filzstift**	ighnern filtsshtift
fountain pen	**einen Füllfeder-halter**	ighnern fewlfayderrhahlterr
glue	**Leim**	lighm
grammar book	**eine Grammatik**	ighner grahmahtik
guidebook	**einen Reiseführer**	ighnern righzerfewrerr
ink	**Tinte**	tinter
black/red/blue	**schwarz/rot/blau**	shvahrts/roat/blow
(adhesive) labels	**(selbstklebende) Etikette**	(zehlpstklaybernder) ehtikkehter
magazine	**eine Illustrierte**	ighner illustreerter
map	**eine Landkarte**	ighner lahntkahrter
map of the town	**einen Stadtplan**	ighnern shtahtplaan
road map of ...	**eine Straßenkarte von ...**	ighner shtraassernkahrter fon
mechanical pencil	**einen Drehbleistift**	ighnern drayblighshtift
newspaper	**eine Zeitung**	ighner tsightung
American	**amerikanische**	ahmehrikkaanisher
English	**englische**	ehnglisher
notebook	**ein Notizheft**	ighn nottitshehft
note paper	**Briefpapier**	breefpahpeer
paintbox	**einen Malkasten**	ighnern maalkahstern
paper	**Papier**	pahpeer
paperback	**ein Taschenbuch**	ighn tahshernbookh
paperclips	**Büroklammern**	bewroaklahmerrn
paper napkins	**Papierservietten**	pahpeerzehrviehtern
paste	**Klebstoff**	klaypshtof
pen	**eine Feder**	ighner fayderr
pencil	**einen Bleistift**	ighnern blighshtift
pencil sharpener	**einen Bleistift-spitzer**	ighnern blighshtiftshpitserr
playing cards	**Spielkarten**	shpeelkahrtern
pocket calculator	**einen Taschenrechner**	ighnern tahshernrehkhnerr
postcard	**eine Postkarte**	ighner postkahrter
propelling pencil	**einen Drehbleistift**	ighnern drayblighshtift
refill (for a pen)	**eine Ersatzmine**	ighner ehrzahtsmeener
rubber	**einen Radiergummi**	ighnern rahdeergummi
ruler	**ein Lineal**	ighn linnayaal
staples	**Heftklammern**	hehftklahmerrn
string	**Bindfaden/Schnur**	bintfaadern/shnoor
thumbtacks	**Reißzwecken**	righstsvehkern
tissue paper	**Seidenpapier**	zighdernpahpeer
typewriter ribbon	**ein Farbband**	ighn fahrpbahnt
typing paper	**Schreibmaschinen-papier**	shrighpmahsheenern-pahpeer
writing pad	**einen Schreibblock**	ighnern shrighpblok

Camping equipment   *Campingausrüstung*

I'd like a/an/ some ...	Ich hätte gern ...	ikh hehter gehrn
bottle-opener	einen Flaschenöffner	ighnern flahshernurfnerr
bucket	einen Eimer	ighnern ighmerr
butane gas	Butangas	buttaangaass
campbed	ein Feldbett	ighn fehltbeht
can opener	einen Büchsenöffner	ighnern bewksernurfnerr
candles	Kerzen	kehrtsern
chair	einen Stuhl	ighnern shtool
folding chair	Klappstuhl	klahpshtool
charcoal	Holzkohle	holtskoaler
clothes pegs	Wäscheklammern	vehsherklahmerrn
compass	einen Kompaß	ighnern kompahss
cool box	eine Kühltasche	ighner kewltahsher
corkscrew	einen Korkenzieher	ighnern korkerntseeherr
crockery	Geschirr	gershir
cutlery	Besteck	bershtehk
deckchair	einen Liegestuhl	ighnern leegershtool
dishwashing detergent	Spülmittel	shpewlmitterl
first-aid kit	einen Verbandkasten	ighnern fehrbahntkahstern
fishing tackle	Angelzeug	ahngerltsoyg
flashlight	eine Taschenlampe	ighner tahshernlahmper
food box	einen Proviant- behälter	ighnern provviahnt- berhehlterr
frying-pan	eine Bratpfanne	ighner braatpfahner
groundsheet	einen Zeltboden	ighnern tsehltboadern
hammer	einen Hammer	ighnern hahmerr
hammock	eine Hängematte	ighner hehngermahter
haversack	eine Provianttasche	ighner provviahnttahsher
ice pack	einen Kühlbeutel	ighnern kewlboyterl
kerosene	Petroleum	paytroalayum
lamp	eine Lampe	ighner lahmper
lantern	eine Laterne	ighner lahtehrner
matches	Streichhölzer	shtrighkhhurltserr
mattress	eine Matratze	ighner mahtrahtser
methylated spirits	Brennspiritus	brehnshpeerittuss
mosquito net	ein Mückennetz	ighn mewkernnehts
pail	einen Eimer	ighnern ighmerr
paper napkins	Papierservietten	pahpeerzehrviehtern
paraffin	Petroleum	paytroalayum
penknife	ein Taschenmesser	ighn tahshernmehsserr
picnic basket	einen Picknickkorb	ighnern piknikkorp
plastic bag	einen Plastikbeutel	ighnern plahstikboyterl

CAMPING, see page 32

rope	ein Seil	ighn zighl
rucksack	einen Rucksack	ighnern rukzahk
saucepan	einen Kochtopf	ighnern kokhtopf
scissors	eine Schere	ighner shayrer
screwdriver	einen Schrauben-zieher	ighnern shrowbern-tseeherr
sleeping bag	einen Schlafsack	ighnern shlaafzahk
stew pot	einen Schmortopf	ighnern shmoartopf
table	einen Tisch	ighnern tish
folding table	Klapptisch	klahptish
tent	ein Zelt	ighn tsehlt
tent pegs	Heringe	hayringer
tent pole	eine Zeltstange	ighner tsehltshtahnger
tinfoil	Aluminiumfolie	ahlumeeniumfoalier
tin opener	einen Büchsenöffner	ighnern bewksernurfnerr
tongs	eine Zange	ighner tsahnger
torch	eine Taschenlampe	ighner tahshernlahmper
vacuum flask	eine Thermosflasche	ighner tehrmosflahsher
washing powder	Waschpulver	vahshpulferr
washing-up liquid	Spülmittel	shpewlmitterl
water carrier	einen Wasserkanister	ighnern vahsserkahnisterr
water flask	eine Feldflasche	ighner fehltflahsher
wood alcohol	Brennspiritus	brehnshpeerittuss

Crockery *Geschirr*

cups	Tassen	tahssern
mugs	Becher	behkherr
plates	Teller	tehlerr
saucers	Untertassen	unterrtahssern
tumblers	Wassergläser	vahsserrglaizerr

Cutlery *Besteck*

forks	Gabeln	gaaberln
knives	Messer	mehsserr
dessert knives	Dessertmesser	dehssayrmehsserr
spoons	Löffel	lurferl
teaspoons	Teelöffel	taylurferl
made of plastic	aus Plastik	owss plahstik
made of stainless steel	aus rostfreiem Stahl	owss rostfrigherm shtaal

Chemist's (drugstore) *Apotheke*

In German, a chemist's is called *Apotheke* (ahpot**tay**ker). They don't sell cameras, books and the like. At night and on Sundays all chemists' display the address of the nearest one open. If you're looking for toiletries, household articles or film, try a *Drogerie* (droge**hree**). You'll also find non-prescription medicine available in a *Drogerie*.

This section has been divided into two parts:

1. Pharmaceutical—medicine, first-aid, etc.
2. Toiletry—toilet articles, cosmetics

General *Allgemeines*

Where's the nearest (all-night) chemist's?	**Wo ist die nächste Apotheke (mit Nachtdienst)?**	voa ist dee **naikh**ster ahpot**tay**ker (mit **nahkht**deenst)
What time does the chemist's open/ close?	**Um wieviel Uhr öffnet/schließt die Apotheke?**	um **vee**feel oor **urf**nert/**shleest** dee ahpot**tay**ker

1—Pharmaceutical *Arzneien*

I want something for ...	**Ich möchte etwas gegen ...**	ikh **murkh**ter **eht**vahss **gay**gern
a cold	**eine Erkältung**	**igh**ner ehr**kehl**tung
a cough	**Husten**	**hoo**stern
a hangover	**einen Kater**	**igh**nern **kaa**terr
hay fever	**Heuschnupfen**	**hoy**shnupfern
insect bites	**Insektenstiche**	in**zehk**ternshtikher
sunburn	**Sonnenbrand**	**zon**nernbrahnt
travel sickness	**Reisekrankheit**	**righ**zerkrahnk-hight
an upset stomach	**Magenverstimmung**	**maa**gernfehrshtimmung
Can you make up this prescription for me?	**Können Sie mir dieses Rezept machen?**	**kur**nern zee meer **dee**zerss reht**sehpt** **mahkh**ern
Can I get it without a prescription?	**Kann ich das ohne Rezept bekommen?**	kahn ikh dahss **oa**ner reht**sehpt** ber**kom**mern
Shall I wait?	**Soll ich warten?**	zol ikh **vahr**tern

DOCTOR, see page 137

Do you have homoeo-pathic remedies?	**Haben Sie homöo-pathische Mittel?**	haabern zee hommurop-pahtisher mitterl
Can I have a/an/some ...?	**Kann ich ... haben?**	kahn ikh ... haabern
analgesic	**ein Schmerzmittel**	ighn **shmehrts**mitterl
antiseptic cream	**eine Wundsalbe**	**igh**ner vuntzahlber
aspirin	**Aspirin**	ahspi**reen**
bandage	**einen Verband**	**igh**nern fehr**bahnt**
elastic bandage	**eine elastische Binde**	**igh**ner ehlahstisher binder
Band-Aids	**Heftpflaster**	hehftpflahsterr
contraceptives	**ein Verhütungs-mittel**	ighn fehr**hew**tungsmitterl
corn plasters	**Hühneraugen-pflaster**	hewnerrowgernpflahsterr
cotton wool (absorbent cotton)	**Watte**	vahter
cough drops	**Hustenpastillen**	hoosternpahstillern
disinfectant	**ein Desinfektions-mittel**	ighn dehsinfehk**tsioans**-mitterl
ear drops	**Ohrentropfen**	oarerntropfern
Elastoplast	**Heftpflaster**	hehftpflahsterr
eye drops	**Augentropfen**	owgerntropfern
gauze	**Verbandmull**	fehr**bahnt**mul
insect repellent/spray	**einen Insektenschutz/ein Insektizid**	**igh**nern inzehk**tern**shuts/ighn inzehkt**it**seet
iodine	**Jod**	yoat
laxative	**ein Abführmittel**	ighn ahp**few**rmitterl
mouthwash	**Mundwasser**	muntvahsserr
nose drops	**Nasentropfen**	naazerntropfern
painkiller	**ein Schmerzmittel**	ighn **shmehrts**mitterl
sanitary napkins	**Damenbinden**	daamernbindern
sleeping pills	**Schlaftabletten**	shlaaftahblehtern
suppositories	**Zäpfchen**	tsehpfkhern
... tablets	**...tabletten**	...tah**bleh**tern
tampons	**Tampons**	tahmpongs
thermometer	**ein Thermometer**	ighn tehrmom**may**terr
throat lozenges	**Halspastillen**	hahlspahstillern
tranquillizers	**Beruhigungsmittel**	berr**oo**iggungsmitterl
vitamin pills	**Vitamintabletten**	vittahm**een**tahblehtern

GIFT	POISON
NICHT EINNEHMEN	FOR EXTERNAL USE ONLY

2—Toiletry *Toilettenartikel*

I'd like a/an/some ...	Ich hätte gern ...	ikh **heh**ter gehrn
acne cream	eine Aknesalbe	**igh**ner **ahk**nerzahlber
after-shave lotion	ein Rasierwasser	ighn rah**zeer**vahsserr
astringent	ein Adstringens	ighn ahd**string**ehns
bath salts	Badesalz	**baad**erzahlts
bubble bath	ein Schaumbad	ighn **show**mbaat
cologne	ein Kölnischwasser	ighn kurl**nish**vahsserr
cream	eine Creme	**igh**ner kraym
cleansing cream	Reinigungscreme	**righ**niggungskraym
for greasy/	für fettige/normale/	fewr **feh**tigger/nor**mah**ler/
normal/dry skin	trockene Haut	**trokk**ehner howt
foundation cream	Grundierungs-creme	grun**deer**ungskraym
moisturizing cream	Feuchtigkeitscreme	**foykh**tikhkightskraym
night cream	Nachtcreme	**nahkht**kraym
cuticle remover	Nagelhautentferner	**naag**erlhowtehntfehrnerr
deodorant	ein Deodorant	ighn dehoddoa**rahnt**
depilatory cream	Haarentfernungs-mittel	**haa**rehntfehrnungsmitterl
emery board	eine Sandpapierfeile	**igh**ner **zahnt**pahpeerfighler
eye liner	einen Lidstift	**igh**nern **leed**shtift
eye pencil	einen Augenbrauen-stift	**igh**nern **ow**gernbrowern-shtift
eye shadow	einen Lidschatten	**igh**nern **leed**shahtern
face powder	Gesichtspuder	ger**zikhts**pooderr
foot cream	Fußcreme	**foos**kraym
foot powder	Fußpuder	**foos**pooderr
hand cream	Handcreme	**hahnt**kraym
interdental cleaners	medizinische Zahn-stocher	maydit**see**nisher **tsaan**-shtokherr
lipsalve	eine Lippenpomade	**igh**ner **lip**pernpommaader
lipstick	einen Lippenstift	**igh**nern **lip**pernshtift
make-up remover pads	Abschminkwatte	**ahp**shminkvahter
mascara	Wimperntusche	**vim**perrntusher
nail brush	eine Nagelbürste	**igh**ner **naa**gerlbewrster
nail clippers	eine Nagelzange	**igh**ner **naa**gerltsahnger
nail file	eine Nagelfeile	**igh**ner **naa**gerlfighler
nail polish	Nagellack	**naa**gerllahk
nail polish remover	Nagellackentferner	**naa**gerllahkehntfehrnerr
nail scissors	eine Nagelschere	**igh**ner **naa**gerlshayrer
perfume	ein Parfüm	ighn pahr**fewm**
powder	Puder	**poo**derr
razor	einen Rasierapparat	**igh**nern rah**zeer**ahpahraat
razor blades	Rasierklingen	rah**zeer**klingern

rouge	**Rouge**	roozh
safety pins	**Sicherheitsnadeln**	zikherrhightsnaaderln
shaving brush	**einen Rasierpinsel**	ighnern rahzeerpinzerl
shaving cream	**Rasiercreme**	rahzeerkraym
soap	**eine Seife**	ighner zighfer
sponge	**einen Schwamm**	ighnern shvahm
sun-tan cream	**Sonnencreme**	zonnernkraym
sun-tan oil	**Sonnenöl**	zonnernurl
talcum powder	**Körperpuder**	kurrperrpooderr
tissues	**Papiertücher**	pahpeertewkherr
toilet paper	**Toilettenpapier**	toahlehternpahpeer
toilet water	**ein Toilettenwasser**	ighn toahlehternvahsserr
toothbrush	**eine Zahnbürste**	ighner tsaanbewrster
toothpaste	**Zahnpasta**	tsaanpahstah
towel	**ein Handtuch**	ighn hahnttukh
tweezers	**eine Pinzette**	ighner pintsehter

For your hair *Für Ihr Haar*

bobby pins	**Haarklemmen**	haarklehmern
colour shampoo	**ein Tönungsshampoo**	ighn turnungsshahmpoo
comb	**einen Kamm**	ighnern kahm
curlers	**Lockenwickler**	lokkernviklerr
dry shampoo	**ein Trockenshampoo**	ighn trokkernshahmpoo
hairbrush	**eine Haarbürste**	ighner haarbewrster
hair dye	**ein Haarfärbemittel**	ighn haarfehrbermitterl
hairgrips	**Haarklemmen**	haarklehmern
hair lotion	**Haarwasser**	haarvahsserr
hairpins	**Haarnadeln**	haarnaaderln
hair slide	**eine Haarspange**	ighner haarshpahnger
hair spray	**einen Haarspray**	ighnern haarshpray
setting lotion	**einen Haarfestiger**	ighnern haarfehstiggerr
shampoo	**ein Haarwaschmittel**	ighn haarvahshmitterl
for dry/greasy	**für trockenes/**	fewr trokkernerss/
(oily) hair	**fettiges Haar**	fehtiggerss haar
tint	**ein Tönungsmittel**	ighn turnungsmitterl
wig	**eine Perücke**	ighner pehrewker

For the baby *Für den Säugling*

baby food	**Säuglingsnahrung**	zoyglingsnaarung
dummy (pacifier)	**einen Schnuller**	ighnern shnullerr
feeding bottle	**eine Saugflasche**	ighner zowgflahsher
nappies (diapers)	**Windeln**	vinderln

Clothing *Bekleidung*

If you want to buy something specific, prepare yourself in advance. Look at the list of clothing on page 116. Get some idea of the colour, material and size you want. They're all listed on the next few pages.

General *Allgemeines*

I'd like ...	**Ich möchte ...**	ikh murkhter
I want ... for a 10-year-old boy/girl.	**Ich möchte ... für einen Jungen/ ein Mädchen von 10 Jahren.**	ikh murkhter ... fewr ighnern yungern/ ighn maitkhern fon 10 yaarern
I want something like this.	**Ich möchte etwas in dieser Art.**	ikh murkhter ehtvahss in deezerr aart
I like the one in the window.	**Das im Schaufenster gefällt mir.**	dahss im showfehnsterr gerfehlt meer
How much is that per metre?	**Wieviel kostet der Meter?**	veefeel kostert derr mayterr

1 centimetre (cm.)	= 0.39 in.	1 inch	= 2.54 cm.
1 metre (m.)	= 39.37 in.	1 foot	= 30.5 cm.
10 metres	= 32.81 ft.	1 yard	= 0.91 m.

Colour *Farbe*

I want something in ...	**Ich möchte etwas in ...**	ikh murkhter ehtvahss in
I want a darker/ lighter shade.	**Ich möchte es etwas dunkler/heller.**	ikh murkhter ehss ehtvahss dunklerr/hehlerr
I want something to match this.	**Ich möchte etwas hierzu Passendes.**	ikh murkhter ehtvahss heertsoo pahssernderss
I don't like the colour.	**Die Farbe gefällt mir nicht.**	dee fahrber gerfehlt meer nikht
Is it colour fast?	**Ist es farbecht?**	ist ehss fahrpehkht

NUMBERS, see page 147

beige	**beige**	bayzh
black	**schwarz**	shvahrts
blue	**blau**	blow
brown	**braun**	brown
fawn	**hellbraun**	**hehl**brown
golden	**golden**	**gold**ern
green	**grün**	grewn
grey	**grau**	grow
mauve	**lila**	**lee**lah
orange	**orange**	o**rrahng**zher
pink	**rosa**	**roa**zah
purple	**violett**	vio**lleht**
red	**rot**	roat
scarlet	**scharlachrot**	**shahr**lahkhroat
silver	**silbern**	**zil**berrn
turquoise	**türkisfarben**	tewr**kees**fahrbern
white	**weiß**	vighss
yellow	**gelb**	gehlp
light ...	**hell ...**	hehl
dark ...	**dunkel ...**	**dunk**erl

uni	gestreift	gepunktet	kariert	gemustert
(unni)	(ger**shtright**ft)	(ger**punk**tert)	(kah**reert**)	(ger**musterr**t)

Fabric *Stoff*

Do you have anything in ...?	**Haben Sie etwas in ...?**	**haa**bern zee **eht**vahss in
Is that ...?	**Ist das ...?**	ist dahss
handmade	**Handarbeit**	**hahn**tahrbight
imported	**importiert**	import**eert**
made here	**inländisches Fabrikat**	**in**lehndisherss fahbrik**kaat**
I want something thinner.	**Ich möchte etwas Dünneres.**	ikh **murkh**ter **eht**vahss **dew**nerrerss
Do you have any better quality?	**Haben Sie eine bessere Qualität?**	**haa**bern zee **igh**ner **behs**serer kvahlit**tait**

cambric	**Batist**	bahtist
camel-hair	**Kamelhaar**	kahmaylhaar
chiffon	**Chiffon**	shiffoan
corduroy	**Kordsamt**	kortzahmt
cotton	**Baumwolle**	bowmvoller
crepe	**Krepp**	krehp
denim	**Drillich**	drillikh
felt	**Filz**	filts
flannel	**Flanell**	flahnehl
gabardine	**Gabardine**	gahbahrdin
lace	**Spitze**	shpitser
leather	**Leder**	layderr
linen	**Leinen**	lighnern
poplin	**Popeline**	popperleen
rayon	**Kunstseide**	kunstzighder
satin	**Satin**	zahtehng
silk	**Seide**	zighder
suede	**Wildleder**	viltlayderr
terrycloth	**Frottee**	frottay
velvet	**Samt**	zahmt
velveteen	**Manchester**	mahnshehsterr
wool	**Wolle**	voller
worsted	**Kammgarn**	kahmgahrn

Is it ...?	**Ist es ...?**	ist ehss
pure cotton/wool	**reine Baumwolle**	righner bowmvoller
synthetic	**synthetisch**	zewntaytish
wash and wear	**bügelfrei**	bewgerlfrigh
wrinkle resistant	**knitterfrei**	knitterrfrigh
Is it hand washable/ machine washable?	**Kann man es mit der Hand/in der Maschine waschen?**	kahn mahn ehss mit derr hahnt/in derr mahsheener **vah**shern
Will it shrink?	**Läuft es beim Waschen ein?**	loyft ehss bighm **vah**shern ighn

Size *Größe*

I take size 38.	**Ich habe Größe 38.**	ikh **haa**ber grursser 38
Could you measure me?	**Können Sie mir Maß nehmen?**	kurnern zee meer maass naymern
I don't know the German sizes.	**Ich kenne die deutschen Größen nicht.**	ikh **keh**ner dee **doy**chern grursserr nikht

Sizes can vary somewhat from one manufacturer to another, so be sure to try on shoes and clothing before you buy.

Women   *Damen*

Dresses/Suits					
American	8	10	12	14	16	18
British	10	12	14	16	18	20
Continental	36	38	40	42	44	46

Stockings							Shoes			
American	8	8½	9	9½	10	10½	6	7	8	9
British							4½	5½	6½	7½
Continental	0	1	2	3	4	5	37	38	40	41

Men   *Herren*

Suits/Overcoats							Shirts			
American	36	38	40	42	44	46	15	16	17	18
British										
Continental	46	48	50	52	54	56	38	41	43	45

Shoes									
American	5	6	7	8	8½	9	9½	10	11
British									
Continental	38	39	41	42	43	43	44	44	45

A good fit?   *Paßt es?*

Can I try it on?	**Kann ich es anprobieren?**	kahn ikh ehss ahnprobbeerern
Where's the fitting room?	**Wo ist die Umkleidekabine?**	voa ist dee umklighderkahbeener
Is there a mirror?	**Gibt es einen Spiegel?**	gipt ehss ighnern shpeegerl
It fits very well.	**Es paßt sehr gut.**	ehss pahst zayr goot
It doesn't fit.	**Es paßt nicht.**	ehss pahst nikht

NUMBERS, see page 147

It's too ...	**Es ist zu ...**	ehss ist tsu
short/long	**kurz/lang**	koorts/lahng
tight/loose	**eng/weit**	ehng/vight
How long will it take to alter?	**Wie lange brauchen Sie, um es zu ändern?**	vee lahnger browkhern zee um ehss tsoo ehnderrn

Clothes and accessories *Kleidungsstücke und Zubehör*

I would like a/an/some ...	**Ich hätte gern ...**	ikh hehter gehrn
bathrobe	**einen Bademantel**	ighnern baadermahnterl
bathing cap	**eine Badekappe**	ighner baaderkahper
bathing suit	**einen Badeanzug**	ighnern baaderahntsook
blouse	**eine Bluse**	ighner bloozer
bow tie	**eine Fliege**	ighner fleeger
bra	**einen Büstenhalter**	ighnern bewsternhahlterr
braces	**Hosenträger**	hoazerntraigerr
briefs	**eine Unterhose**	ighner unterrhoazer
cap	**eine Mütze**	ighner mewtser
cardigan	**eine Wolljacke**	ighner volyahker
coat	**einen Mantel**	ighnern mahnterl
dress	**ein Kleid**	ighn klight
dressing gown	**einen Morgenrock**	ighnern morgernrok
evening dress (woman's)	**ein Abendkleid**	ighn aaberntklight
frock	**ein Kleid**	ighn klight
fur coat	**einen Pelzmantel**	ighnern pehltsmahnterl
girdle	**einen Hüfthalter**	ighnern hewfthahlterr
gloves	**Handschuhe**	hahntshooer
handbag	**eine Handtasche**	ighner hahnttahsher
handkerchief	**ein Taschentuch**	ighn tahsherntookh
hat	**einen Hut**	ighnern hoot
jacket	**ein Jackett/eine Jacke**	ighn zhahkeht/ighner yahker
jeans	**Jeans**	"jeans"
jersey	**eine Strickjacke**	ighner shtrikyahker
jumper (Br.)	**einen Pullover**	ighnern pulloaverr
leather trousers	**eine Lederhose**	ighner layderrhoazer
nightdress	**ein Nachthemd**	ighn nahkhthehmt
pair of ...	**ein Paar ...**	ighn paar
panties	**einen Schlüpfer**	ighnern shlewpferr
pants (Am.)	**eine Hose**	ighner hoazer
panty girdle	**ein Strumpf-halterhöschen**	ighn shtrumpfhahlterr-hurskhern
panty hose	**eine Strumpfhose**	ighner shtrumpfhoazer

pullover	einen Pullover	ighnern pulloaverr
roll-neck (turtle-neck)	mit Rollkragen	mit rolkraagern
round-neck	mit rundem Ausschnitt	mit runderm owsshnit
V-neck	mit V-Ausschnitt	mit fowowsshnit
with long/short sleeves	mit langen/kurzen Ärmeln	mit lahngern/koortsern ehrmerln
without sleeves	ärmellos	ehrmerlloass
pyjamas	einen Schlafanzug	ighnern shlaafahntsoog
raincoat	einen Regenmantel	ighnern raygernmahnterl
scarf	ein Halstuch	ighn hahlstookh
shirt	ein Hemd	ighn hehmt
shorts	Shorts	"shorts"
skirt	einen Rock	ighnern rok
slip	einen Unterrock	ighnern unterrrok
socks	Socken	zokkern
stockings	Strümpfe	shtrewmpfer
suit (man's)	einen Anzug	ighnern ahntsoog
suit (woman's)	ein Kostüm	ighn kostewm
suspenders (Am.)	Hosenträger	hoazerntraigerr
sweater	einen Pullover	ighnern pulloaverr
sweatshirt	ein Sweatshirt	ighn "sweatshirt"
swimming trunks	eine Badehose	ighner baaderhoazer
swimsuit	einen Badeanzug	ighnern baaderahntsoog
T-shirt	ein T-Shirt	ighn "T-shirt"
tie	eine Krawatte	ighner krahvahter
tights	eine Strumpfhose	ighner shtrumpfhoazer
tracksuit	einen Trainingsanzug	ighnern trainingsahntsoog
trousers	eine Hose	ighner hoazer
umbrella	einen Regenschirm	ighnern raygernshirm
underpants	eine Unterhose/ einen Slip	ighner unterrhoazer/ ighnern "slip"
undershirt	ein Unterhemd	ighn unterrhehmt
vest (Am.)	eine Weste	ighner vehster
vest (Br.)	ein Unterhemd	ighn unterrhehmt
waistcoat	eine Weste	ighner vehster

belt	der Gürtel	derr gewrterl
buckle	die Schnalle	dee shnahler
button	der Knopf	derr knopf
pocket	die Tasche	dee tahsher
press stud (snap fastener)	der Druckknopf	derr drukknopf
zip (zipper)	der Reißverschluß	derr righsfehrshluss

Shoes *Schuhe*

I'd like a pair of ...	Ich möchte ein Paar ...	ikh murkhter ighn paar
boots	Stiefel	shteeferl
moccasins	Mokassins	mokkahssins
plimsolls (sneakers)	Turnschuhe	toornshooer
rain boots	Gummistiefel	gummishteeferl
sandals	Sandalen	zahndaalern
shoes	Schuhe	shooer
flat	flache	flahkher
with a heel	mit hohen Absätzen	mit hoaern ahpzehtsern
with leather soles	mit Ledersohlen	mit layderzoalern
with rubber soles	mit Gummisohlen	mit gummizoalern
slippers	Hausschuhe	howsshooer
These are too ...	Diese sind zu ...	deezer zint tsu
narrow/wide	eng/weit	ehng/vight
large/small	groß/klein	groass/klighn
Do you have a larger/ smaller size?	Haben Sie eine größere/kleinere Nummer?	haabern zee ighner grursserrer/klighnerrer nummerr
Do you have the same in black?	Haben Sie die gleichen in Schwarz?	haabern zee dee glighkhern in shvahrts
cloth/leather	Stoff/Leder	shtof/layderr
rubber/suede	Gummi/Wildleder	gummi/viltlayderr
Is it genuine leather?	Ist es echtes Leder?	ist ehss ehkhters layderr
I need some shoe polish/shoelaces.	Ich brauche Schuhcreme/ Schnürsenkel.	ikh browkher shookraym/ shnewrzehnkerl

Shoes worn out? Here's the key to getting them fixed again:

Can you repair these shoes?	Können Sie diese Schuhe reparieren?	kurnern zee deezer shooer rehpahreerern
Can you stitch this?	Können Sie das nähen?	kurnern zee dahss naiern
I want new soles and heels.	Ich möchte neue Sohlen und Absätze.	ikh murkhter noyer zoalern unt ahpzehtser
When will they be ready?	Wann sind sie fertig?	vahn zint zee fehrtikh

COLOURS, see page 113

Electrical appliances *Elektrische Geräte*

220 volt, 50-cycle A.C. is almost universal in Germany as well as in Austria and Switzerland.

What's the voltage?	**Welche Spannung haben Sie hier?**	vehlkher shpahnung haabern zee heer
Do you have a battery for this?	**Haben Sie eine Batterie hierfür?**	haabern zee ighner bahterree heerfewr
This is broken. Can you repair it?	**Das ist kaputt. Können Sie es reparieren?**	dahss ist kahput. kurnern zee ehss rehpahreerern
Can you show me how it works?	**Können Sie mir zeigen, wie es funktioniert?**	kurnern zee meer tsighgern vee ehss funktsionneert
I'd like a video cassette.	**Ich möchte eine Videokassette.**	ikh murkhter ighner veedehokkahssehter
I'd like a/an/ some ...	**Ich möchte ...**	ikh murkhter
adaptor	**einen Zwischen-stecker**	ighnern tsvishern-shtehkerr
amplifier	**einen Verstärker**	ighnern fehrshtairkerr
bulb	**eine Glühbirne**	ighner glewbeerner
clock-radio	**einen Radiowecker**	ighnern raadiovehkerr
electric toothbrush	**eine elektrische Zahnbürste**	ighner aylehktrisher tsaanbewrster
extension lead (cord)	**eine Verlängerungs-schnur**	ighner fehrlehngerrungs-shnoor
hair dryer	**einen Haartrockner**	ighnern haartroknerr
headphones	**einen Kopfhörer**	ighnern kopfhurrerr
(travelling) iron	**ein (Reise)bügeleisen**	ighn (righzer)bewgerlighzern
lamp	**eine Lampe**	ighner lahmper
plug	**einen Stecker**	ighnern shtehkerr
portable ...	**Koffer- ...**	kofferr
radio	**ein Radio**	ighn raadio
car radio	**Autoradio**	owtorraadio
record player	**einen Plattenspieler**	ighnern plahternshpeelerr
shaver	**einen Rasierapparat**	ighnern rahzeerahpahraat
speakers	**Lautsprecher**	lowtshprehkherr
(cassette) tape recorder	**einen Kassetten-recorder**	ighnern kahssehtern-rehkorderr
(colour) television	**einen (Farb)fernseher**	ighnern (fahrp)fehrnzayerr
transformer	**einen Transformator**	ighnern trahnsformaator
video-recorder	**einen Videorecorder**	ighnern veedehorrehkorderr

Grocery *Lebensmittelgeschäft*

I'd like some bread, please.	**Ich möchte ein Brot, bitte.**	ikh **murkh**ter ighn broat **bitter**
What sort of cheese do you have?	**Welche Käsesorten haben Sie?**	**vehl**kher **kai**zerzortern **haa**bern zee
A piece of ...	**Ein Stück von ...**	ighn shtewk fon
this one	**diesem**	**dee**zerm
the one on the shelf	**dem auf dem Regal**	daym owf daym **reh**gaal
I'll have one of those, please.	**Ich möchte einen von denen, bitte.**	ikh **murkh**ter **igh**nern fon **day**nern **bitter**
May I help myself?	**Kann ich mich selbst bedienen?**	kahn ikh mikh **zehl**pst ber**dee**nern
I'd like ...	**Ich möchte ...**	ikh **murkh**ter
a kilo of apples	**ein Kilo Äpfel**	ighn **kee**lo **ehp**ferl
half a kilo of tomatoes	**ein halbes Kilo Tomaten**	ighn **hahl**bers **kee**lo tom**maa**tern
100 grams of butter	**100 Gramm Butter**	100 grahm **butterr**
a litre of milk	**einen Liter Milch**	**igh**nern **lee**terr milkh
half a dozen of eggs	**ein halbes Dutzend Eier**	ighn **hahl**bers **dut**sernd **igh**err
4 slices of ham	**4 Scheiben Schinken**	4 **shigh**bern **shin**kern
a box of chocolate	**eine Schachtel Schokolade**	**igh**ner **shahkh**terl shok**kol**laader
a jar of jam	**ein Glas Marmelade**	ighn glaass mahrmer**laa**der
a tin (can) of peaches	**eine Büchse Pfirsiche**	**igh**ner **bewk**ser **pfeer**ziker
a tube of mustard	**eine Tube Senf**	**igh**ner **too**ber zehnf
a packet of tea	**eine Packung Tee**	**igh**ner **pah**kung tay

Weights and measures		
1 kilogram or kilo (kg.) = 1000 grams (g.)		
100 g. = 3.5 oz.	½ kg. = 1.1 lb.	
200 g. = 7.0 oz.	1 kg. = 2.2 lb.	
1 oz. = 28.35 g.		
1 lb. = 453.60 g.		

1 litre (l.) = 0.88 imp. quarts = 1.06 U.S. quarts		
1 imp. quart = 1.14 l.	1 U.S. quart = 0.95 l.	
1 imp. gallon = 4.55 l.	1 U.S. gallon = 3.8 l.	

FOOD, see also page 64

Einkaufsführer

Jeweller's—Watchmaker's   *Juwelier – Uhrmacher*

I want a small present for ...	**Ich möchte ein kleines Geschenk für ...**	ikh **murkh**ter ighn **kligh**nerss ger**shehnk** fewr
Could I please see that?	**Könnte ich das bitte sehen?**	**kurn**ter ikh dahss **bitt**er **zay**ern
Do you have anything in gold?	**Haben Sie etwas in Gold?**	**haab**ern zee **eht**vahss in golt
How many carats is this?	**Wieviel Karat hat es?**	vee**feel** kah**raat** haht ehss
Is this real silver?	**Ist das Echtsilber?**	ist dahss **ekht**zilberr
Can you repair this watch?	**Können Sie diese Uhr reparieren?**	**kurn**ern zee **dee**zer oor rehpah**ree**rern
I'd like a/an/some ...	**Ich möchte ...**	ikh **murkh**ter
alarm clock	**einen Wecker**	**igh**nern **veh**kerr
bangle	**einen Armreif**	**igh**nern **ahrm**righf
battery	**eine Batterie**	**igh**ner bahter**ree**
bracelet	**ein Armband**	ighn **ahrm**bahnt
chain bracelet	**Gliederarmband**	**glee**derrahrmbahnt
charm bracelet	**Amulettarmband**	ahmu**leht**ahrmbahnt
brooch	**eine Brosche**	**igh**ner **brosh**er
chain	**eine Kette**	**igh**ner **keht**er
charm	**ein Amulett**	ighn ahmu**leht**
cigarette case	**ein Zigarettenetui**	ighn tsiggah**reh**ternehtvee
cigarette lighter	**ein Feuerzeug**	ighn **foy**errtsoyg
clip	**einen Klipp**	**igh**nern klip
clock	**eine Uhr**	**igh**ner oor
cross	**ein Kreuz**	ighn kroyts
cuckoo clock	**eine Kuckucksuhr**	**igh**ner **kuk**kuksoor
cuff links	**Manschettenknöpfe**	mahn**sheh**ternknurpfer
cutlery	**Tafelbesteck**	**taa**ferlbershtehk
earrings	**Ohrringe**	**oar**ringer
gem	**einen Edelstein**	**igh**nern **ayd**erlshtighn
jewel box	**ein Schmuckkästchen**	ighn **shmuk**kehstkhern
music box	**eine Spieldose**	**igh**ner **shpeel**doazer
necklace	**eine Halskette**	**igh**ner **hahls**kehter
pendant	**einen Anhänger**	**igh**nern **ahn**hehngerr
pin	**eine Anstecknadel**	**igh**ner **ahn**shtehknaaderl
pocket watch	**eine Taschenuhr**	**igh**ner **tahsh**ernoor
powder compact	**eine Puderdose**	**igh**ner **pood**errdoazer

ring	einen Ring	ighnern ring
engagement ring	**Verlobungsring**	fehrloabungsring
signet ring	**Siegelring**	zeegerlring
wedding ring	**Ehering**	ayerring
rosary	einen Rosenkranz	ighnern roazernkrahnts
silverware	Tafelsilber	taaferlzilberr
tie clip	einen Krawatten-klipp	ighnern krahvahternklip
tie pin	eine Krawatten-nadel	ighner krahvahternnaaderl
watch	eine Uhr	ighner oor
automatic	**automatische**	owtomaatisher
digital	**Digital-**	diggitaal
quartz	**Quarz-**	kvahrts
with a second hand	**mit Sekundenzeiger**	mit zehkunderntsighgerr
waterproof	**wasserdicht**	wahsserrdikht
watchstrap	ein Uhrarmband	ighn oorahrmbahnt
wristwatch	eine Armbanduhr	ighner ahrmbahntoor

amber	**Bernstein**	behrnshtighn
amethyst	**Amethyst**	ahmehtist
chromium	**Chrom**	kroam
copper	**Kupfer**	kupferr
coral	**Koralle**	korrahler
crystal	**Kristall**	kristahl
cut glass	**geschliffenes Glas**	gershliffernerss glahss
diamond	**Diamant**	diahmahnt
emerald	**Smaragd**	smahrahgt
enamel	**Email**	ehmahi
gold	**Gold**	golt
gold-plated	**vergoldet**	fehrgoldert
ivory	**Elfenbein**	ehlfernbighn
jade	**Jade**	yaader
onyx	**Onyx**	oaniks
pearl	**Perle**	pehrler
pewter	**Zinn**	tsin
platinum	**Platin**	plaateen
ruby	**Rubin**	rubeen
sapphire	**Saphir**	zahfeer
silver	**Silber**	zilberr
silver-plated	**versilbert**	fehrzilbert
stainless steel	**rostfreier Stahl**	rostfrigherr shtaal
topaz	**Topas**	toppaass
turquoise	**Türkis**	tewrkeess

Optician *Optiker*

| I've broken my glasses. | Meine Brille ist zerbrochen. | mighner briller ist tsehrbrokhern |
| I've broken my glasses. | Meine Brille ist zerbrochen. | mighner briller ist tsehrbrokhern |

English	German	Pronunciation
I've broken my glasses.	**Meine Brille ist zerbrochen.**	**migh**ner **bril**ler ist tsehr**brokh**ern
Can you repair them for me?	**Können Sie sie reparieren?**	**kur**nern zee zee rehpah**ree**rern
When will they be ready?	**Wann ist sie fertig?**	vahn ist zee **fehr**tikh
Can you change the lenses?	**Können Sie die Gläser auswechseln?**	**kur**nern zee dee **glai**zerr **ows**vehk**serl**n
I want tinted lenses.	**Ich möchte getönte Gläser.**	ikh **murkh**ter ger**turn**ter **glai**zerr
The frame is broken.	**Das Gestell ist zerbrochen.**	dahss ger**shtehl** ist tsehr**brokh**ern
I'd like a spectacle case.	**Ich möchte ein Brillenetui.**	ikh **murkh**ter ighn **bril**lerneh**tvee**
I'd like to have my eyesight checked.	**Ich möchte meine Augen kontrollieren lassen.**	ikh **murkh**ter **migh**ner **ow**gern kontro**lee**rern **lahs**sern
I'm short-sighted/long-sighted.	**Ich bin kurzsichtig/weitsichtig.**	ikh bin **kurts**zikhtikh/**vight**zikhtikh
I want some contact lenses.	**Ich möchte Kontaktlinsen.**	ikh **murkh**ter kon**tahkt**linzern
I've lost one of my contact lenses.	**Ich habe eine Kontaktlinse verloren.**	ikh **haab**er **igh**ner kon**tahkt**linzer fehr**loar**ern
Could you give me another one?	**Können Sie mir eine Ersatzlinse geben?**	**kur**nern zee meer **igh**ner err**zahts**linzer **gay**bern
I have hard/soft lenses.	**Ich habe harte/weiche Linsen.**	ikh **haab**er **hahr**ter/**vigh**kher **lin**zern
Have you any contact-lens liquid?	**Haben Sie eine Flüssigkeit für Kontaktlinsen?**	**haab**ern zee **igh**ner **flew**ssikhkight fewr kon**tahkt**linzern
I'd like to buy a pair of sunglasses.	**Ich hätte gern eine Sonnenbrille.**	ikh **heh**ter gehrn **igh**ner **zon**nernbriller
May I look in a mirror?	**Kann ich mich im Spiegel sehen?**	kahn ikh mikh im **shpee**gerl **zay**ern
I'd like to buy a pair of binoculars.	**Ich hätte gern ein Fernglas.**	ikh **heh**ter gehrn ighn **fehrn**glaass

Photography *Fotogeschäft*

I want a(n) ... camera.	**Ich möchte einen ... Fotoapparat.**	ikh murkhter ighnern ... foatoahpahraat
automatic	**automatischen**	owtommaatishern
inexpensive	**billigen**	billiggern
simple	**einfachen**	ighnfahkhern
Show me some cine (movie) cameras, please.	**Zeigen Sie mir bitte einige Filmkameras.**	tsighgern zee meer bitter ighnigger filmkahmehraass
Show me that one in the window.	**Zeigen Sie mir die im Schaufenster.**	tsighgern zee meer dee im showfehnsterr
I'd like to have some passport photos taken.	**Ich möchte Paßbilder machen lassen.**	ikh murkhter pahssbilderr mahkhern lahssern

Film *Filme*

I'd like a film for this camera.	**Ich hätte gern einen Film für diese Kamera.**	ikh hehter gehrn ighnern film fewr deezer kahmehraa
black and white	**Schwarzweißfilm**	shvahrtsvighsfilm
colour	**Farbfilm**	fahrpfilm
colour negative	**Farbnegativfilm**	fahrpnehgahteeffilm
colour slide	**Film für Farbdias**	film fewr fahrpdeeahss
cartridge	**eine Kassette**	ighner kahssehter
roll film	**ein Rollfilm**	ighn rolfilm
24/36 exposures	**vierundzwanzig/ sechsunddreißig Aufnahmen**	feerunttsvahntsikh/ zehksuntdrighssikh owfnaamern
this size	**dieses Format**	deezers formaat
this ASA/DIN number	**diese ASA/DIN-Zahl**	deezer aazaa/deen tsaal
artificial light type	**Kunstlichtfilm**	kunstlikhtfilm
daylight type	**Tageslichtfilm**	taagerslikhtfilm
fast (high speed)	**hochempfindlich**	hoakhehmpfintlikh
fine grain	**Feinkorn**	fighnkorn

Processing *Entwickeln*

How much do you charge for developing?	**Was kostet das Entwickeln?**	vahss kostert dahss ehntvikkerln

NUMBERS, see page 147

I want ... prints of each negative.	Ich möchte ... Abzüge von jedem Negativ.	ikh murkhter ... ahptsewger fon yayderm nehgahteef
with a mat finish	matt	maht
with a glossy finish	Hochglanz	hokhglahnts
Will you please enlarge this?	Können Sie das bitte vergrößern?	kurnern zee dahss bitter fehrgrursserrn
When will the photos be ready?	Wann sind die Fotos fertig?	vahn zint dee foatoss fehrtikh

Accessories and repairs *Zubehör und Reparaturen*

I want a/an/some ...	Ich möchte ...	ikh murkhter
battery	eine Batterie	ighner bahterree
cable release	einen Drahtauslöser	ighnern draatowslurzer
camera case	eine Fototasche	ighner foatotahsher
(electronic) flash	einen (Elektronen) blitz	ighnern (aylehktroanern) blits
filter	einen Filter	ighnern filterr
for black and white	für schwarzweiß	fewr shvahrtsvighss
for colour	für Farbe	fewr fahrber
lens	ein Objektiv	ighn obyehkteef
telephoto lens	ein Teleobjektiv	ighn taylerobyehkteef
wide-angle lens	ein Weitwinkel- objektiv	ighn vightvinkerlobyehkteef
lens cap	einen Objektivdeckel	ighnern obyehkteefdehkerl
Can you repair this camera?	Können Sie diesen Fotoapparat repa- rieren?	kurnern zee deezern foatoahpahraat rehpah- reerern
The film is jammed.	Der Film klemmt.	derr film klehmt
There's something wrong with the ...	Mit ... stimmt etwas nicht.	mit ... shtimt ehtvahss nikht
exposure counter	dem Bildzählwerk	daym bilttsailvehrk
film winder	dem Filmtransport	daym filmtrahnsport
flash attachment	dem Blitzgerät	daym blitsgerrait
lens	dem Objektiv	daym obyehkteef
light meter	dem Belichtungs- messer	daym berlikhtungsmehsserr
rangefinder	dem Entfernungs- messer	daym ehntfehrnungsmehsser
shutter	dem Verschluß	daym fehrshluss

Tobacconist's *Tabakladen*

Cigarettes are sold in specialized tobacco shops, at kiosks and from vending machines. In Switzerland you can also buy cigarettes in restaurants, supermarkets, etc.

A packet of cigarettes, please.	**Eine Schachtel Zigaretten, bitte.**	ighner shahkhterl tsiggahrehtern bitter
Do you have any American/English cigarettes?	**Haben Sie amerikanische/ englische Zigaretten?**	haabern zee ahmehrikkaanisher ehnglisher tsiggahrehtern
I'd like a carton.	**Ich möchte eine Stange.**	ikh murkhter ighner shtahnger
Give me a/some ..., please.	**Geben Sie mir bitte ...**	gaybern zee meer bitter
candy	**Bonbons**	bongbongs
chewing gum	**Kaugummi**	kowgummi
chewing tobacco	**Kautabak**	kowtahbahk
chocolate	**Schokolade**	shokkollaader
cigarette case	**ein Zigarettenetui**	ighn tsiggahrehternehtvee
cigarette holder	**eine Zigarettenspitze**	ighner tsiggahrehternshpitser
cigarettes	**Zigaretten**	tsiggahrehtern
filter-tipped	**mit Filter**	mit filterr
without filter	**ohne Filter**	oaner filterr
light/dark tobacco	**heller/dunkler Tabak**	hehlerr/dunklerr tahbahk
mild/strong	**milder/starker**	milderr/shtahrkerr
menthol	**Menthol-**	mehntoal
king-size	**extra lang**	ehkstraa lahng
cigars	**Zigarren**	tsiggahrern
lighter	**ein Feuerzeug**	ighn foyerrtsoyg
lighter fluid/gas	**Benzin/Gas fürs Feuerzeug**	behntseen/gaass fewrs foyerrtsoyg
matches	**Streichhölzer**	shtrighkhhurltserr
pipe	**eine Pfeife**	ighner pfighfer
pipe cleaners	**Pfeifenreiniger**	pfighfernrighniggerr
pipe tobacco	**Pfeifentabak**	pfighferntahbahk
pipe tool	**ein Pfeifenbesteck**	ighn pfighfernbershtehk
postcard	**eine Postkarte**	ighner postkahrter
snuff	**Schnupftabak**	shnupftahbahk
stamps	**Briefmarken**	breefmahrkern
sweets	**Bonbons**	bongbongs
wick	**einen Docht**	ighnern dokht

Miscellaneous   *Verschiedenes*

Souvenirs   *Andenken*

Here are some suggestions for articles which you might like
to bring back as a souvenir or a gift from Germany.

Bavarian peasant dress	**das Dirndl(kleid)**	dahss **deerndl**(klight)
beer stein	**der Bierkrug**	derr **beerkroog**
glassware	**die Glaswaren**	dee **glahs**vaarern
leather goods	**die Lederwaren**	dee **lay**derrvaarern
music box	**die Spieldose**	dee **shpeel**doazer
porcelain	**das Porzellan**	dahss portsehlaan
waterproof woollen overcoat	**der Lodenmantel**	derr **loa**dernmahnterl
wood carving	**die Holzschnitzarbeit**	dee **holts**shnitsahrbight

The high quality of Austrian and Swiss winter sports equipment is well known. But petit-point embroidery and porcelain in Austria and linens and organdies in Switzerland are
also good buys. Consider leather goods and *Lederhosen*
(knee-length leather trousers) in Austria, and don't miss the
fabulous array of watches and luscious chocolate in Switzerland.

chocolate	**die Schokolade**	dee shokkollaader
cuckoo clock	**die Kuckucksuhr**	dee kukkuksoor
embroidery	**die Stickerei**	dee shtikkerrigh
linen	**das Leinenzeug**	dahss **lighn**erntsoyg
ski equipment	**die Skiausrüstung**	dee **shee**owsrewstung
Swiss army knife	**Schweizer Armee-messer**	**shvight**serr ahrmay-mehsserr
Tyrolean hat	**der Tirolerhut**	derr **teeroa**lerrhoot
Tyrolean pipe	**die Tiroler Pfeife**	dee **teeroa**lerr pfighfer
watch	**die Uhr**	dee oor

Records—Cassettes   *Schallplatten – Kassetten*

Do you have any records by ...?	**Haben Sie Schall-platten von ...?**	haabern zee **shahl-**plahtern fon
Can I listen to this record?	**Kann ich diese Platte hören?**	kahn ikh **dee**zer **plah**ter hurrern

L.P. (33 rpm)	die Langspielplatte (33 UpM)	dee lahngshpeelplahter (drighuntdrighssik oo pay ehm)
E.P. (45 rpm)	45 UpM	fewnfuntfeertsikh oo pay ehm
single	die Single	dee "single"

Have you any songs by ...?	Haben Sie Lieder von ...?	haabern zee leederr fon
I'd like a ...	Ich hätte gern ...	ikh hehter gehrn
cassette	eine Kassette	ighner kahssehter
video cassette	eine Videokassette	ighner veedehokkahssehter
compact disc	eine Compact Disc	ighner "compact disc"
chamber music	die Kammermusik	dee kahmerrmuzeek
classical music	die klassische Musik	dee klahssisher muzeek
folk music	die Volksmusik	dee folksmuzeek
instrumental music	die Instrumental-musik	dee instrumehntaalmuzeek
jazz	der Jazz	derr dzhaiss
light music	die Unterhaltungs-musik	dee unterrhahltungsmuzeek
orchestral music	die Orchestermusik	dee orkehsterrmuzeek
pop music	die Popmusik	dee popmuzeek

Toys *Spielwaren*

I'd like a toy/ game ...	Ich möchte ein Spiel-zeug/Spiel ...	ikh murkhter ighn shpeel-tsoyg/shpeel
for a boy	für einen Jungen	fewr ighnern yungern
for a 5-year-old girl	für ein 5-jähriges Mädchen	fewr ighn 5yairiggerss maitkhern
ball	einen Ball	ighnern bahl
bucket and spade (pail and shovel)	Eimer und Schaufel	ighmerr unt showferl
building blocks	einen Baukasten	ighnern bowkahstern
card game	ein Kartenspiel	ighn kahrternshpeel
chess set	ein Schachspiel	ighn shahkhshpeel
doll	eine Puppe	ighner pupper
electronic game	ein elektronisches Spiel	ighn aylektroanishers shpeel
roller skates	Rollschuhe	rolshooer

NUMBERS, see page 147

Your money: banks—currency

Banking hours in Germany are usually from 8.30 a.m. to 1 p.m. and from 2.30 to 4 p.m., Monday to Friday (Thursday until 5.30 p.m.). Hours are slightly different in Austria and Switzerland. Small currency-exchange offices, indicated by the words *Geldwechsel* or *Wechselstube* are sometimes open outside regular banking hours.

The *Deutsche Mark* (abbreviated to *DM* and called *D-Mark* —**day** mahrk) is the unit of currency in Germany. It's divided into 100 *Pfennig* (**pfeh**nikh), abbreviated *Pf*.
Coins: 1, 2 and 5 marks; 1, 2, 5, 10 and 50 pfennigs.
Banknotes: 5, 10, 20, 50, 100, 500 and 1,000 marks.

In Austria, the basic unit is the *Schilling* (**shil**ling), abbreviated *S*. It's divided into 100 *Groschen* (**gro**shern), abbreviated *g*.
Coins: 1, 5, 10 and 20 schillings; 10 and 50 groschen.
Banknotes: 20, 50, 100, 500 and 1,000 schillings.

The *Franken* (**frahn**kern), usually abbreviated *Fr.*, is the Swiss unit of currency. There are 100 *Rappen* (**rah**pern), abbreviated *Rp.*, to a franc.
Coins: 1, 2 and 5 francs; 5, 10, 20 and 50 Rappen.
Banknotes: 10, 20, 50, 100, 500 and 1,000 francs.

Credit cards may be used in an increasing number of hotels, restaurants, shops, etc. Signs are posted indicating which cards are accepted.

Traveller's cheques are accepted by hotels, travel agents and many shops, although the exchange rate is invariably better at a bank. Eurocheques are also accepted.

| Where's the nearest bank? | **Wo ist die nächste Bank?** | voa ist dee **naikh**ster bahnk |
| Where is the currency exchange? | **Wo ist die Wechselstube?** | voa ist dee **vehk**sel-shtoober |

At the bank *In der Bank*

I want to change some dollars/pounds.	**Ich möchte Dollar/Pfund wechseln.**	ikh murkhter dollahr/pfunt vehkserln
I want to cash a traveller's cheque.	**Ich möchte einen Reisescheck einlösen.**	ikh murkhter ighnern righzershehk ighnlurzern
What's the exchange rate?	**Wie ist der Wechselkurs?**	vee ist derr vehkserlkoorss
How much commission do you charge?	**Welche Gebühr erheben Sie?**	vehlkher gerbewr ehrhaybern zee
Can you telex my bank in London?	**Können Sie meiner Bank in London ein Telex schicken?**	kurnern zee mighnerr bahnk in london ighn taylehks shikkern
I have a/an/some ...	**Ich habe ...**	ikh haaber
bank card	**eine Kontokarte**	ighner kontokkahrter
credit card	**eine Kreditkarte**	ighner krayditkahrter
Eurocheques	**Eurocheques**	oyroshehks
introduction from ...	**einen Empfehlungsbrief von ...**	ighnern ehmpfaylungsbreef fon
letter of credit	**einen Kreditbrief**	ighnern krayditbreef
I'm expecting some money from New York. Has it arrived yet?	**Ich erwarte Geld aus New York. Ist es schon angekommen?**	ikh ehrvahrter gehlt owss "New York". ist ehss shoan ahngerkommern
Please give me ... notes (bills) and some small change.	**Geben Sie mir bitte ... Scheine und etwas Kleingeld.**	gaybern zee meer bitter ... shighner unt ehtvahss klighngehlt
Give me ... large notes and the rest in small notes.	**Geben Sie mir ... große Scheine und den Rest in kleinen Scheinen.**	gaybern zee meer ... groasser shighner unt dayn rehst in klighnern shighnern

Depositing—Withdrawing *Einzahlen – Abheben*

I want to ...	**Ich möchte ...**	ikh murkhter
open an account	**ein Konto eröffnen**	ighn konto ehrurfnern
withdraw ...	**... abheben**	... ahphaybern
Where should I sign?	**Wo muß ich unterschreiben?**	voa muss ikh unterrshrighbern

NUMBERS, see page 147

| I want to deposit this in my account. | Ich möchte das auf mein Konto einzahlen. | ikh **murkh**ter dahss owf mighn **konto ighnt**saalern |

Business terms *Geschäftsausdrücke*

My name is ...	Ich heiße ...	ikh **high**sser
Here's my card.	Hier ist meine Karte.	heer ist **mighn**er **kahr**ter
I have an appointment with Mr./Mrs. ...	Ich bin mit Herrn/Frau ... verabredet.	ikh bin mit hehrn/frow ... fehr**ah**praydert
Can you give me an estimate of the cost?	Können Sie mir einen Kostenvoranschlag machen?	**kur**nern zee meer **igh**nern **kostern**foarahnshlaak **mahkh**ern
What's the rate of inflation?	Wie hoch ist die Inflationsrate?	vee hoakh ist dee inflah**tsioans**raater
Can you provide me with an interpreter/a secretary?	Können Sie mir einen Dolmetscher/eine Sekretärin besorgen?	**kur**nern zee meer **igh**nern **dolmehts**herr/**igh**ner zaykray**tair**in ber**zoar**gern
Where can I make photocopies?	Wo kann ich Fotokopien machen?	voa kahn ikh **foato**kope**eern mahkh**ern

amount	der Betrag	derr ber**traag**
balance	die Bilanz	dee bil**lahnts**
capital	das Kapital	dahss kahpit**taal**
cheque book	das Scheckbuch	dahss **shehk**bookh
contract	der Vertrag	derr fehr**traag**
expenses	die Unkosten	dee **oon**kostern
interest	die Zinsen	dee **tsin**zern
investment	die Kapitalanlage	dee kahpit**taal**ahnlaager
invoice	die Rechnung	dee **rehkh**nung
loss	der Verlust	derr fehr**lust**
mortgage	die Hypothek	dee hippo**tayk**
payment	die Zahlung	dee **tsaa**lung
percentage	der Prozentsatz	derr pro**tsehnt**zahts
profit	der Gewinn	derr ger**vin**
purchase	der Kauf	derr kowf
sale	der Verkauf	derr fehr**kowf**
share	die Aktie	dee **ahkt**sier
transfer	die Überweisung	dee ewberr**vigh**zung
value	der Wert	derr vayrt

At the post office

The offices of Germany's *Bundespost* are open from 8 a.m. to 6 p.m. They close at noon on Saturdays. Swiss post offices are open from 7.30 a.m. to midday and from 1.30 to 6.30 p.m. (8 to 11 a.m. on Saturdays). In Austria, post offices are open from 8 a.m. to midday and from 2 to 5 p.m. (8 to 10 or noon on Saturdays). Letter boxes (mailboxes) are painted yellow in Germany and Switzerland and yellow or blue in Austria. In principal cities, some post offices are open outside the normal hours. Remember that for telephoning and cables you should go to the post office—there are no separate telephone or cable offices.

Where's the nearest post office?	**Wo ist das nächste Postamt?**	voa ist dahss **naikh**ster **post**ahmt
What time does the post office open/ close?	**Wann öffnet/schließt das Postamt?**	vahn **urf**nert/**shleest** dahss **post**ahmt
A stamp for this letter/postcard, please.	**Eine Briefmarke für diesen Brief/diese Postkarte, bitte.**	**igh**ner **breef**maarker fewr **dee**zern breef/**dee**zer **post**kaarter **bit**ter
A ...-pfennig stamp, please.	**Eine Briefmarke zu ... Pfennig, bitte.**	**igh**ner **breef**maarker tsoo ... **pfeh**nikh **bit**ter
What's the postage for a letter to London?	**Was kostet ein Brief nach London?**	vahss **kos**tert ighn breef naakh **london**
What's the postage for a postcard to Los Angeles?	**Was kostet eine Postkarte nach Los Angeles?**	vahss **kos**tert **igh**ner **post**kaarter naakh los **ehnd**zehrlerss
Where's the letter box (mailbox)?	**Wo ist der Brief- kasten?**	voa ist derr **breef**kahstern
I want to send this by ...	**Ich möchte dies ... senden.**	ikh **murkh**ter deess ... **zehn**dern
airmail	**per Luftpost**	pehr **luft**post
express (special delivery)	**per Expreß**	pehr **ehks**prehss
registered mail	**per Einschreiben**	pehr **ighn**shrighbern

I want to send this parcel.	**Ich möchte dieses Paket schicken.**	ikh **murkh**ter **dee**zers pah**kayt shikk**ern
At which counter can I cash an international money order?	**An welchem Schalter kann ich eine internationale Postanweisung einlösen?**	ahn **vehl**kherm **shahl**terr kahn ikh **igh**ner interr**nahts**ioa**naa**ler **post**ahnvighzung **ighn**lurzern
Where's the poste restante (general delivery)?	**Wo ist der Schalter für postlagernde Sendungen?**	voa ist derr **shahl**terr fewr **post**laagerrnder **zehn**dungern
Is there any mail for me? My name is ...	**Ist Post für mich da? Ich heiße ...**	ist post fewr mikh daa? ikh **high**sser

BRIEFMARKEN	STAMPS
PAKETE	PARCELS
POSTANWEISUNGEN	MONEY ORDERS

Telegrams *Telegramme*

For telegrams you should go to the post-office—there are no separate cable offices.

I want to send a telegram/telex. May I please have a form?	**Ich möchte ein Telegramm/Telex aufgeben. Kann ich bitte ein Formular haben?**	ikh **murkh**ter ighn taylay**grahm**/**tay**lehks **owf**gaybern. kahn ikh **bitt**er ighn formul**laar haa**bern
How much is it per word?	**Was kostet es pro Wort?**	vahss **kost**ert ehss proa vort
How long will a cable to Chicago take?	**Wie lange braucht ein Telegramm nach Chicago?**	vee **lahn**ger browkht ighn taylay**grahm** naakh tshikk**aa**go

Telephoning *Telefonieren*

The telephone networks of Germany, Austria and Switzerland are almost entirely automated. Coin-operated booths are to be found on the street, with instructions posted inside, often in English.

International calls can be made from almost all public telephones in Germany and in Switzerland. In Austria, only some are equipped for long-distance calls. If you need assistance in placing the call, go to the post office or ask at your hotel.

Phone numbers are given in pairs. Note that, in telephoning, *zwei* becomes *zwo* (tsvoa).

Where's the telephone?	**Wo ist das Telefon?**	voa ist dahss taylayfoan
Where's the nearest telephone booth?	**Wo ist die nächste Telefonzelle?**	voa ist dee **naikh**ster taylayfoantsehler
May I use your phone?	**Darf ich Ihr Telefon benutzen?**	dahrf ikh eer taylay**foan** bernutsern
Do you have a telephone directory for Bonn?	**Haben Sie ein Telefonbuch von Bonn?**	**haa**bern zee ighn taylayfoanbukh fon bon
What's the dialling (area) code for ...?	**Wie ist die Vorwählnummer von ...?**	vee ist dee **foar**vailnummerr fon
How do I get the international operator?	**Welche Nummer hat die (internationale) Vermittlung?**	**vehl**kher nummerr haht dee (interrnahtsionnaaler) fehr**mit**lung

Operator *Vermittlung*

Good morning, I want Hamburg 12 34 56.	**Guten Morgen. Ich möchte Hamburg 12 34 56.**	**goo**tern morgern. ikh **murkh**ter hahmboorg 12 34 56
Can you help me get this number?	**Können Sie mir helfen, diese Nummer zu bekommen?**	**kur**nern zee meer **hehl**fern deezer nummerr tsoo berkommern
I want to place a personal (person-to-person) call.	**Ich möchte ein Gespräch mit Voranmeldung.**	ikh **murkh**ter ighn gershpraikh mit **foar**ahnmehldung
I want to reverse the charges (call collect).	**Ich möchte ein R-Gespräch anmelden.**	ikh **murkh**ter ighn **ehr**-gershpraikh **ahn**mehldern

NUMBERS, see page 147

Speaking *Am Apparat*

Hello. This is ... speaking.	**Hallo. Hier spricht ...**	hahloa. heer shprikht
I want to speak to ...	**Ich möchte ... sprechen.**	ikh murkhter ... shprehkhern
I want extension ...	**Ich möchte Nebenanschluß ...**	ikh murkhter naybern-ahnshluss
Speak louder/more slowly, please.	**Sprechen Sie bitte etwas lauter/lang-samer.**	shprehkhern zee bitter ehtvahss lowterr/lahng-zaamerr

Bad luck *Pech gehabt*

Would you please try again later?	**Würden Sie es bitte später noch einmal versuchen?**	vewrdern zee ehss bitter shpaiterr nokh ighnmaal fehrzookhern
Operator, you gave me the wrong number.	**Fräulein, Sie haben mich falsch verbunden.**	froylighn zee haabern mikh fahlsh fehrbundern
We were cut off.	**Wir sind unter-brochen worden.**	veer zint unterrbrokhern vordern

Telephone alphabet *Buchstabiertabelle*

A	**Anton**	ahntoan	O	**Otto**	otto
Ä	**Ärger**	ehrgerr	Ö	**Ökonom**	urkonnoam
B	**Berta**	behrtah	P	**Paula**	powlah
C	**Caesar**	tsaizahr	Q	**Quelle**	kvehler
CH	**Charlotte**	shahrlotter	R	**Richard**	rikhahrt
D	**Dora**	doarah	S	**Samuel**	zaamuehl
E	**Emil**	aymeel	SCH	**Schule**	shooler
F	**Friedrich**	freedrikh	T	**Theodor**	tayoddoar
G	**Gustav**	gustahf	U	**Ulrich**	ulrikh
H	**Heinrich**	highnrikh	Ü	**Übel**	ewberl
I	**Ida**	eedah	V	**Viktor**	viktor
J	**Julius**	yooliuss	W	**Wilhelm**	vilhehlm
K	**Kaufmann**	kowfmahn	X	**Xanthippe**	ksahntipper
L	**Ludwig**	loodvikh	Y	**Ypsilon**	ewpseelon
M	**Martha**	mahrtah	Z	**Zacharias**	tsahkhahreeahss
N	**Nordpol**	nortpoal			

Not there *Nicht da*

When will he/she be back?	**Wann ist er/sie zurück?**	vahn ist ehr/zee tsoorewk
Will you tell him/her I called?	**Würden Sie ihm/ihr sagen, daß ich angerufen habe?**	vewrdern zee eem/eer zaagern dahss ikh ahngerroofern haaber?
My name's ...	**Mein Name ist ...**	mighn naamer ist
Would you ask him/her to call me?	**Würden Sie ihn/sie bitten, mich anzurufen?**	vewrdern zee een/zee bittern mikh ahntsooroofern
Would you please take a message?	**Würden Sie bitte etwas ausrichten?**	vewrdern zee bitter ehtvahss owsrikhtern

Charges *Gebühren*

| What was the cost of that call? | **Was hat das Gespräch gekostet?** | vahss haht dahss gershpraikh gerkostert |
| I want to pay for the call. | **Ich möchte das Gespräch bezahlen.** | ikh murkhter dahss gershpraikh bertsaalern |

Ein Anruf für Sie.	There's a telephone call for you.
Welche Nummer haben Sie gewählt?	What number are you calling?
Die Linie ist besetzt.	The line's engaged.
Es meldet sich niemand.	There's no answer.
Sie sind falsch verbunden.	You've got the wrong number.
Das Telefon funktioniert nicht.	The phone is out of order.
Einen Augenblick, bitte.	Just a moment.
Bitte bleiben Sie am Apparat.	Hold on, please.
Er/Sie ist im Augenblick nicht da.	He's/She's out at the moment.

Doctor

To be at ease, make sure your health insurance policy covers any illness or accident while on holiday. If not, ask your insurance representative, automobile association or travel agent for details of special health insurance.

General   *Allgemeines*

Can you get me a doctor?	**Können Sie einen Arzt holen?**	kurnern zee **igh**nern ahrtst **hoa**lern
Is there a doctor here?	**Gibt es hier einen Arzt?**	gipt ehss heer **igh**nern ahrtst
I need a doctor quickly.	**Ich brauche schnell einen Arzt.**	ikh **brow**kher shnehl **igh**nern ahrtst
Where's there a doctor who speaks English?	**Wo gibt es einen Arzt, der Englisch spricht?**	voa gipt ehss **igh**nern ahrtst derr **ehn**glish shprikht
Where's the surgery (doctor's office)?	**Wo ist die Arztpraxis?**	voa ist dee **ahrtst**prahksiss
What are the surgery (office) hours?	**Wann sind die Sprechstunden?**	vahn zint dee **shprekh**shtundern
Could the doctor come to see me here?	**Könnte der Arzt mich behandeln?**	**kurn**ter derr ahrtst mikh heer ber**hahn**derln
What time can the doctor come?	**Wann kann der Arzt kommen?**	vahn kahn derr ahrtst **kom**mern
Can you recommend a/an ...?	**Können Sie mir ... angeben?**	kurnern zee meer ... **ahn**gaybern
general practitioner	**einen praktischen Arzt**	**igh**nern **prahk**tishern ahrtst
children's doctor	**einen Kinderarzt**	**igh**nern **kin**derrahrtst
eye specialist	**einen Augenarzt**	**igh**nern **ow**gernahrtst
gynaecologist	**einen Frauenarzt**	**igh**nern **frow**ernahrtst
Can I have an appointment ...?	**Kann ich ... einen Termin haben?**	kahn ikh ... **igh**nern teh**meen haa**bern
tomorrow	**morgen**	**mor**gern
as soon as possible	**so bald wie möglich**	zo bahlt vee **murg**likh

CHEMIST'S, see page 108

DOCTOR

Arzt

Parts of the body *Körperteile*

appendix	der Blinddarm	derr blintdahrm
arm	der Arm	derr ahrm
artery	die Arterie	dee ahrtayrier
back	der Rücken	derr rewkern
bladder	die Blase	dee blaazer
bone	der Knochen	derr knokhern
bowel	der Darm	derr dahrm
breast	die Brust	dee brust
chest	der Brustkorb	derr brustkorp
ear	das Ohr	dahss oar
eye	das Auge	dahss owger
face	das Gesicht	dahss gerzikht
finger	der Finger	derr fingerr
foot	der Fuß	derr fooss
gland	die Drüse	dee drewzer
hand	die Hand	dee hahnt
head	der Kopf	derr kopf
heart	das Herz	dahss hehrts
jaw	der Kiefer	derr keeferr
joint	das Gelenk	dahss gerlehnk
kidney	die Niere	dee neerer
knee	das Knie	dahss knee
leg	das Bein	dahss bighn
lip	die Lippe	dee lipper
liver	die Leber	dee layberr
lung	die Lunge	dee lunger
mouth	der Mund	derr munt
muscle	der Muskel	derr muskerl
neck	der Hals	derr hahls
nerve	der Nerv	derr nehrf
nervous system	das Nervensystem	dahss nehrfernzewstaym
nose	die Nase	dee naazer
rib	die Rippe	dee ripper
shoulder	die Schulter	dee shulterr
skin	die Haut	dee howt
spine	die Wirbelsäule	dee veerberlzoyler
stomach	der Magen	derr maagern
tendon	die Sehne	dee zayner
thigh	der Schenkel	derr shehnkerl
throat	der Hals	derr hahls
thumb	der Daumen	derr dowmern
toe	die Zehe	dee tsayer
tongue	die Zunge	dee tsunger
tonsils	die Mandeln	dee mahnderln
vein	die Vene	dee vayner

Accident — Injury *Unfall – Verletzung*

There has been an accident.	**Es ist ein Unfall passiert.**	ehss ist ighn **unfahl** pah**sseert**
My child has had a fall.	**Mein Kind ist hingefallen.**	mighn kint ist **hin**gerfahlern
He/She has hurt his/her head.	**Er/Sie ist am Kopf verletzt.**	ehr/zee ist ahm kopf fehr**lehtst**
He's/She's unconscious.	**Er/Sie ist bewußtlos.**	ehr/zee ist ber**vusst**loass
He's/She's bleeding (heavily).	**Er/Sie blutet (stark).**	ehr/zee **bloo**tert (shtahrk)
He's/She's (seriously) injured.	**Er/Sie ist (schwer) verletzt.**	ehr/zee ist (shvayr) fehr**lehtst**
His/Her arm is broken.	**Sein/Ihr Arm ist gebrochen.**	zighn/eer ahrm ist ger**brokhen**
His/Her ankle is swollen.	**Sein/Ihr Knöchel ist geschwollen.**	zighn/eer **knurkherl** ist ger**shvollern**
I've been stung.	**Ich bin gestochen worden.**	ikh bin ger**shtokhern voardern**
I've got something in my eye.	**Ich habe etwas im Auge.**	ikh **haaber ehtvahss** im **owger**
I've got a/an ...	**Ich habe ...**	ikh **haaber**
blister	**eine Blase**	**igh**ner **blaazer**
boil	**einen Furunkel**	**igh**nern **foor**unkerl
bruise	**eine Quetschung**	**igh**ner **kveht**shung
burn	**eine Brandwunde**	**igh**ner **brahnt**vunder
cut	**eine Schnittwunde**	**igh**ner **shnit**vunder
graze	**eine Abschürfung**	**igh**ner **ahp**shewrfung
insect bite	**einen Insektenstich**	**igh**nern in**zehk**ternshtikh
lump	**eine Beule**	**igh**ner **boyler**
rash	**einen Ausschlag**	**igh**nern **owss**shlaag
sting	**einen Stich**	**igh**nern **shtikh**
strained muscle	**eine Muskelzerrung**	**igh**nern **musk**erltsehrrung
swelling	**eine Schwellung**	**igh**ner **shvehl**lung
wound	**eine Wunde**	**igh**ner **vun**der
Could you have a look at it?	**Sehen Sie es bitte mal an.**	**zay**ern zee ehss **bitter** maal ahn
I can't move my ... It hurts.	**Ich kann den/die/das ... nicht bewegen. Es tut weh.**	ikh kahn dayn/dee/dahss ... nikht ber**vaygern**. ehss toot vay

👉	👈
Wo haben Sie Schmerzen?	Where does it hurt?
Was für Schmerzen haben Sie?	What kind of pain is it?
dumpfe/stechende pulsierende/anhaltende unregelmäßig auftretende	dull/sharp throbbing/constant on and off
Es ist ...	It's ...
gebrochen/verstaucht verrenkt/gerissen	broken/sprained dislocated/torn
Sie müssen geröntgt werden.	I want you to have an X-ray taken.
Sie bekommen einen Gipsverband.	You'll get a plaster.
Es ist infiziert.	It is infected.
Sind Sie gegen Wundstarrkrampf geimpft?	Have you been vaccinated against tetanus?
Ich gebe Ihnen ein Antiseptikum/Schmerzmittel.	I'll give you an antiseptic/ a painkiller.
In ... Tagen möchte ich Sie wiedersehen.	I'd like you to come back in ... days.

Illness *Krankheit*

I'm not feeling well.	**Ich fühle mich nicht wohl.**	ikh **few**ler mikh nikht voal
I'm ill.	**Ich bin krank.**	ikh bin krahnk
I feel dizzy/ sick.	**Mir ist schwindlig/ übel.**	meer ist **shvind**likh/ **ew**berl
I've got a fever.	**Ich habe Fieber.**	ikh **haa**berr **fee**berr
My temperature is 38 degrees.	**Ich habe 38° Fieber.**	ikh **haa**ber 38 graat **fee**berr
I've been vomiting.	**Ich habe mich übergeben.**	ikh **haa**ber mikh **ew**berr**gay**bern
I'm constipated.	**Ich habe Verstopfung.**	ikh **haa**ber fehr**shtopf**ung
I've got diarrhoea.	**Ich habe Durchfall.**	ikh **haa**ber **doorkh**fahl
My ... hurts.	**Mein ... tut weh.**	mighn ... toot vay

I've got (a/an) ...	Ich habe ...	ikh **haa**ber
asthma	**Asthma**	**ahst**mah
backache	**Rückenschmerzen**	**rew**kernshmehrtsern
cold	**eine Erkältung**	**igh**ner ehr**kehl**tung
cough	**Husten**	**hoos**tern
cramps	**Krämpfe**	**krehm**pfer
earache	**Ohrenschmerzen**	**oar**ernshmehrtsern
headache	**Kopfschmerzen**	**kopf**shmehrtsern
indigestion	**eine Magen-verstimmung**	**igh**ner **maa**gern-fehrshtimmung
nosebleed	**Nasenbluten**	**naa**zernblootern
palpitations	**Herzklopfen**	**hehrts**klopfern
rheumatism	**Rheumatismus**	roy**mah**tismuss
sore throat	**Halsschmerzen**	**hahls**shmehrtsern
stiff neck	**einen steifen Nacken**	**igh**nern **shtigh**fern **nahk**ern
stomach ache	**Magenschmerzen**	**maa**gernshmehrtsern
sunstroke	**einen Sonnenstich**	**igh**nern **zonn**ernshtikh
I have difficulties breathing.	**Ich habe Atembeschwerden.**	ikh **haa**ber **aa**term-bershvayrdern
I have a pain in my chest.	**Ich habe Schmerzen in der Brust.**	ikh **haa**ber **shmehrts**ern in derr brust
I had a heart attack ... years ago.	**Ich hatte vor ... Jahren einen Herzanfall.**	ikh **hah**ter vor ... **yaa**rern **igh**nern **hehrts**ahnfahl
My blood pressure is too high/too low.	**Mein Blutdruck ist zu hoch/zu niedrig.**	mighn **bloot**druk ist tsu **hoakh**/tsu **need**rikh
I'm allergic to ...	**Ich bin gegen ... allergisch.**	ikh bin **gay**gern ... ah**lehr**gish
I'm a diabetic.	**Ich bin Diabetiker.**	ikh bin diah**bay**tikkerr

Women's complaints *Frauenbeschwerden*

I have period pains.	**Ich habe Menstruationsbeschwerden.**	ikh **haa**ber mehnstruah-tsioansbershvayrdern
I have a vaginal infection.	**Ich habe eine Scheidenentzündung.**	ikh **haa**ber **igh**ner **shigh**dernehntsewndung
I'm on the pill.	**Ich nehme die Pille.**	ikh **nay**mer dee **pill**er
I haven't had my period for 2 months.	**Ich habe seit zwei Monaten meine Periode nicht mehr gehabt.**	ikh **haa**ber zight tsvigh **moa**nahtern **migh**ner pe**hrioa**der nikht mayr ge**hahpt**
I'm pregnant.	**Ich bin schwanger.**	ikh bin **shvahn**gerr

☞   ☜

Wie lange fühlen Sie sich schon so?	How long have you been feeling like this?
Haben Sie das zum ersten Mal?	Is it the first time you've had this?
Ich werde Ihre Temperatur/ Ihren Blutdruck messen.	I'll take your temperature/ blood pressure.
Streifen Sie bitte den Ärmel hoch.	Roll up your sleeve, please.
Bitte machen Sie den Oberkörper frei.	Please undress down to the waist.
Legen Sie sich bitte hierhin.	Please lie down over here.
Machen Sie den Mund auf.	Open your mouth.
Tief atmen, bitte.	Breathe deeply.
Husten Sie bitte.	Cough, please.
Wo haben Sie Schmerzen?	Where do you feel the pain?
Sie haben ...	You've got (a/an) ...
Blasenentzündung	cystitis
Blinddarmentzündung	appendicitis
... entzündung	inflammation of ...
Gelbsucht	jaundice
eine Geschlechtskrankheit	venereal disease
Grippe	flu
Lebensmittelvergiftung	food poisoning
Lungenentzündung	pneumonia
Magenschleimhautentzündung	gastritis
Masern	measles
Ich gebe Ihnen eine Spritze.	I'll give you an injection.
Ich brauche eine Blutprobe/ Stuhlprobe/Urinprobe.	I want a specimen of your blood/stools/urine.
Sie müssen ... Tage im Bett bleiben.	You must stay in bed for ... days.
Sie sollten einen Spezialisten aufsuchen.	I want you to see a specialist.
Sie müssen zu einer General- untersuchung ins Krankenhaus.	I want you to go to the hos- pital for a general check-up.

Prescription—Treatment   *Rezept – Behandlung*

This is my usual medicine.	**Gewöhnlich nehme ich dieses Medikament.**	gervurnlikh naymer ikh deezerss maydikahmehnt
Can you give me a prescription for this?	**Können Sie mir dafür ein Rezept geben?**	kurnern zee meer dah**fewr** ighn reht**sehpt** gay**bern**
Can you prescribe some sleeping pills/ an antidepressant?	**Können Sie mir Schlaftabletten/ein Mittel gegen Depressionen verschreiben?**	kurnern zee mir shlaaftahblehtern/ighn mitterl gaygern dayprehssioanern fehrshrighbern
I'm allergic to antibiotics/penicilline.	**Ich bin allergisch gegen Antibiotika/ Penizillin.**	ikh bin ah**lehr**gish gaygern ahntibbioatikkah/ pehnitsillin
I don't want anything too strong.	**Ich möchte kein zu starkes Mittel.**	ikh murkhter kighn tsu shtahrkers mitterl
How many times a day should I take it?	**Wie oft täglich soll ich es nehmen?**	vee oft taiglikh zol ikh ehss naymern
Must I swallow them whole?	**Muß ich sie ganz schlucken?**	muss ikh zee gahnts shlukkern

---

🖝   🗲

Wie werden Sie behandelt?	What treatment are you having?
Welches Medikament nehmen Sie?	What medicine are you taking?
Als Spritze oder Tabletten?	Injection or oral?
Nehmen Sie von dieser Medizin ... Teelöffel ...	Take ... teaspoons of this medicine ...
Nehmen Sie eine Tablette mit einem Glas Wasser ...	Take one pill with a glass of water ...
alle ... Stunden	every ... hours
... mal täglich	... times a day
vor/nach jeder Mahlzeit	before/after each meal
morgens/abends	in the morning/at night
wenn Sie Schmerzen haben	in case of pain
während ... Tagen	for ... days

CHEMIST'S, see page 108

Arzt

Fee *Honorar*

How much do I owe you?	**Wieviel bin ich Ihnen schuldig?**	veefeel bin ikh eenern shuldikh
May I have a receipt for my health insurance?	**Kann ich bitte eine Quittung für meine Krankenkasse haben?**	kahn ikh bitter ighner kvittung fewr mighner krahnkernkahssar haabern
Can I have a medical certificate?	**Können Sie mir ein ärztliches Zeugnis ausstellen?**	kurnern zee meer ighn ehrtstlikhers tsoygniss owsshtehlern
Would you fill in this health insurance form, please?	**Würden Sie bitte dieses Krankenkassen-Formular ausfüllen?**	vewrdern zee bitter deezers krahnkernkahssern-formullaar owsfewlern

Hospital *Krankenhaus*

Please notify my family.	**Benachrichtigen Sie bitte meine Familie.**	bernahkhrikhtiggern zee bitter mighner fahmeelier
What are the visiting hours?	**Wann ist Besuchs-zeit?**	vahn ist berzookhstsight
When can I get up?	**Wann darf ich auf-stehen?**	vahn dahrf ikh owf-shtayern
When will the doctor come?	**Wann kommt der Arzt?**	vahn komt derr ahrtst
I'm in pain.	**Ich habe Schmerzen.**	ikh haaber shmehrtsern
I can't eat/sleep.	**Ich kann nicht essen/ schlafen.**	ikh kahn nikht ehssern/ shlaafern
Where is the bell?	**Wo ist die Klingel?**	voa ist dee klingerl

nurse	**die Kranken-schwester**	dee krahnkernshvehsterr
patient	**der Patient/die Patientin**	derr pahtsiehnt/dee pahtsiehntin
anaesthesia	**die Narkose**	dee nahrkoazer
blood transfusion	**die Bluttransfusion**	dee bloottrahnsfuzioan
injection	**die Spritze**	dee shpritser
operation	**die Operation**	dee oppehrahtsioan
bed	**das Bett**	dahss beht
bedpan	**die Bettpfanne**	dee behtpfahner
thermometer	**das Thermometer**	dahss tehrmommayterr

Dentist *Zahnarzt*

Can you recommend a good dentist?	**Können Sie mir einen guten Zahnarzt empfehlen?**	kurnern zee meer **igh**nern gootern tsaanahrtst ehmpfaylern
Can I make an (urgent) appointment to see Dr ...?	**Kann ich einen (dringenden) Termin bei Herrn/Frau Dr. ... haben?**	kahn ikh **igh**nern (dringerndern) tehr**meen** bigh hehrn/frow **dok**tor ... **haa**bern
Can't you possibly make it earlier than that?	**Geht es wirklich nicht eher?**	gayt ehss **virk**likh nikht ayer
I have toothache.	**Ich habe Zahnschmerzen.**	ikh **haa**ber **tsaans**hmehrtsern
Is it an abscess/ infection?	**Ist es ein Abszeß/ eine Infektion?**	ist ehss ighn ahp**stsehss**/ **igh**ner infehk**tsioan**
This tooth hurts.	**Dieser Zahn schmerzt.**	**dee**zerr tsaan shmehrtst
at the top	**oben**	**oa**bern
at the bottom	**unten**	**un**tern
in the front	**vorne**	**for**ner
at the back	**hinten**	**hin**tern
Can you fix it temporarily?	**Können Sie ihn provisorisch behandeln?**	kurnern zee een provvi**zoa**rish ber**hahn**derln
I don't want it extracted.	**Ich möchte ihn nicht ziehen lassen.**	ikh **murkh**ter een nikht **tseeern** lahssern
Could you give me an anaesthetic?	**Können Sie mir eine Spritze geben?**	kurnern zee meer **igh**ner **shprit**ser **gay**bern
I've lost a filling.	**Ich habe eine Plombe verloren.**	ikh **haa**ber **igh**ner **plom**ber fehr**loa**rern
The gum ...	**Das Zahnfleisch ...**	dahss **tsahn**flighsh
is very sore	**ist wund**	ist vunt
is bleeding	**blutet**	**bloo**tert
I've broken this denture.	**Mein Gebiß ist zerbrochen.**	mighn ger**biss** ist tsehr**bro**khern
Can you repair this denture?	**Können Sie das Gebiß reparieren?**	kurnern zee dahss ger**biss** rehpah**ree**rern
When will it be ready?	**Wann ist es fertig?**	vahn ist ehss **fehr**tikh

Reference section

Where do you come from?   *Woher kommen Sie?*

I'm from ...	Ich komme aus ...	ikh **kom**mer ows
Africa	**Afrika**	ah**frik**kah
Asia	**Asien**	**aa**ziern
Australia	**Australien**	ow**straa**liern
Europe	**Europa**	oy**roa**pah
North America	**Nordamerika**	**nort**ahmay**rik**kah
South America	**Südamerika**	**zewd**ahmay**rik**kah
Austria	**Österreich**	**urs**terrighkh
Belgium	**Belgien**	**behl**giern
Canada	**Kanada**	**kah**nahdah
Czechoslovakia	**der Tschechoslo-**	derr chehkhoslov**vah**kigh
	wakei	
China	**China**	**khee**nah
Denmark	**Dänemark**	**dai**nermahrk
England	**England**	**ehng**lahnt
Finland	**Finnland**	**fin**lahnt
France	**Frankreich**	**frahnk**righkh
Germany	**Deutschland**	**doych**lahnt
East Germany	**der DDR**	derr day day ehr
West Germany	**der Bundesrepublik**	derr **bun**dersrehpublik
Great Britain	**Großbritannien**	**groas**brittahniern
Greece	**Griechenland**	**greek**hernlahnt
Ireland	**Irland**	**eer**lahnt
Israel	**Israel**	**iz**rahayl
Italy	**Italien**	i**taa**liern
Japan	**Japan**	**yaa**pahn
Liechtenstein	**Liechtenstein**	**likh**ternshtighn
Luxembourg	**Luxemburg**	**luks**ermboorg
Netherlands	**den Niederlanden**	dayn **nee**derrlahndern
Norway	**Norwegen**	**nor**vaygern
Poland	**Polen**	**poa**lern
Portugal	**Portugal**	**por**tuggahl
Scotland	**Schottland**	**shot**lahnt
South Africa	**Südafrika**	**zewd**ah**frik**kah
Soviet Union	**der Sowjetunion**	derr **zov**yeht**un**nioan
Spain	**Spanien**	**shpaa**niern
Sweden	**Schweden**	**shvay**dern
Switzerland	**der Schweiz**	derr **shvights**
United States	**den Vereinigten**	dayn feh**righ**nigtern
	Staaten	**shtaa**tern
Wales	**Wales**	"Wales"

Numbers *Zahlen*

0	**null**	nul
1	**eins**	**ighns**
2	**zwei**	**tsvigh**
3	**drei**	**drigh**
4	**vier**	**feer**
5	**fünf**	**fewnf**
6	**sechs**	**zehks**
7	**sieben**	**zee**bern
8	**acht**	**ahkht**
9	**neun**	**noyn**
10	**zehn**	**tsayn**
11	**elf**	**ehlf**
12	**zwölf**	**tsvurlf**
13	**dreizehn**	**drigh**tsayn
14	**vierzehn**	**feer**tsayn
15	**fünfzehn**	**fewnf**tsayn
16	**sechzehn**	**zehkh**tsayn
17	**siebzehn**	**zeep**tsayn
18	**achtzehn**	**ahkht**tsayn
19	**neunzehn**	**noyn**tsayn
20	**zwanzig**	**tsvahnt**sikh
21	**einundzwanzig**	**ighn**unttsvahntsikh
22	**zweiundzwanzig**	**tsvigh**unttsvahntsikh
23	**dreiundzwanzig**	**drigh**unttsvahntsikh
24	**vierundzwanzig**	**feer**unttsvahntsikh
25	**fünfundzwanzig**	**fewnf**unttsvahntsikh
26	**sechsundzwandzig**	**zehks**unttsvahntsikh
27	**siebenundzwanzig**	**zeebern**unttsvahntsikh
28	**achtundzwanzig**	**ahkht**unttsvahntsikh
29	**neunundzwanzig**	**noyn**unttsvahntsikh
30	**dreißig**	**drighs**sikh
31	**einunddreißig**	**ighn**untdrighssikh
32	**zweiunddreißig**	**tsvigh**untdrighssikh
33	**dreiunddreißig**	**drigh**untdrighssikh
40	**vierzig**	**feert**sikh
50	**fünfzig**	**fewnf**tsikh
60	**sechzig**	**zehkht**sikh
70	**siebzig**	**zeept**sikh
80	**achtzig**	**ahkht**sikh
90	**neunzig**	**noynt**sikh
100	**(ein)hundert**	**(ighn)h**underrt
101	**hunderteins**	hunderrt**ighnss**
102	**hundertzwei**	hunderrt**tsvigh**
110	**hundertzehn**	hunderrt**tsayn**
120	**hundertzwanzig**	hunderrt**tsvahn**tsikh

200	**zwei**hundert	**tsvigh**hunderrt
300	**drei**hundert	**drigh**hunderrt
400	**vier**hundert	**feer**hunderrt
500	**fünf**hundert	**fewnf**hunderrt
600	**sechs**hundert	**zehks**hunderrt
700	**sieben**hundert	**zeebern**hunderrt
800	**acht**hundert	**ahkht**hunderrt
900	**neun**hundert	**noyn**hunderrt
1000	**(ein)**tausend	**(ighn)tow**zernt
1100	**tausendeinhundert**	towzern**tighn**hunderrt
1200	**tausendzweihundert**	towzernt**tsvigh**hunderrt
2000	**zwei**tausend	**tsvigh**towzernt
10,000	**zehn**tausend	**tsayn**towzernt
50,000	**fünfzig**tausend	**fewnftsikh**towzernt
100,000	**hundert**tausend	**hunderrt**towzernt
1,000,000	**eine Million**	**igh**ner milli**oan**
1,000,000,000	**eine Milliarde**	**igh**ner milli**ahr**der
first	**erste**	**ehr**ster
second	**zweite**	**tsvigh**ter
third	**dritte**	**drit**ter
fourth	**vierte**	**feer**ter
fifth	**fünfte**	**fewnf**ter
sixth	**sechste**	**zehks**ter
seventh	**siebte**	**zeeb**ter
eighth	**achte**	**ahkh**ter
ninth	**neunte**	**noyn**ter
tenth	**zehnte**	**tsayn**ter
once	**einmal**	**ighn**maal
twice	**zweimal**	**tsvigh**maal
three times	**dreimal**	**drigh**maal
a half	**eine Hälfte**	**igh**ner **hehlf**ter
half a ...	**ein halber ...**	ighn **hahl**berr
half of ...	**die Hälfte von ...**	dee **hehlf**ter fon
half (adj.)	**halb**	hahlp
a quarter	**ein Viertel**	ighn **feer**terl
one third	**ein Drittel**	ighn **drit**terl
a pair of	**ein Paar**	ighn paar
a dozen	**ein Dutzend**	ighn **dut**sernd
3.4%	**3,4 Prozent**	drigh **kom**mah feer pro**tsehnt**
1981	**neunzehnhundert-** **einundachtzig**	noyntsaynhunderrt- **ighn**untahkhtsikh
1992	**neunzehnhundert-** **zweiundneunzig**	noyntsaynhunderrt- **tsvigh**undnoyntsikh
2003	**zweitausenddrei**	tsvightowzernt**drigh**

Year and age *Jahre und Alter*

year	**das Jahr**	dahss yaar
leap year	**das Schaltjahr**	dahss **shahlt**yaar
decade	**das Jahrzehnt**	dahss **yaart**saynt
century	**das Jahrhundert**	dahss **yaar**hundert
this year	**dieses Jahr**	**dee**zers yaar
last year	**letztes Jahr**	**leht**sters yaar
next year	**nächstes Jahr**	**naikh**sters yaar
each year	**jedes Jahr**	**yay**ders yaar
2 years ago	**vor 2 Jahren**	foar tsvigh **yaar**ern
in one year	**in einem Jahr**	in **igh**nerm yaar
in the eighties	**in den achtziger Jahren**	in dayn **ahkht**siggerr **yaar**ern
from the 19th century	**vom 19. Jahrhundert**	fom **noynt**sayntern **yaar**hunderrt
in the 20th century	**im 20. Jahrhundert**	im **tsvahnt**sikhstern **yaar**hunderrt
old/young	**alt/jung**	ahlt/yung
old/new	**alt/neu**	ahlt/noy
How old are you?	**Wie alt sind Sie?**	vee ahlt zint zee
I'm 30 years old.	**Ich bin 30 Jahre alt.**	ikh bin **drigh**ssikh **yaar**er ahlt
He/She was born in 1960.	**Er/Sie ist 1960 geboren.**	ehr/zee ist noyntsaynhun- derrt**zehkht**sikh ger**boar**ern
What is his/her age?	**Wie alt ist er/sie?**	vee ahlt ist ehr/zee
Children under 16 are not admitted.	**Kindern unter 16 Jahren ist der Zutritt verboten.**	**kind**errn **unt**err **zehkht**sayn **yaar**ern ist derr **tsutrit** fehr**boat**ern

Seasons *Jahreszeiten*

spring	**der Frühling**	derr **frew**ling
summer	**der Sommer**	derr **zomm**err
autumn	**der Herbst**	derr **hehrp**st
winter	**der Winter**	derr **vint**err
in spring	**im Frühling**	im **frew**ling
during the summer	**während des Sommers**	**vair**ernt dehss **zomm**errs
high season	**die Hauptsaison**	dee **howpt**zehzong
low season (before/ after season)	**die Vorsaison/ die Nachsaison**	dee **foar**zehzong/ dee **nahkh**zehzong

Months *Monate*

January	**Januar**	yahnuaar
February	**Februar**	faybruaar
March	**März**	mehrts
April	**April**	ahpril
May	**Mai**	migh
June	**Juni**	yooni
July	**Juli**	yooli
August	**August**	owgust
September	**September**	sehptehmberr
October	**Oktober**	oktoaberr
November	**November**	novvehmberr
December	**Dezember**	daytsehmberr
after June	**nach Juni**	nahkh yooni
before July	**vor Juli**	foar yooli
during the month of August	**während des Monats August**	vairernt dehss moanahts owgust
in September	**im September**	im zehptehmberr
until October	**bis Oktober**	biss oktoaberr
not until November	**nicht vor November**	nikht foar novehmberr
since December	**seit Dezember**	zight dehtsehmberr
last month	**im letzten Monat**	im lehtstern moanaht
next month	**im nächsten Monat**	im naikhstern moanaht
the month before	**der vorhergehende Monat**	derr foarhayrgayernder moanaht
the month after	**der folgende Monat**	derr folgernder moanaht
the beginning of January	**Anfang Januar**	ahnfahnk yahnuaar
the middle of February	**Mitte Februar**	miterr faybruaar
the end of March	**Ende März**	ehnder mehrts

Days and date *Tage – Datum*

What day is it today?	**Welchen Tag haben wir heute?**	vehlkhern taag haabern veer hoyter
Sunday	**Sonntag**	zontaag
Monday	**Montag**	moantaag
Tuesday	**Dienstag**	deenstaag
Wednesday	**Mittwoch**	mitvokh
Thursday	**Donnerstag**	donnerrstaag
Friday	**Freitag**	frightaag
Saturday	**Samstag/Sonnabend**	zahmstaag/zonnaabernt

What's the date today?	**Den wievielten haben wir heute?**	dayn veefeeltern haabern veer hoyter
It's ...	**Es ist ...**	ehss ist
July 1	**der 1. Juli**	derr ehrster yooli
March 10	**der 10. März**	derr tsaynter mehrts
When's your birthday?	**Wann haben Sie Geburtstag?**	vahn haabern zee gerburtstaag
August 2nd.	**Am 2. August.**	ahm tsvightern owgust
in the morning	**am Morgen**	ahm morgern
during the day	**tagsüber**	taagsewberr
in the afternoon	**am Nachmittag**	ahm nahkhmittaag
in the evening	**am Abend**	ahm aabernt
at night	**nachts**	nahkhts
the day before yesterday	**vorgestern**	foargehsterrn
yesterday	**gestern**	gehsterrn
today	**heute**	hoyter
tomorrow	**morgen**	morgern
the day after tomorrow	**übermorgen**	ewberrmorgern
the day before	**der vorhergehende Tag**	derr foarhayrgayernder taag
the next day	**der Tag danach**	derr taag dahnaakh
two days ago	**vor zwei Tagen**	foar tsvigh taagern
in three days' time	**in drei Tagen**	in drigh taagern
last week	**letzte Woche**	lehtster vokher
next week	**nächste Woche**	naikhster vokher
for a fortnight (two weeks)	**zwei Wochen lang**	tsvigh vokhern lahng
day off	**der freie Tag**	derr frigher taag
holiday	**der Feiertag**	derr figherrtaag
holidays (vacation)	**die Ferien/der Urlaub**	dee fayriern/derr oorlowp
week	**die Woche**	dee vokher
weekend	**das Wochenende**	dahss vokhernehnder
working day	**der Werktag**	derr vehrktaag

Greetings and wishes *Grüße und Wünsche*

| Merry Christmas! | **Fröhliche Weihnachten!** | frurlikher vighnahkhtern |
| Happy New Year! | **Glückliches Neues Jahr!** | glewklikhers noyers yaar |

Happy Easter!	**Frohe Ostern!**	froaer oasterrn
Happy birthday!	**Alles Gute zum Geburtstag!**	ahlerss gooter tsum gerburtstaag
Best wishes!	**Alles Gute!**	ahlers gooter
Congratulations!	**Herzlichen Glück-wunsch!**	hehrtslikhern glewkvunsh
Good luck/All the best!	**Viel Glück!**	feel glewk
Have a nice trip!	**Gute Reise!**	gooter righzer
Have a nice holiday!	**Schöne Ferien!**	shurner fayriern
Best regards from ...	**Herzliche Grüße von ...**	hehrtslikher grewsser fon
My regards to ...	**Beste Grüße an ...**	behster grewsser ahn

Public holidays *Feiertage*

Only national holidays in Germany (D), Austria (A) or Switzerland (CH) are cited below.

Jan. 1	**Neujahr**	New Year's Day	D A CH
Jan. 2			CH*
Jan. 6	**Dreikönigstag**	Epiphany	A
May 1	**Tag der Arbeit**	Labour Day	D A
June 17	**Tag der Deutschen Einheit**	National Unity Day	D
Aug. 1	**Nationalfeiertag**	National Day	CH*
Aug. 15	**Mariä Himmelfahrt**	Assumption Day	A
Oct. 26	**Nationalfeiertag**	National Day	A
Nov. 1	**Allerheiligen**	All Saints' Day	A
Dec. 8	**Mariä Empfängnis**	Immaculate Conception	A
Dec. 25	**1. Weihnachtstag**	Christmas Day	D A CH
Dec. 26	**2. Weihnachtstag**	St. Stephen's Day	D A CH*
Movable dates:	**Karfreitag**	Good Friday	D CH*
	Ostermontag	Easter Monday	D A CH*
	Christi Himmelfahrt	Ascension	D A CH
	Pfingstmontag	Whit Monday	D A CH*
	Fronleichnam	Corpus Christi	A

*Most cantons

What time is it? *Wie spät ist es?*

Excuse me. Can you tell me the time?	Verzeihung. Können Sie mir bitte sagen, wie spät ist es?	fehrtsighung. kurnern zee meer bitter zaagern vee shpait ehss ist
It's ...	Es ist ...	ehss ist
five past one	fünf nach eins*	fewnf nakh ighns
ten past two	zehn nach zwei	tsayn nakh tsvigh
a quarter past three	viertel nach drei	feerterl nahkh drigh
twenty past four	zwanzig nach vier	tsvahntsikh nahkh feer
twenty-five past five	fünf vor halb sechs	fewnf foar hahlp zehks
half past six	halb sieben	hahlp zeebern
twenty-five to seven	fünf nach halb sieben	fewnf nakh hahlp zeebern
twenty to eight	zwanzig vor acht	tsvahntsikh foar ahkht
a quarter to nine	viertel vor neun	feerterl foar noyn
ten to ten	zehn vor zehn	tsayn foar tsayn
five to eleven	fünf vor elf	fewnf foar ehlf
twelve o'clock (noon/midnight)	zwölf Uhr (Mittag/Mitternacht)	tsvurlf oor (mittaag/mitterrnahkht)
in the morning	morgens	morgerns
in the afternoon	nachmittags	nahkhmittaags
in the evening	abends	aabernds
The train leaves at ...	Der Zug fährt um ...	derr tsoog fairt um
13.04 (1.04 p.m.)	dreizehn Uhr vier	drightsayn oor feer
0.40 (0.40 a.m.)	null Uhr vierzig	nul oor feertsikh
in five minutes	in fünf Minuten	in fewnf minnootern
in a quarter of an hour	in einer Viertelstunde	in ighnerr feerterlshtunder
half an hour ago	vor einer halben Stunde	foar ighnerr hahlbern shtunder
about two hours	ungefähr zwei Stunden	ungerfair tsvigh shtundern
more than 10 minutes	über 10 Minuten	ewberr tsayn minnootern
less than 30 seconds	weniger als 30 Sekunden	vayniggerr ahlss drighssikh zehkundern
The clock is fast/slow.	Die Uhr geht vor/nach.	dee oor gayt foar/nahkh

---

* In ordinary conversation, time is expressed as shown here. However, official time uses a 24-hour clock which means that after noon hours are counted from 13 to 24.

Common abbreviations *Gebräuchliche Abkürzungen*

ACS	Automobil-Club der Schweiz	Automobile Association of Switzerland
ADAC	Allgemeiner Deutscher Automobil-Club	General Automobile Association of Germany
a.M.	am Main	on the river Main
a.Rh.	am Rhein	on the river Rhine
AvD	Automobil-Club von Deutschland	Automobile Club of Germany
Bhf	Bahnhof	railway station
BRD	Bundesrepublik Deutschland	Federal Republic of Germany (West Germany)
DB	Deutsche Bundesbahn	Federal German Railway
DDR	Deutsche Demokratische Republik	German Democratic Republic (East Germany)
d.h.	das heißt	i.e. (that is)
DIN	Deutsche Industrie-Norm	German Industrial Standard
Frl.	Fräulein	Miss
G.	Gasse	lane
Hbf.	Hauptbahnhof	main railway station
Hr.	Herr	Mr.
LKW	Lastkraftwagen	lorry/truck
MEZ	Mitteleuropäische Zeit	Central European Time
Mio.	Million	million
Mrd.	Milliarde	1000 millions (billion)
n.Chr.	nach Christus	A.D.
ÖAMTC	Österreichischer Automobil-Motorrad- und Touring-Club	Austrian Automobile, Motorcycle and Touring Association
ÖBB	Österreichische Bundesbahnen	Austrian Federal Railways
PKW	Personenkraftwagen	motor car
Pl.	Platz	square
PS	Pferdestärke	horsepower
PTT	Post, Telephon, Telegraph	Post, Telephone and Telegraph Office
SBB	Schweizerische Bundesbahnen	Swiss Federal Railways
St.	Stock	floor
Str.	Straße	street
TCS	Touring-Club der Schweiz	Swiss Touring Club
usw.	und so weiter	etc.
v.Chr.	vor Christus	B.C.
z.B.	zum Beispiel	e.g. (for example)
z.Z.	zur Zeit	at present

Signs and notices *Aufschriften und Hinweise*

Achtung	Caution
Aufzug	Lift (elevator)
Ausgang	Exit
Auskunft	Information
Außer Betrieb	Out of order
Ausverkauf	Sale
Ausverkauft	Sold out
Belegt	Full/No vacancies
Besetzt	Occupied
Bitte klingeln	Please ring
Bitte nicht stören	Do not disturb
Damen	Ladies
Drücken	Push
Eingang	Entrance
Eintreten ohne zu klopfen	Enter without knocking
Eintritt frei	No admission charge
Frei	Vacant
Frisch gestrichen	Wet paint
Für Unbefugte verboten	No trespassing
Gefahr	Danger
Geschlossen	Closed
Heiß	Hot
Herren	Men
Kalt	Cold
Kasse	Cash desk
Kein Zutritt	No entrance
Lebensgefahr	Danger of death
Lift	Lift (elevator)
Nicht berühren	Do not touch
Notausgang	Emergency exit
Notruf	Emergency
Nur für Anlieger	Residents only
Privatweg	Private road
Radweg	Cycle path
Rauchen verboten	No smoking
Reserviert	Reserved
Unbefugtes Betreten verboten	No trespassing
... verboten	... forbidden/prohibited
Vorsicht	Caution
Vorsicht, bissiger Hund	Beware of the dog
Ziehen	Pull
Zimmer frei	Vacancies
Zu verkaufen	For sale
Zu vermieten	To let (for hire)

Emergency *Notfall*

Call the police	**Rufen Sie die Polizei**	**roo**fern zee dee **pol**litsigh
DANGER	**GEFAHR**	ger**faar**
FIRE	**FEUER**	**foy**err
Gas	**Gas**	gaass
Get a doctor	**Holen Sie einen Arzt**	**hoa**lern zee **igh**nern **ahrtst**
Go away	**Gehen Sie weg**	**gay**ern zee vehk
HELP	**HILFE**	**hil**fer
Get help	**Holen Sie Hilfe**	**hoa**lern zee **hil**fer
I'm ill	**Ich bin krank**	ikh bin krahnk
I'm lost	**Ich habe mich verirrt**	ikh **haa**ber mikh feh**reert**
LOOK OUT	**VORSICHT**	**foar**zikht
POLICE	**POLIZEI**	**pol**litsigh
Quick	**Schnell**	shnehl
STOP	**HALT**	hahlt
Stop that man/woman	**Haltet den Mann/die Frau**	**hahl**tert dayn mahn/dee frow
STOP THIEF	**HALTET DEN DIEB**	**hahl**tert dayn deep

Emergency telephone numbers *Notrufnummern*

	Austria	Germany	Switzerland
Fire	122	112	118
Ambulance	144	112	
Police	133	110	117

Lost property—Theft *Fundsachen – Diebstahl*

Where's the ...?	**Wo ist ...?**	voa ist
lost-property (lost and found) office	**das Fundbüro**	dahss **funt**bewroa
police station	**die Polizeiwache**	dee pol**lit**sighvahkher
I want to report a theft.	**Ich möchte einen Diebstahl anzeigen.**	ikh **murkh**ter **igh**nern **deep**shtaal **ahn**tsighgern
My ... has been stolen.	**Mein(e) ... ist mir gestohlen worden.**	mighn(er) ... ist meer ger**shtoa**lern **voar**dern
I've lost my wallet.	**Ich habe meine Brieftasche verloren.**	ikh **haa**ber **migh**ner **breef**tahsher fehr**loa**rern

CAR ACCIDENTS, see page 78

Conversion tables

Centimetres and inches

To change centimetres into inches, multiply by .39.

To change inches into centimetres, multiply by 2.54.

	in.	feet	yards
1 mm.	0.039	0.003	0.001
1 cm.	0.39	0.03	0.01
1 dm.	3.94	0.32	0.10
1 m.	39.40	3.28	1.09

	mm.	cm.	m.
1 in.	25.4	2.54	0.025
1 ft.	304.8	30.48	0.305
1 yd.	914.4	91.44	0.914

(32 metres = 35 yards)

Temperature

To convert centigrade into degrees Fahrenheit, multiply centigrade by 1.8 and add 32.

To convert degrees Fahrenheit into centigrade, subtract 32 from Fahrenheit and divide by 1.8.

Kilometres into miles

1 kilometre (km.) = 0.62 miles

km.	10	20	30	40	50	60	70	80	90	100	110	120	130
miles	6	12	19	25	31	37	44	50	56	62	68	75	81

Miles into kilometres

1 mile = 1.609 kilometres (km.)

miles	10	20	30	40	50	60	70	80	90	100
km.	16	32	48	64	80	97	113	129	145	161

Fluid measures

1 litre (l.) = 0.88 imp. quart or 1.06 U.S. quart

1 imp. quart = 1.14 l.	1 U.S. quart = 0.95 l.
1 imp. gallon = 4.55 l.	1 U.S. gallon = 3.8 l.

litres	5	10	15	20	25	30	35	40	45	50
imp. gal.	1.1	2.2	3.3	4.4	5.5	6.6	7.7	8.8	9.9	11.0
U.S. gal.	1.3	2.6	3.9	5.2	6.5	7.8	9.1	10.4	11.7	13.0

Weights and measures

1 kilogram or kilo (kg.) = 1000 grams (g.)

100 g. = 3.5 oz.	½ kg. = 1.1 lb.
200 g. = 7.0 oz.	1 kg. = 2.2 lb.

1 oz. = 28.35 g.
1 lb. = 453.60 g.

CLOTHING SIZES, see page 115/YARDS AND INCHES, see page 112

Basic Grammar

Here is a brief outline of some essential features of German grammar.

Articles

All nouns in German are either masculine, feminine or neuter, and they are classified by the article which precedes them.

1. **Definite article** (the):

			Plural:
masc.	*der* **Mann**	the man	*die* **Männer**
fem.	*die* **Frau**	the woman	*die* **Frauen**
neut.	*das* **Kind**	the child	*die* **Kinder**

2. **Indefinite article** (a/an):

masc.	*ein* **Zug**	a train
fem.	*eine* **Reise**	a trip
neut.	*ein* **Flugzeug**	a plane

Nouns and adjectives

1. All nouns are written with a capital letter. The rules for constructing the plural are very complex.

2. **Declension:** According to their use in the sentence, German articles, nouns and modifying adjectives undergo related changes. The tables below show the declension of all three parts of speech.

	masc. sing.	masc. plur.
subject	der reiche Mann	die reichen Männer
direct object	den reichen Mann	die reichen Männer
possessive	des reichen Mannes	der reichen Männer
indirect object	dem reichen Mann	den reichen Männern

	fem. sing.	fem. plur.
subject	**die schöne Frau**	**die schönen Frauen**
direct object	**die schöne Frau**	**die schönen Frauen**
possessive	**der schönen Frau**	**der schönen Frauen**
indirect object	**der schönen Frau**	**den schönen Frauen**

	neuter sing.	neuter plur.
subject	**das kleine Kind**	**die kleinen Kinder**
direct object	**das kleine Kind**	**die kleinen Kinder**
possessive	**des kleinen Kindes**	**der kleinen Kinder**
indirect object	**dem kleinen Kind**	**den kleinen Kindern**

The indefinite article is declined in a slightly different way, as is the modifying adjective.

	masc.	fem.
subject	**ein reicher Mann**	**eine schöne Frau**
direct object	**einen reichen Mann**	**eine schöne Frau**
possessive	**eines reichen Mannes**	**einer schönen Frau**
indirect object	**einem reichen Mann**	**einer schönen Frau**

	neuter	plur.
subject	**ein kleines Kind**	**keine* großen Leute**
direct object	**ein kleines Kind**	**keine großen Leute**
possessive	**eines kleinen Kindes**	**keiner großen Leute**
indirect object	**einem kleinen Kind**	**keinen großen Leuten**

If declined without an article the adjectives take the endings of the definite article, except in the possessive, which you'll hardly use: **guter Wein** (good wine), **kalte Milch** (cold milk), **warmes Wasser** (hot water).

3. **Demonstrative adjectives:** In spoken German "that" is usually expressed by the definite article, but contrary to the

---

* **ein** has no plural, but the negative **kein** (declined in singular like **ein**) does.

article, it is stressed. "This" **dieser, diese, dieses** and plural **diese** is declined like the definite article.

das Buch (that book)   **dieser Platz** (this seat)

4. **Possessive adjectives:** These agree in number and gender with the noun they modify, i.e., with the thing possessed and not the possessor. In singular they are declined like the indefinite article, and in plural like the definite. Note that **Ihr** meaning "your" in the polite form is capitalized.

	masc. or neut.	fem. or plur.
my	**mein**	**meine**
your	**dein**	**deine**
his/its	**sein**	**seine**
her	**ihr**	**ihre**
our	**unser**	**unsere**
your	**euer**	**eure**
their	**ihr**	**ihre**
your (pol.)	**Ihr**	**Ihre**

5. **Comparatives and superlatives:** These are formed by adding **-er (-r)** and **-est (-st)** respectively, very often together with an umlaut.

alt (old)   **kurz** (short)
älter (older)   **kürzer** (shorter)
ältest (oldest)   **kürzest** (shortest)

Adverbs

Many adjectives are used in their undeclined form as adverbs.

schnell   quick, quickly
gut   good, well

There are a few irregularities:

glücklich – glücklicherweise happy—happily
anders   differently
besonders   especially
gleichfalls   as well, (the) same

Viel indicates quantity and **sehr** intensity:

| Er arbeitet viel. | He works a lot. |
| Er ist sehr müde. | He's very tired. |

Personal pronouns

	subject	direct object	indirect object
I	**ich**	**mich**	**mir**
you	**du**	**dich**	**dir**
he	**er**	**ihn**	**ihm**
she	**sie**	**sie**	**ihr**
it	**es**	**es**	**ihm**
we	**wir**	**uns**	**uns**
you	**ihr**	**euch**	**euch**
they	**sie**	**sie**	**ihnen**
you	**Sie**	**Sie**	**Ihnen**

Note: There are two forms for "you" in German: **du** and **Sie; du** (plur.: **ihr**) is used when talking to relatives, close friends and children (and between young people); **Sie** (both sing. and plur.) in all other cases. **Sie** is written with a capital **S**. The verb has the same form as that of the 3rd person plural.

Verbs

Here we are concerned only with the infinitive, the present tense, and the imperative.

Learn these two important **auxiliary verbs:**

sein (to be)	**haben** (to have)
ich bin (I am)	**ich habe** (I have)
du bist (you are)	**du hast** (you have)
er, sie, es ist (he, she, it is)	**er, sie, es hat** (he, she, it has)
wir sind (we are)	**wir haben** (we have)
ihr seid (you are)	**ihr habt** (you have)
sie sind (they are)	**sie haben** (they have)
Sie sind (you are)	**Sie haben** (you have)

The infinitive of practically all verbs ends in **-en.** Here are the endings for the present tense:

ich lieb*e*	I love
du lieb*st*	you love
er, sie, es lieb*t*	he, she, it loves
wir lieb*en*	we love
ihr lieb*t*	you love
sie, Sie lieb*en*	they, you love

Here are four useful irregular verbs in the present tense:

	können (to be able)	gehen (to go)	sehen (to see)	tun (to do)
ich	kann	gehe	sehe	tue
du	kannst	gehst	siehst	tust
er/sie/es	kann	geht	sieht	tut
wir	können	gehen	sehen	tun
ihr	könnt	geht	seht	tut
sie/Sie	können	gehen	sehen	tun

For both regular and irregular verbs, the **imperative** is formed by reversing the order of the verb and the personal pronoun.

Gehen wir!	Let's go!
Gehen Sie!	Go!

Negatives

Negatives are formed with **nicht.**

Er ist nicht hier.	He is not here.

Questions

These are formed by inverting the subject and the verb (putting the verb first, the subject second).

Sprechen Sie English?	Do you speak English?

Dictionary
and alphabetical index

English–German

f feminine	m masculine	nt neuter	pl plural

anywhere irgendwo
apartment *(flat)* Wohnung f 22
aperitif Aperitif m 59
appendicitis Blinddarmentzündung f 142
appendix Blinddarm m 138
appetizer Vorspeise f 41
apple Apfel m 53, 64, 120
apple juice Apfelsaft m 61
appliance Gerät nt 119
appointment Verabredung f 131; Termin m 137, 145
apricot Aprikose f 53
April April m 150
archaeology Archäologie f 83
architect Architekt m 83
area code Vorwählnummer f 134
arm Arm m 138, 139
arrangement *(set price)* Pauschale f 20
arrival Ankunft f 16, 65, 68
arrive, to ankommen 68, 130
art Kunst f 83
artery Arterie f 138
art gallery Kunstgalerie f 81, 98
artichoke Artischocke f 41
artificial künstlich 124
artist Künstler(in) m/f 83
ashtray Aschenbecher m 27, 36
Asia Asien *(nt)* 146
ask, to fragen 35, 76; bitten 136
asparagus Spargel m 41, 50
aspirin Aspirin nt 109
asthma Asthma nt 141
at an, bei 14
at least mindestens 26
at once sofort 31
aubergine Aubergine f 49
August August m 150
aunt Tante f 93
Australia Australien *(nt)* 146
Austria Österreich *(nt)* 146
Austrian österreichisch 18
automatic automatisch 122, 124; mit Automatik 20
autumn Herbst m 149
avalanche Lawine f 79
awful scheußlich 84, 94

B

baby Baby nt 24; Säugling m 111
baby food Säuglingsnahrung f 111
babysitter Babysitter m 27
back Rücken m 138

backache Rückenschmerzen m/pl 141
bacon Speck m 38, 46
bad schlecht 14, 95
bag Tasche f 17, 18; Tragetasche f 103
baggage Gepäck nt 17, 18, 26, 31, 71
baggage cart Kofferkuli m 18, 71
baggage check Gepäckaufbewahrung f 67, 71
baked gebacken 44, 47
baker's Bäckerei f 98
balance *(account)* Bilanz f 131
balcony Balkon m 23
ball *(inflated)* Ball m 128
ballet Ballett nt 88
ball-point pen Kugelschreiber m 104
banana Banane f 53, 64
bandage Verband m 109
Band-Aid Heftpflaster nt 109
bangle Armreif m 121
bank *(finance)* Bank f 98, 129, 130
bank card Kontokarte f 130
banknote Schein m 130
bar *(chocolate)* Tafel f 64
barber's Friseur m 30, 98
basil Basilikum nt 51
basketball Basketball m 89
bass *(fish)* Barsch m 44
bath *(hotel)* Bad nt 23, 24, 27
bathing cap Badekappe f 116
bathing suit Badeanzug m 116
bathrobe Bademantel m 116
bathroom Bad nt 27
bath towel Badetuch nt 27
battery Batterie f 75, 78, 119, 121, 125
bay leaf Lorbeer m 50
be, to sein 10, 162
beach Strand m 90
bean Bohne f 49
beard Bart m 31
beautiful schön 13, 84
beauty salon Kosmetiksalon m 30, 98
be back, to zurück sein 21, 136
bed Bett nt 24, 142, 144
bed and breakfast Übernachtung mit Frühstück f 24
bedpan Bettpfanne f 144
beef Rindfleisch nt 45
beer Bier nt 56, 64
beer stein Bierkrug m 127
beet(root) rote Beete f 50
before vor 14
begin, to beginnen 80, 87, 88

beginner Anfänger(in) *m/f* 91
beginning Anfang *m* 150
behind hinter 15, 77
beige beige 113
Belgium Belgien *(nt)* 146
bell *(electric)* Klingel *f* 144
bellboy Page *m* 26
below unten 15
belt Gürtel *m* 117
berth Schlafplatz *m* 69, 70, 71
best beste 152
better besser 13, 25, 101, 113
between zwischen 15
beverage Getränk *nt* 61
bicycle Fahrrad *nt* 74
big groß 13, 25
bilberry Blaubeere *f*, Heidelbeere *f* 54
bill Rechnung *f* 31, 63
billion *(Am.)* Milliarde *f* 148
binoculars Fernglas *nt* 123
bird Vogel *m* 85
birthday Geburtstag *m* 151, 152
biscuit *(Br.)* Keks *m* 64
bitter bitter 62
black schwarz 38, 105, 113
black and white Schwarzweißfilm *m* 124, 125
blackberry Brombeere *f* 53
blackcurrant schwarze Johannisbeere *f* 53
bladder Blase *f* 138
blade Klinge *f* 110
blanket Decke *f* 27
bleach Aufhellung *f* 30
bleed, to bluten 139, 145
blind *(window)* Rollo *nt* 29
blister Blase *f* 139
blood Blut *nt* 142
blood pressure Blutdruck *m* 141, 142
blood transfusion Bluttransfusion *f* 144
blouse Bluse *f* 116
blow-dry Fönen *nt* 30
blue blau 113
blueberry Blaubeere *f*, Heidelbeere *f* 53
boar *(wild)* Wildschwein *nt* 48
boarding house Pension *f* 19, 22
boat Schiff *nt*, Boot *nt* 74
bobby pin Haarklemme *f* 111
body Körper *m* 138
boil Furunkel *m* 139
boiled gekocht 47, 51
bone Knochen *m* 138

book Buch *nt* 11, 104
book, to reservieren (lassen)
booking office Reservierungsschalter *m* 19; Platzreservierung *f* 67
booklet *(of tickets)* Fahrscheinheft *nt* 72
bookshop Buchhandlung *f* 98, 104
boot Stiefel *m* 118
born geboren 149
botanical gardens Botanischer Garten *m* 81
botany Botanik *f* 83
bottle Flasche *f* 17, 56, 59
bottle-opener Flaschenöffner *m* 106
bowel Darm *m* 138
bow tie Fliege *f* 116
box Schachtel *f* 120
boxing Boxen *nt* 89
boy Junge *m* 112, 128
boyfriend Freund *m* 93
bra Büstenhalter *m* 116
bracelet Armband *nt* 121
braces *(suspenders)* Hosenträger *m/pl* 116
braised geschmort 47
brake Bremse *f* 78
brake fluid Bremsflüssigkeit *f* 75
brandy Weinbrand *m*, Kognak *m* 59
bread Brot *m* 36, 38, 64, 120
breaded paniert 44
break, to zerbrechen 123, 145;
(sich) brechen 139
breakdown van Abschleppwagen *m* 78
breakfast Frühstück *nt* 24, 34, 38
breast Brust *f* 138
breathe, to atmen 141, 142
bridge Brücke *f* 85
briefs Unterhose *f* 116
bring, to bringen 12, 71
bring down, to herunterbringen 31
British Brite (Britin) *m/f* 93
broiled vom Rost 40; gegrillt 47
broken kaputt 29, 119; gebrochen 140
brooch Brosche *f* 121
brother Bruder *m* 93
brown braun 113
bruise Quetschung *f* 139
brush Bürste *f* 111
Brussels sprouts Rosenkohl *m* 50
bubble bath Schaumbad *nt* 110
bucket Eimer *m* 106, 128
buckle Schnalle *f* 117
build, to (er)bauen 83

building Gebäude *nt* 81, 82, 83
building blocks/bricks Baukasten *m* 128
bulb (Glüh)birne *f* 28, 75, 119
burn Brandwunde *f* 139
bus Bus *m* 18, 19, 65, 72, 73, 80
business Geschäft *nt* 131
business trip Geschäftsreise *f* 93
bus stop Bushaltestelle *f* 72, 73
busy beschäftigt 96
but aber 15
butane gas Butangas *nt* 32, 106
butcher's Fleischerei *f*, Metzgerei *f* 98
butter Butter *f* 36, 38, 64
button Knopf *m* 29, 117
buy, to kaufen 82, 100

C

cabbage Kohl *m* 50
cabin (*ship*) Kabine *f* 74
cable Telegramm *nt* 133
cable car Seilbahn *f* 74
café Café *nt* 33
caffein-free koffeinfrei 28, 61
cake Kuchen *m* 37, 54, 64
cake shop Konditorei *f* 33, 98
calculator Rechner *m* 105
calendar Kalender *m* 104
call (*phone*) (Telefon)gespräch *nt* 135, 136; Anruf *m* 136
call, to (*give name*) heißen 10; (*summon*) rufen 78, 79, 156; (*phone*) anrufen 136; (*wake*) wecken 71
call at, to (*boat*) anlegen 74
calm ruhig 90
camel-hair Kamelhaar *nt* 114
camera Fotoapparat *m* 124, 125
camera case Fototasche *f* 125
camera shop Fotogeschäft *nt* 98
camp, to zelten 32
campbed Feldbett *nt* 106
camping Camping *nt* 32
camping equipment Camping-ausrüstung *f* 106
camp site Campingplatz *m* 32
can (*of peaches*) Büchse *f* 120
can (*to be able*) können 11, 12, 163
Canada Kanada (*nt*) 146
Canadian Kanadier(in) *m/f* 93
cancel, to annullieren 65
candle Kerze *f* 106
candy Bonbon *nt* 126
can opener Büchsenöffner *m* 106

cap Mütze *f* 116
caper Kaper *f* 51
capital (*finance*) Kapital *nt* 131
car Auto *nt*, Wagen *m* 19, 20, 26, 32, 75, 76, 78
carat Karat *nt* 121
caravan Wohnwagen *m* 32
caraway Kümmel *m* 51
carbon paper Durchschlagpapier *nt* 104
carbonated mit Kohlensäure 61
carburetor Vergaser *m* 78
card Karte *f* 93, 131
card game Kartenspiel *nt* 128
cardigan Wolljacke *f* 116
car hire Autoverleih *m* 19, 20
car number Kraftfahrzeugnummer *f* 25
car park Parkplatz *m* 77
car racing Autorennen *nt* 89
car radio Autoradio *nt* 119
car rental Autoverleih *m* 19, 20
carrot Karotte *f* 50
carry, to tragen 21
carton (*of cigarettes*) Stange (Zigaretten) *f* 17, 126
cartridge (*camera*) Kassette *f* 124
case (*cigarettes, glasses*) Etui *nt* 121, 123
cash, to einlösen 130, 133
cash desk Kasse *f* 103, 155
cassette Kassette *f* 119, 127, 128
castle Schloß *nt*, Burg *f* 85
catalogue Katalog *m* 82
cathedral Kathedrale *f*, Dom *m* 81
Catholic katholisch 84
cauliflower Blumenkohl *m* 49
caution Vorsicht *f* 79, 155; Achtung *f* 155
cave Höhle *f* 81
celery Sellerie *m* 50
cellophane tape Klebstreifen *m* 104
cemetery Friedhof *m* 81
centimetre Zentimeter *m* 112
centre Zentrum *nt* 19, 21, 76
century Jahrhundert *nt* 149
ceramics Keramik *f* 83
cereal Getreideflocken *f/pl* 38
certificate Zeugnis *nt* 144
chain (*jewellery*) Kette *f* 121
chair Stuhl *m* 106
chamber music Kammermusik *f* 128
champagne (*German*) Sekt *m* 59
change (*money*) Kleingeld *nt* 77, 130

change, to wechseln 18, 123, 130; *(train)* umsteigen 65, 68, 73; *(reservation)* umbuchen 65
chapel Kapelle f 81
charcoal Holzkohle f 106
charge Gebühr f 32, 136; Rechnung f 28
charge, to berechnen 24; *(commission)* erheben 130
cheap billig 14, 24, 25, 101
check Scheck m 130; *(restaurant)* Rechnung f 63
check, to kontrollieren 75, 123; prüfen 75; *(luggage)* aufgeben 71
check book Scheckbuch nt 131
check in, to *(airport)* einchecken 65
check out, to abreisen 31
checkup *(medical)* Untersuchung f 142
cheers! Prost! 60
cheese Käse m 37, 38, 52, 64
chef Küchenchef m 40
chemist's Apotheke f 98, 108
cheque Scheck m 130
cheque book Scheckbuch nt 131
cherry Kirsche f 53
chess Schach nt 93
chess set Schachspiel nt 128
chest Brust(korb) m 138, 141
chewing gum Kaugummi m 126
chicken Huhn nt 48
chicory Endivie f; *(Am.)* Chicorée f 49
child Kind nt 24, 62, 82, 93, 139, 149, 159
children's doctor Kinderarzt m 137
China China *(nt)* 146
chips Pommes frites f/pl 49; *(Am.)* Kartoffelchips m/pl 64
chives Schnittlauch m 51
chocolate Schokolade f 38, 61, 64, 120, 126, 127
choice Wahl f 40
chop Kotelett nt 46
Christmas Weihnachten nt 151
church Kirche f 81, 84
cider Apfelwein m 59
cigar Zigarre f 126
cigarette Zigarette f 17, 95, 126
cigarette lighter Feuerzeug nt 121
cine camera Filmkamera f 124
cinema Kino nt 86, 96
cinnamon Zimt m 51
circle *(theatre)* Rang m 87
city Stadt f 81, 92

clam Muschel f 44
classical klassisch 128
clean sauber 62
clean, to reinigen 29, 76
cleansing cream Reinigungscreme f 110
cloakroom Garderobe f 87
clock Uhr f 119, 121, 153
clock-radio Radiowecker m 119
clog, to verstopfen 28
close *(near)* nahe 78, 98
close, to schließen 10, 82, 108, 132
closed geschlossen 155
cloth Stoff m 118
clothes Kleider nt/pl 29, 116
clothes peg Wäscheklammer f 106
clothing Bekleidung f 112
cloud Wolke f 94
clove Nelke f 50
coach *(bus)* Bus m 72
coat Mantel m 116
coconut Kokosnuß f 54
cod Kabeljau m, Dorsch m 44
coffee Kaffee m 38, 61, 64
cognac Kognak m 59
coin Münze f 83
cold kalt 13, 24, 38, 62, 155
cold *(illness)* Erkältung f 108, 141
cold cuts Aufschnitt m 64
collect call R-Gespräch nt 134
cologne Kölnischwasser nt 110
colour Farbe f 103, 112, 124, 125
colour chart Farbtabelle f 30
colour fast farbecht 112
colour film Farbfilm m 124
colour negative Farbnegativ nt 124
colour shampoo Tönungsshampoo nt 111
colour slide Farbdia nt 124
colour television *(set)* Farbfernseher m 119
comb Kamm m 111
come, to kommen 36, 59, 92, 95, 137, 144, 146
comedy Komödie f 86
commission Gebühr f 86
common *(frequent)* gebräuchlich 154
compact disc Compact Disc f 127
compartment Abteil nt 70
compass Kompaß m 106
complaint Reklamation f 62
concert Konzert nt 88
concert hall Konzerthalle f 81, 88
conductor *(orchestra)* Dirigent m 88

confirm, to bestätigen 65
confirmation Bestätigung f 23
congratulation Glückwunsch m 152
connection *(train)* Anschluß m 65, 68
constipation Verstopfung f 140
contact lens Kontaktlinse f 123
contain, to enthalten 37
contraceptive Verhütungsmittel nt 109
contract Vertrag m 131
control Kontrolle f 16
convent Kloster nt 81
convention hall Kongreßhalle f 81
conversion Umrechnung f 157
cookie Keks m 64
cool box Kühltasche f 106
copper Kupfer nt 122
corduroy Kordsamt m 114
cork Korken m 62
corkscrew Korkenzieher m 106
corn *(Am.)* Mais m 50; *(foot)* Hühnerauge nt 109
corner Ecke f 21, 36, 77
corn plaster Hühneraugenpflaster nt 109
cost Kosten pl 131
cost, to kosten 10, 20, 80, 133
cotton Baumwolle f 114
cotton wool Watte f 109
cough Husten m 108, 141
cough, to husten 142
cough drops Hustenpastillen f/pl 109
counter Schalter m 133
country Land nt 93
countryside Landschaft f, Land nt 85
court house Gericht(sgebäude) nt 81
cousin Cousin(e) m/f 93
cramp Krampf m 141
cranberry Preiselbeere f 53
crayfish *(river)* Krebs m 41, 44
crayon Buntstift m 104
cream Sahne f 54, 61; *(toiletry)* Creme f 110
credit Kredit m 130
credit card Kreditkarte f 20, 31, 63, 102, 130
cress Kresse f 51
crisps Kartoffelchips m/pl 64
crockery Geschirr nt 106, 107
croissant Hörnchen nt 38
cross Kreuz nt 121
cross-country skiing Langlauf m 91
crossing *(by sea)* Überfahrt f 74
crossroads Kreuzung f 77

cruise Kreuzfahrt f 74
crystal Kristall m 122
cuckoo clock Kuckucksuhr f 121, 127
cucumber Gurke f 50
cuff link Manschettenknopf m 121
cuisine Küche f 35
cup Tasse f 36, 61, 107
curler Lockenwickler m 111
currency Währung f 129
currency exchange Wechselstube f 18, 67, 129
current Strömung f 90
curtain Vorhang m 28
customs Zoll m 16, 102
cut *(wound)* Schnittwunde f 139
cut, to schneiden 30
cut off, to *(phone)* unterbrechen 135
cut glass geschliffenes Glas nt 122
cutlery Besteck nt 106, 107; Tafelbesteck nt 121
cutlet Kotelett nt 45
cycling Radfahren nt 89
cystitis Blasenentzündung f 142
Czechoslovakia Tschechoslowakei f 146

D

dairy Milchhandlung f 98
dance, to tanzen 88, 96
danger Gefahr f 155, 156
dangerous gefährlich 90
dark dunkel 24, 56, 101, 112, 113, 126
date *(day)* Datum nt 25, 150; *(appointment)* Verabredung f 95; *(fruit)* Dattel f 53
daughter Tochter f 93
day Tag m 16, 20, 26, 32, 80, 150, 151
daylight Tageslicht nt 124
day off freier Tag m 151
decade Jahrzehnt nt 149
December Dezember m 150
decision Entscheidung f 24, 102
deck *(ship)* Deck nt 74
deck-chair Liegestuhl m 91, 106
declare, to *(customs)* verzollen 17
deep tief 142
delay Verspätung f 69
delicatessen Delikatessengeschäft nt 98
deliver, to liefern 102
delivery Lieferung f 102
Denmark Dänemark *(nt)* 146

dentist Zahnarzt m 98, 145
denture Gebiß nt 145
deodorant Deodorant nt 110
department Abteilung f 83, 100
department store Warenhaus nt 98
departure Abflug m 65; Abfahrt f 69
depilatory cream Haarentfernungs-mittel nt 110
deposit, to *(bank)* einzahlen 130, 131; *(car hire)* hinterlegen 20
dessert Nachtisch m, Nachspeise f, Süßspeise f 37, 40, 54
detour *(traffic)* Umleitung f 79
develop, to entwickeln 124
diabetic Diabetiker(in) m/f 37, 41
dialling code Vorwählnummer f 134
diamond Diamant m 122
diaper Windel f 111
diarrhoea Durchfall m 140
dictionary Wörterbuch nt 104
diesel Diesel(öl) nt 75
diet Diät f 37
difficult schwierig 13
difficulty Schwierigkeit f 28, 102, 141
digital Digital- 122
dill Dill m 51
dining-car Speisewagen m 66, 68, 71
dining-room Speisesaal m 27
dinner Abendessen nt 34, 94
direct direkt 65
direct, to den Weg zeigen 12
direction Richtung f 76
director *(film)* Regisseur m 86
directory *(phone)* Telefonbuch nt 134
disabled Behinderte m/f 82
discotheque Diskothek f 88, 96
disease Krankheit f 142
dish Gericht nt 36, 37, 40
dishwashing detergent Spülmittel nt 106
disinfectant Desinfektionsmittel nt 109
dislocate, to verrenken 140
display case Vitrine f 100
dissatisfied unzufrieden 103
district *(town)* Viertel nt 81
disturb, to stören 155
diversion *(traffic)* Umleitung f 79
dizzy schwindlig 140
do, to tun 163
doctor Arzt m, Ärztin f 79, 98, 137; Herr(Frau) Doktor m/f 145
doctor's office Arztpraxis f 137
dog Hund m 155

doll Puppe f 128
dollar Dollar m 18, 102, 130
door Tür(e) f 28
double bed Doppelbett nt 23
double cabin Zweierkabine f 74
double room Doppelzimmer nt 19, 23
down hinunter 15
downhill skiing Abfahrtslauf m 91
downstairs unten 69
downtown Innenstadt f 81
dozen Dutzend nt 120, 149
draught beer Bier vom Faß nt 56
drawing paper Zeichenpapier nt 104
drawing pin Reißzwecke f 104
dress Kleid nt 116
dress shop Modengeschäft nt 99
dressing gown Morgenrock m 116
drink Getränk nt 40, 59, 61, 62
drink, to trinken 35, 36
drinking water Trinkwasser nt 32
drip, to *(tap)* tropfen 28
drive, to fahren 21, 76
driving licence Führerschein m 20, 79
drop *(liquid)* Tropfen m 109
drugstore Apotheke f 98, 108
dry trocken 30, 59, 110, 111
dry cleaner's chemische Reinigung f 29, 98
dry shampoo Trockenshampoo nt 111
duck Ente f 48
dummy Schnuller m 111
during während 14, 150
duty *(customs)* Zoll m 17
duty-free shop Duty-free-Shop m 19
dye, to färben 30

E

each jede(r/s) 125, 143, 149
ear Ohr nt 138
earache Ohrenschmerzen m/pl 141
ear drops Ohrentropfen m/pl 109
early früh 14, 31
earring Ohrring m 121
east Ost(en) m 77
Easter Ostern nt 152
East Germany DDR f 146
easy leicht 14
eat, to essen 36, 37, 144
eel Aal m 41, 43
egg Ei nt 38, 40, 64
eggplant Aubergine f 49
eight acht 147

eighteen achtzehn 147
eighth achte 148
eighty achtzig 147
elastic elastisch 109
elastic bandage elastische Binde f 109
Elastoplast Heftpflaster nt 109
electric(al) elektrisch 119
electrician Elektriker m 98
electricity (facilities) Stromanschluß m 32
electronic elektronisch 125, 128
elevator Fahrstuhl m 27, 100; Aufzug m 155
eleven elf 147
embarkation point Anlegeplatz m 74
embroidery Stickerei f 127
emerald Smaragd m 122
emergency Notfall m 156; (phone) Notruf m 155, 156
emergency exit Notausgang m 27, 99, 155
emery board Sandpapierfeile f 110
empty leer 13
enamel Email nt 122
end Ende nt 69, 150
endive Chicorée f; (Am.) Endivie f 49
engaged (phone) besetzt 136
engagement ring Verlobungsring m 122
engine (car) Motor m 78
England England (nt) 146
English englisch 104, 126
English Englisch nt 11, 16, 84, 137
English Engländer(in) m/f 93
enjoyable angenehm 31
enjoy oneself, to sich gut unterhalten 96
enlarge, to vergrößern 125
enough genug 14
enquiry Auskunft f 68
entrance Eingang m 67, 99; Zutritt m 155
entrance fee Eintritt m 82
envelope Briefumschlag m 27, 104
equipment Ausrüstung f 91, 106
eraser Radiergummi m 105
escalator Rolltreppe f 100
especially besonders 21
estimate (cost) Kostenvoranschlag m 131
Europe Europa (nt) 146
evening Abend m 9, 87, 95, 96, 151, 153

evening dress Abendgarderobe f 88; (woman) Abendkleid nt 116
everything alles 31
exchange, to umtauschen 103
exchange rate Wechselkurs m 18, 130
excursion Ausflug m 80
excuse me Entschuldigung 26, 78; Verzeihung 70, 153
exercise book Schreibheft nt 104
exhaust pipe Auspuff m 78
exhibition Ausstellung f 81
exit Ausgang m 67, 99, 155; (motorway) Ausfahrt f 79
expect, to erwarten 130
expenses Unkosten pl 131
expensive teuer 13, 19, 24, 101
exposure (photography) Aufnahme f 124
express per Expreß 133
expression Ausdruck m 9; Redewendung f 100
expressway Autobahn f 76
extension (phone) Nebenanschluß m 135
extension cord/lead Verlängerungsschnur f 119
extra zusätzlich 24
extract, to (tooth) ziehen 145
eye Auge nt 123, 138, 139
eye drops Augentropfen m/pl 109
eye liner Lidstift m 110
eye pencil Augenbrauenstift m 110
eye shadow Lidschatten m 110
eye specialist Augenarzt m 137

F
fabric Stoff m 113
face Gesicht nt 138
face-pack Gesichtsmaske f 30
face powder Gesichtspuder m 110
factory Fabrik f 81
fair Messe f 81
fall (autumn) Herbst m 149
family Familie f 93, 144
fan Ventilator m 28
fan belt Keilriemen m 75
far weit 14, 21, 100
fare Fahrpreis m 21, 68, 73
farm Bauernhof m 85
fast (film) hochempfindlich 124
fat Fett nt 37
father Vater m 93
February Februar m 150

fruit Obst *nt* 37, 53
fruit cocktail Obstsalat *m* 53, 54
fruit juice Fruchtsaft *m* 37, 61
frying-pan Bratpfanne *f* 106
full voll 13; belegt 155
full board Vollpension *f* 24
full insurance Vollkaskoversicherung *f* 20
fur coat Pelzmantel *m* 116
furniture Möbel *nt/pl* 83
furrier's Pelzgeschäft *nt* 98

G

gallery Galerie *f* 81
game Spiel *nt* 128; *(food)* Wild *nt* 40
garage *(parking)* Garage *f* 26; *(repairs)* Reparaturwerkstatt *f* 78
garden Garten *m* 85
gardens Grünanlage *f* 81
garlic Knoblauch *m* 51
gas Gas *nt* 156
gasoline Benzin *nt* 75, 78
gastritis Magenschleimhautentzündung *f* 142
gauze Verbandmull *m* 109
gem Edelstein *m* 121
general allgemein 26, 100
general delivery postlagernd 133
general practitioner praktischer Arzt *m* 137
gentleman Herr *m* 155
genuine echt 118
geology Geologie *f* 83
German deutsch 114
German Deutsch *nt* 11, 95
Germany Deutschland *(nt)* 146
get, to *(find)* finden 19, 21; *(obtain)* bekommen 10, 32, 90, 108, 134; *(taxi)* bestellen 31; *(fetch)* holen 137, 156
get back, to zurück sein 80
get off, to aussteigen 73
get to, to kommen nach/zu 19, 100; ankommen in 70
get up, to aufstehen 144
gherkin Essiggurke *f* 50, 64
gift *(present)* Geschenk *nt* 17
ginger Ingwer *m* 51
girdle Hüfthalter *m* 116
girl Mädchen *nt* 112, 128
girlfriend Freundin *f* 93, 95
give, to geben 12, 13, 123, 126
give way *(traffic)* Vorfahrt gewähren 79

glad *(to know you)* sehr erfreut 92
gland Drüse *f* 138
glass Glas *nt* 36, 56, 59, 60, 62, 143
glasses Brille *f* 123
glassware Glaswaren *f/pl* 127
gloomy düster 84
glove Handschuh *m* 116
glue Leim *m* 105
go, to gehen 96, 163
go away, to weggehen 156
go out, to ausgehen 96
gold Gold *nt* 121, 122
golden golden 113
gold-plated vergoldet 122
golf Golf *nt* 89
golf course Golfplatz *m* 89
good gut 13, 101
good-bye auf Wiedersehen 9
Good Friday Karfreitag *m* 152
goods Waren *f/pl* 16
goose Gans *f* 48
gooseberry Stachelbeere *f* 53
gram Gramm *nt* 120
grammar book Grammatik *f* 105
grape (Wein)traube *f* 53, 64
grape juice Traubensaft *m* 61
grapefruit Grapefruit *f*, Pampelmuse *f* 53
grapefruit juice Grapefruitsaft *m* 38
gravy Soße *f* 48
gray grau 113
graze Abschürfung *f* 139
greasy fettig 30, 110, 111
great *(excellent)* prima 95
Great Britain Großbritannien *(nt)* 146
Greece Griechenland *(nt)* 146
green grün 113
green bean grüne Bohne *f* 49
greengrocer's Gemüsehandlung *f* 98
green salad grüner Salat *m* 50
greeting Begrüßung *f* 9; Gruß *m* 151
grey grau 113
grilled gegrillt 44, 47; vom Rost 40
grocery Lebensmittelgeschäft *nt* 98, 120
groundsheet Zeltboden *m* 106
group Gruppe *f* 82
guide Fremdenführer(in) *m/f* 80
guidebook (Reise)führer *m* 82, 104, 105
gum *(teeth)* Zahnfleisch *nt* 145
gynaecologist Frauenarzt *m* 137

H

habit Gewohnheit f 34
haddock Schellfisch m 44
hair Haar nt 30, 111
hairbrush Haarbürste f 111
haircut Haarschnitt m 30
hairdresser's Friseur m 27, 30, 99
hair dryer Haartrockner m 119
hair dye Haarfärbemittel nt 111
hairgrip Haarklemme f 111
hair lotion Haarwasser nt 111
half Hälfte f 148
half a dozen halbes Dutzend nt 120
half an hour halbe Stunde f 153
half board Halbpension f 24
half price (ticket) zum halben Preis 69
halibut Heilbutt m 44
hall (large room) Halle f 81, 88
ham Schinken m 38, 41, 46, 64
hammer Hammer m 106
hand Hand f 138
handbag Handtasche f 116
hand cream Handcreme f 110
handicrafts Kunsthandwerk nt 83
handkerchief Taschentuch nt 116
handmade Handarbeit f 113
hanger Kleiderbügel m 27
hangover Kater m 108
happy glücklich, froh 151, 152
harbour Hafen m 74, 81
hard hart 52, 123
hard-boiled (egg) hartgekocht 38
hardware shop Eisenwarenhandlung f 98
hare Hase m 48
hat Hut m 116, 127
have, to haben 162
hay fever Heufieber nt 108
hazelnut Haselnuß f 53
he er 162
head Kopf m 138, 139
headache Kopfschmerzen m/pl 141
headphones Kopfhörer m 119
head waiter Oberkellner m 62
health food shop Reformhaus nt 98
health insurance Krankenkasse f 144
health insurance form Kranken-
    kassenformular nt 144
heart Herz nt 138
heart attack Herzanfall m 141
heat, to heizen 90
heating Heizung f 28
heavy schwer 13, 101
heel Absatz m 118

helicopter Hubschrauber m 74
hello! (phone) Hallo! 135
help Hilfe f 156
help, to helfen 12, 21, 71, 100,
    134; (oneself) sich bedienen 120
her ihr 161
herb Kraut nt 51
herb tea Kräutertee m 60
here hier 15
herring Hering m 41, 44
high hoch 85, 141
high season Hauptsaison f 149
high-speed (photo) hochempfindlich
    124
high tide Flut f 90
hike, to wandern 74
hill Hügel m 85
hire Verleih m 20, 74
hire, to mieten 19, 20, 74, 89, 91;
    vermieten 155
his sein 161
history Geschichte f 83
hitchhike, to trampen 74
hole Loch nt 29
holiday Feiertag m 151
holidays Ferien pl, Urlaub m 151
home address Wohnort m 25; Wohn-
    adresse f 31
home-made hausgemacht 40
homeopathic homöopathisch 109
honey Honig m 38
horse racing Pferderennen nt 89
horseback riding Reiten nt 89
horseradish Meerrettich m 51
hospital Krankenhaus nt 142, 144
hot heiß 14, 24, 38, 61, 155
hotel Hotel nt 19, 21, 22, 80
hotel guide Hotelverzeichnis nt 19,
    22
hotel reservation Hotelreservierung f
    20
hot water warmes Wasser nt 23, 28
hot-water bottle Wärmflasche f 27
hour Stunde f 153
house Haus nt 83, 85
how wie 10
how far wie weit 10, 76, 85
how long wie lange 10, 24
how many wie viele 10
how much wieviel 10, 24
hundred (ein)hundert 147
hungry hungrig 35; (to be) Hunger
    haben 12, 35
hurry (to be in a) es eilig haben 21, 31

hurt, to weh tun 139; schmerzen 145; *(oneself)* sich verletzen 139
husband Mann *m* 93
hydrofoil Tragflächenboot *nt* 74

I

I ich 162
ice Eis *nt* 94
ice-cream Eis *nt* 54, 64
ice cube Eiswürfel *m* 27
iced tea Eistee *m* 61
ice pack Kühlbeutel *m* 106
ill krank 140, 156
illness Krankheit *f* 140
important wichtig 12
imported importiert 113
impressive eindrucksvoll 84
in in 14
included inbegriffen 20, 24, 31, 32, 40, 63, 80
indigestion Magenverstimmung *f* 141
inexpensive preiswert 35; billig 124
infect, to infizieren 140
infection Infektion *f* 145
inflammation Entzündung *f* 142
inflation Inflation *f* 131
inflation rate Inflationsrate *f* 131
influenza Grippe *f* 142
information Auskunft *f* 67, 155
injection Spritze *f* 142, 144, 145
injure, to verletzen 139
injured verletzt 79, 139
injury Verletzung *f* 139
ink Tinte *f* 105
inn Gasthaus *nt*, Gasthof *m* 22, 33
inquiry Auskunft *f* 68
insect bite Insektenstich *m* 108, 139
insect repellent Insektenschutz *m* 109
insect spray Insektizid *nt* 109
inside drinnen 15
instead statt 37
insurance Versicherung *f* 20, 79
insurance company Versicherungs-gesellschaft *f* 79
interest *(on investment)* Zinsen *m/pl* 131
interested, to be sich interessieren 83, 96
interesting interessant 84
international international 133, 134
interpreter Dolmetscher *m* 131
intersection Kreuzung *f* 77
introduce, to vorstellen 92

introduction *(social)* Vorstellung *f* 92; *(letter)* Empfehlungsbrief *m* 130
investment Kapitalanlage *f* 131
invitation Einladung *f* 94
invite, to einladen 94
invoice Rechnung *f* 131
iodine Jod *nt* 109
Ireland Irland *(nt)* 146
Irish Ire (Irin) *m/f* 93
iron *(laundry)* Bügeleisen *nt* 119
iron, to bügeln 29
ironmonger's Eisenwarenhandlung *f* 99
Italy Italien *(nt)* 146
its sein 161
ivory Elfenbein *nt* 122

J

jacket Jackett *nt*, Jacke *f* 116
jade Jade *f* 122
jam Marmelade *f* 38, 120
jam, to klemmen 28, 125
January Januar *m* 150
Japan Japan *(nt)* 146
jar Glas *nt* 120
jaundice Gelbsucht *f* 142
jaw Kiefer *m* 138
jeans Jeans *pl* 116
jersey Strickjacke *f* 116
jewel Edelstein *m* 121
jeweller's Juwelier *m* 99, 121
joint Gelenk *nt* 138
journey Fahrt *f* 72
juice Saft *m* 38, 61
July Juli *m* 150
jumper *(sweater)* Pullover *m* 116
June Juni *m* 150
juniper Wacholder *m* 51
just *(only)* nur 16, 37, 100

K

kerosene Petroleum *nt* 106
ketchup Tomatenketchup *nt* 51
key Schlüssel *m* 26
kidney Niere *f* 138
kilogram Kilo(gramm) *nt* 120
kilometre Kilometer *m* 20
kind nett, freundlich 95
king-size extra lang 126
knee Knie *nt* 138
knife Messer *m* 36, 61, 107
knock, to klopfen 155
know, to wissen 16, 26; kennen 96, 114

L

label Etikett nt 105
lace Spitze f 114
lady Dame f 155
lake See m 23, 81, 85, 90
lamb Lamm(fleisch) nt 45
lamp Lampe f 29, 106, 119
landmark Wahrzeichen nt 85
landscape Landschaft f 92
lane (in town) Gasse f 154
lantern Laterne f 106
large groß 20, 101, 118, 130
last letzte 13, 68, 72, 149, 150, 151
last name (Familien)name m 25
late spät 13
later später 135
laugh, to lachen 95
launderette Waschsalon m 99
laundry (place) Wäscherei f 29, 99;
(clothes) Wäsche f 29
laundry service Wäschedienst m 23
laxative Abführmittel nt 109
lead (theatre) Hauptrolle f 86
lead-free bleifrei 75
leap year Schaltjahr nt 149
leather Leder nt 114, 118
leather goods Lederwaren f/pl 127
leather trousers Lederhose f 116
leave, to lassen 26, 96, 156; (go
away) abreisen 31; abfahren 68, 74
leek Lauch m 50
left linke 13; links 21, 30, 63, 69,
77, 79
left-luggage office Gepäckaufbewahrung f 67, 71
leg Bein nt 138
lemon Zitrone f 37, 38, 53, 54, 60
lemonade Limonade f 61
lens (glasses) Glas nt 123; (camera)
Objektiv nt 125
lentil Linse f 43
less weniger 14
let, to (hire out) vermieten 155
letter Brief m 132
letter box Briefkasten m 132
letter of credit Kreditbrief m 130
lettuce Lattich m 50
library Bibliothek f 81, 99
licence (for driving) Führerschein m
20, 79
lie down, to sich hinlegen 142
life belt Rettungsring m 74
life boat Rettungsboot nt 74
lifeguard Rettungsdienst m 90

lift Fahrstuhl m 27, 100; Aufzug m
155
light leicht 13, 54, 59, 101; (colour)
hell 101, 112, 113, 126
light Licht nt 28, 124; (cigarette)
Feuer nt 95
lighter Feuerzeug nt 126
lighter fluid Benzin fürs Feuerzeug nt
126
lighter gas Gas fürs Feuerzeug nt 126
light meter Belichtungsmesser m 125
light music Unterhaltungsmusik f
128
lightning Blitz m 94
like, to (want) gerne haben 12, 23;
mögen 20, 38; (take pleasure)
gefallen 24, 92, 102, 112
line Linie f 73
linen (cloth) Leinen nt 114
lip Lippe f 138
lipsalve Lippenpomade f 110
lipstick Lippenstift m 110
liqueur Likör m 59, 60
liquid Flüssigkeit f 123
listen, to hören 127
litre Liter m 75, 120
little (a) ein wenig 14
live, to leben 83; (reside) wohnen 83
liver Leber f 46, 138
lobster Hummer m 41, 44
local hiesig 36, 60
local train Nahverkehrszug m 66, 69
long lang 26, 62, 76, 77, 78, 116
long-sighted weitsichtig 123
look, to sehen 123; sich umsehen
100
look for, to suchen 12
look out! Vorsicht! 156
loose (clothes) weit 116
lose, to verlieren 123, 156; (one's
way) sich verirren 12, 156
loss Verlust m 131
lost and found office Fundbüro nt
67, 156
lost property office Fundbüro nt 67,
156
lot (a) eine Menge 14; viel 162
lotion Lotion f 110
loud (voice) laut 135
love, to lieben 163
lovely (wunder)schön 84; herrlich
94
low niedrig 141
lower untere 69, 70

low season Vorsaison f, Nachsaison f 149
low tide Ebbe f 90
luck Glück nt 152
luggage Gepäck nt 18, 26, 31, 71
luggage locker Schließfach nt 18, 67, 71
luggage trolley Kofferkuli m 18, 71
lump (bump) Beule f 139
lunch Mittagessen nt 34, 80, 94
lung Lunge f 138
Luxembourg Luxemburg (nt) 146

M

machine Maschine f 114
mackerel Makrele f 41, 44
magazine Illustrierte f 105
magnificent großartig 84
maid Zimmermädchen nt 26
mail, to aufgeben 28
mail Post f 28, 133
mailbox Briefkasten m 132
main Haupt- 40, 67, 80
make, to machen 131
make a mistake, to (bill) sich verrechnen 31, 63, 102
make up, to machen 28, 71, 108
man Herr m 115, 155; Mann m 159
manager Direktor m 26
manicure Maniküre f 30
many viele 14
map Karte f 76, 105; Plan m 105
March März m 150
marinated mariniert 44
marjoram Majoran m 51
market Markt m 81, 99
marmalade Apfelsinenmarmelade f 38
married verheiratet 93
mass (church) Messe f 84
match Streichholz nt 106, 126; (sport) Wettkampf m 89
match, to (colour) passen 112
material (fabric) Stoff m 113
matinée Nachmittagsvorstellung f 87
mattress Matratze f 106
May Mai m 150
may (can) können 11, 12, 163
meadow Wiese f 85
meal Mahlzeit f 24, 143; Essen nt 34, 63
mean, to bedeuten 10, 25
means Mittel nt 74
measles Masern f/pl 142

measure, to Maß nehmen 114
meat Fleisch nt 40, 45, 46, 62
mechanic Mechaniker m 78
medical ärztlich 144
medical certificate ärztliches Zeugnis nt 144
medicine Medizin f 83; (drug) Medikament nt 143
medium (meat) mittel 47
medium-sized mittlere 20
meet, to treffen 96
melon Melone f 53
memorial Denkmal nt 81
mend, to flicken 75; (clothes) ausbessern 29
menu Gedeck nt 36, 39; Menü nt 39; (printed) Speisekarte f 36, 39, 40
merry fröhlich 151
message Nachricht f 28, 136
metre Meter m 112
middle Mitte f 69, 87, 150
midnight Mitternacht f 153
mild mild 52, 126
mileage Kilometergeld nt 20
milk Milch f 38, 61, 64
milkshake Milchmixgetränk nt 61
million Million f 148
mineral water Mineralwasser nt 61
minister (religion) Pfarrer m 84
mint Pfefferminz(e) f 51
minute Minute f 21, 153
mirror Spiegel m 115, 123
miscellaneous verschieden 127
Miss Fräulein nt 9
miss, to fehlen 18, 29, 62
mistake Irrtum m 62
mixed gemischt 50
modified American plan Halbpension f 24
moment Augenblick m 11, 136
monastery Kloster nt 81
Monday Montag m 150
money Geld nt 129, 130
money order Postanweisung f 133
month Monat m 16, 150
monument Denkmal nt 81
moon Mond m 94
moped Moped nt 74
more mehr 14
morning Morgen m 151, 153
mortgage Hypothek f 131
mosque Moschee f 84
mother Mutter f 93
motorbike Motorrad nt 74

motorboat Motorboot *nt* 91
motorway Autobahn *f* 76
mountain Berg *m* 23, 85
mountaineering Bergsteigen *nt* 89
moustache Schnurrbart *m* 31
mouth Mund *m* 138
mouthwash Mundwasser *nt* 109
move, to bewegen 139
movie Film *m* 86
movie camera Filmkamera *f* 124
movies Kino *nt* 86, 96
Mr. Herr *m* 9, 131
Mrs. Frau *f* 9, 131
much viel 14
mug Becher *m* 107; *(beer)* Maß *f* 56
muscle Muskel *m* 138
museum Museum *nt* 81
mushroom Pilz *m* 41, 50
music Musik *f* 83, 128
musical Musical *nt* 86
music box Spieldose *f* 121, 127
mussel Muschel *f* 41, 44
must, to müssen 23, 31, 95, 101
mustard Senf *m* 37, 51, 64
mutton Hammelfleisch *nt* 45
my mein 161
myself selbst 120

N

nail *(human)* Nagel *m* 110
nail brush Nagelbürste *f* 110
nail clippers Nagelzange *f* 110
nail file Nagelfeile *f* 110
nail polish Nagellack *m* 110
nail polish remover Nagellack-
entferner *m* 110
nail scissors Nagelschere *f* 110
name Name *m* 23, 25, 79, 136
napkin Serviette *f* 36, 105, 106
nappy Windel *f* 111
narrow eng 118
nationality Nationalität *f* 25
natural history Naturkunde *f* 83
near nah 13
nearby in der Nähe 77, 84
nearest nächste 78, 98
neat *(drink)* pur 59
necessary nötig 88
neck Hals *m* 138; *(nape)* Nacken *m* 30
necklace Halskette *f* 121
need, to brauchen 29, 118, 137
needle Nadel *f* 27
negative Negativ *nt* 125

nephew Neffe *m* 93
nerve Nerv *m* 138
nervous system Nervensystem *nt* 138
Netherlands Niederlande *pl* 146
never nie 15
new neu 13
newsagent's Zeitungshändler *m* 99
newspaper Zeitung *f* 104, 105
newsstand Zeitungsstand *m* 19, 67, 99, 104
New Year Neujahr *nt* 151
New Zealand Neuseeland *(nt)* 146
next nächste 13, 65, 68, 73, 76, 149, 150
next time nächstes Mal 95
next to neben 14
nice *(beautiful)* schön 94, 152
niece Nichte *f* 93
night Nacht *f* 9, 24, 151
nightclub Nachtlokal *nt* 88
night cream Nachtcreme *f* 110
nightdress Nachthemd *nt* 116
nine neun 147
nineteen neunzehn 147
ninety neunzig 147
ninth neunte 148
no nein 9
noisy laut 24
nonalcoholic alkoholfrei 61
none kein 15
nonsmoker Nichtraucher *m* 70
non-smoking Nichtraucher- 36
noodle Nudel *f* 49
noon Mittag *m* 153
normal normal 30, 110
north Nord(en) *m* 77
North America Nordamerika *(nt)* 146
Norway Norwegen *(nt)* 146
nose Nase *f* 138
nosebleed Nasenbluten *nt* 141
nose drops Nasentropfen *m/pl* 109
not nicht 15, 163
note *(banknote)* Schein *m* 130
notebook Notizheft *nt* 105
note paper Briefpapier *nt* 105
nothing nichts 15, 17
notice *(sign)* Tafel *f*, Hinweis *m* 155
notify, to benachrichtigen 144
November November *m* 150
now jetzt 15
number Nummer *f* 25, 65, 134, 136; Zahl *f* 124, 147
nurse Krankenschwester *f* 144

O

occupation *(job)* Beruf m 93
occupied besetzt 13, 70, 155
October Oktober m 150
office Büro nt 22, 80
oil Öl nt 51, 75, 111
oily *(greasy)* fettig 30, 111
old alt 13
old town Altstadt f 82
omelet Omelett nt 64
on an, auf 14
once einmal 148
one eins 147
one-way *(ticket)* einfach 69
on foot zu Fuß 76
onion Zwiebel f 50
only nur 15
on time pünktlich 68
onyx Onyx m 122
open offen 13, 82
open, to öffnen 10, 17, 82, 108, 132; *(account)* eröffnen 130
opening hours Öffnungszeiten f/pl 82
opera Oper f 88
opera house Opernhaus nt 82, 88
operation Operation f 144
operator Vermittlung f 134
operetta Operette f 88
opposite gegenüber 77
optician Optiker m 99, 123
or oder 15
orange orange 113
orange Orange f 53, 64; Apfelsine f 53
orange juice Orangensaft m 38, 61
orangeade Orangeade f 61
orchestra Orchester nt 88; *(seats)* Parkett nt 87
orchestral music Orchestermusik f 128
order *(goods, meal)* Bestellung f 40, 102
order, to *(goods, meal)* bestellen 36, 62, 102, 103
ornithology Vogelkunde f 83
other andere 59
our unser 161
out of order außer Betrieb 155
out of stock nicht vorrätig 103
outlet *(electric)* Steckdose f 27
outside draußen 15, 36
oval oval 101
over über 14

over there dort drüben 69
overalls Overall m 116
overdone zu stark gebraten 62
overheat, to *(engine)* heißlaufen 78
overnight *(stay)* eine Nacht 26
overwhelming überwältigend 84
owe, to schulden 144
oyster Auster f 41, 43

P

pacifier Schnuller m 111
packet Packung f 120; Schachtel f 126
page *(hotel)* Page m 26
pail Eimer m 106, 128
pain Schmerz m 140, 141, 144
painkiller Schmerzmittel nt 109
paint Farbe f 155
paint, to malen 83
paintbox Malkasten m 105
painter Maler m 83
painting Malerei f 83
pair Paar nt 116, 118, 149
pajamas Schlafanzug m 117
palace Palast m, Schloß nt 81
palpitation Herzklopfen nt 141
panties Schlüpfer m 116
pants *(trousers)* Hose f 116
panty girdle Strumpfhalterhöschen nt 116
panty hose Strumpfhose f 116
paper Papier nt 105
paperback Taschenbuch nt 105
paperclip Büroklammer f 105
paper napkin Papierserviette f 105
paraffin *(fuel)* Petroleum nt 106
parcel Paket nt 133
pardon? Wie bitte? 10
parents Eltern pl 93
park Park m 82
park, to parken 26, 77
parking Parken nt 77, 79
parking disc Parkscheibe f 77
parking meter Parkuhr f 77
parliament Parlament nt 82
parsley Petersilie f 51
part Teil m 138
parting *(part)* Scheitel m 30
partridge Rebhuhn nt 48
party *(social gathering)* Party f 95
pass *(rail, bus)* Mehrfahrkarte f 72
pass *(mountain)* Paß m 85
passport Paß m 16, 17, 25, 26
passport photo Paßbild nt 124

pass through, to auf der Durchreise sein 16
pasta Teigwaren f/pl 49
paste (glue) Klebstoff m 105
pastry Gebäck nt 54
pastry shop Konditorei f 99
patch, to (clothes) flicken 29
path Weg m 85
patient Patient(in) m/f 144
pay, to (be)zahlen 31, 63, 68, 102, 136
payment Zahlung f 131
pea Erbse f 50
peach Pfirsich m 53
peak Bergspitze f 54
peanut Erdnuß f 53
pear Birne f 53
pearl Perle f 122
pedestrian Fußgänger m 79
peg (tent) Hering m 107
pen Feder f 105
pencil Bleistift m 105
pencil sharpener Bleistiftspitzer m 105
pendant Anhänger m 121
penicilline Penizillin nt 143
penknife Taschenmesser nt 106
pensioner Rentner(in) m/f 82
people Leute pl 93
pepper Pfeffer m 37, 51, 64
per cent Prozent 148
percentage Prozentsatz m 131
perch Barsch m 44
per day pro Tag 20, 32, 89
performance (session) Vorstellung f 87
perfume Parfüm nt 110
perhaps vielleicht 15
per hour pro Stunde 77, 89
period (monthly) Periode f 141
period pains Menstruations-beschwerden f/pl 141
permanent wave Dauerwelle f 30
per night pro Nacht 24
per person pro Person 32
person Person f 32, 36
personal persönlich 17
personal call Gespräch mit Vor-anmeldung nt 134
per week pro Woche 20, 24
petrol Benzin nt 75, 78
pewter Zinn nt 122
pheasant Fasan m 48
phone Telefon nt 28, 78, 79, 134

phone, to telefonieren 134
phone booth Telefonzelle f 134
phone call (Telefon)gespräch nt 135, 136; Anruf m 136
phone number Telefonnummer f 96, 134, 135
photo Foto nt 124, 125
photocopy Fotokopie f 131
photograph, to fotografieren 82
photographer Fotograf m 99
photography Fotografie f 124
phrase Ausdruck m 11
pick up, to (person) abholen 80, 96
picnic Picknick nt 63
picture Bild nt 82; (photo) Foto nt 82
piece Stück nt 29, 52, 64, 120
pigeon Taube f 48
pill Pille f 141; Tablette f 143
pillow Kopfkissen nt 27
pin Nadel f 110; (brooch) Anstecknadel f 121
pineapple Ananas f 53
pink rosa 113
pipe Pfeife f 126, 127
pipe cleaner Pfeifenreiniger m 126
pipe tobacco Pfeifentabak m 126
place Ort m 25, 76
place of birth Geburtsort m 25
plaice Scholle f 44
plane Flugzeug nt 65, 159
plaster (cast) Gipsverband m 140
plastic Plastik nt 107
plastic bag Plastikbeutel m 106
plate Teller m 36, 62, 107
platform (station) Bahnsteig m 67, 68, 69, 70
platinum Platin nt 122
play (theatre) Stück nt 86
play, to spielen 86, 88, 89, 93
playground Spielplatz m 32
playing card Spielkarte f 105
please bitte 9
plimsolls Turnschuhe m/pl 118
plug (electric) Stecker m 29, 119
plum Pflaume f 53
pneumonia Lungenentzündung f 142
pocket Tasche f 117
pocket calculator Taschenrechner m 105
pocket dictionary Taschenwörter-buch nt 104
pocket watch Taschenuhr f 121
point, to (show) zeigen 11
poison Gift nt 109

poisoning Vergiftung f 142
Poland Polen (nt) 146
police Polizei f 78, 156
police station Polizeiwache f 99, 156
pond Teich m 85
pop music Popmusik f 128
poplin Popeline m 114
porcelain Porzellan nt 127
pork Schweinefleisch nt 45
port Hafen m 74; (wine) Portwein m 59
portable tragbar, Koffer- 119
porter Gepäckträger m 18, 71; (hotel) Hausdiener m 26
portion Portion f 37, 54, 62
possible möglich 137
post (letters) Post f 28, 133
post, to aufgeben 28
postage Porto nt 132
postage stamp Briefmarke f 28, 126, 132
postcard Postkarte f 105, 126, 132
poste restante postlagernd 133
post office Postamt nt 99, 132
potato Kartoffel f 48, 49
pottery Töpferei f 83
poultry Geflügel nt 48
pound (money) Pfund nt 18, 102, 130; (weight) Pfund nt 120
powder Puder m 110
powder compact Puderdose f 122
prawn Garnele f 44
pregnant schwanger 141
premium (gasoline) Super nt 75
prescribe, to verschreiben 143
prescription Rezept nt 108, 143
present (gift) Geschenk nt 17, 121
press, to (iron) dampfbügeln 29
press stud Druckknopf m 117
pressure Druck m 75
pretty hübsch 84
price Preis m 40, 69
priest Priester m 84
print (photo) Abzug m 125
private privat 91, 155
private toilet eigene Toilette f 23
processing (photo) Entwickeln nt 124
profession Beruf m 25
profit Gewinn m 131
programme Programm nt 87
prohibit, to verbieten 155
pronunciation Aussprache f 6

Protestant protestantisch, evangelisch 84
provide, to besorgen 131
prune Backpflaume f 53
public holiday Feiertag m 152
pull, to ziehen 155
pullover Pullover m 117
pumpkin Kürbis m 50
puncture Reifenpanne f 75
purchase Kauf m 131
pure rein 114
purple violett 113
push, to (button) drücken 155
put, to stellen 24
put through, to verbinden 28
pyjamas Schlafanzug m 117

Q

quality Qualität f 103, 113
quantity Menge f 14, 103
quarter Viertel nt 148
quarter of an hour Viertelstunde f 153
quartz Quarz m 122
question Frage f 10
quick schnell 13, 156
quickly schnell 79, 137
quiet ruhig 23, 25

R

rabbi Rabbiner m 84
rabbit Kaninchen nt 48
race course/track (Pferde)rennbahn f 90
racket (sport) Schläger m 89
radiator (car) Kühler m 78
radio (set) Radio nt 23, 28, 119
radish Radieschen nt 50
railway station Bahnhof m 19, 21, 67
rain Regen m 94
rain, to regnen 94
rain boot Gummistiefel m 118
raincoat Regenmantel m 117
raisin Rosine f 53
rare (meat) blutig 47
rash Ausschlag m 139
raspberry Himbeere f 53
rate Tarif m 20; (exchange) Kurs m 18, 130; (inflation) Rate f 131
rayon Kunstseide f 114
razor Rasierapparat m 110
razor blade Rasierklinge f 110
ready fertig 29, 118, 123, 125, 145
real echt 121
rear hinten, Hinter- 75

receipt Quittung f 103, 144
reception Empfang m 23
receptionist Empfangschef m 26
recommend, to empfehlen 22, 35, 80, 86, 88, 145
record *(disc)* Schallplatte f 127, 128
record player Plattenspieler m 119
rectangular rechteckig 101
red rot 59, 113
redcurrant rote Johannisbeere f 53
reduction Ermäßigung f 24, 82
refill *(pen)* Ersatzmine f 105
refund Rückerstattung f 103
regards Grüße m/pl 152
register, to *(luggage)* aufgeben 71
registered mail per Einschreiben 132
registration Anmeldung f 25
registration form Anmeldeschein m 25, 26
regular *(petrol)* Normal nt 75
religion Religion f 83
religious service Gottesdienst m 84
rent, to mieten 19, 20, 74, 89, 91; vermieten 155
rental Verleih m 20, 74
repair Reparatur f 125
repair, to reparieren 29, 118, 119, 121, 123, 125, 145
repeat, to wiederholen 11
report, to *(a theft)* anzeigen 156
require, to verlangen 88
reservation Reservierung f 19, 65, 69
reservations office Reservierungs-schalter m 19; Platzreservierung f 67
reserve, to reservieren (lassen) 19, 23, 36
restaurant Restaurant nt 19, 32, 33, 35, 67
return *(ticket)* hin und zurück 69
return, to *(give back)* zurückgeben 103
reverse the charges, to ein R-Ge-spräch anmelden 134
rheumatism Rheumatismus m 141
rhubarb Rhabarber m 53
rib Rippe f 46, 138
ribbon Band nt 105
rice Reis m 49
right rechte 13; rechts 21, 30, 63, 69, 77, 79; *(correct)* richtig 13, 76
ring *(on finger)* Ring m 122
ring, to klingeln 155; telefonieren 134
ripe reif 52

river Fluß m 74, 85, 90; *(major)* Strom m 85
road Straße f 76, 77, 85
road assistance Pannendienst m 78
road map Straßenkarte f 105
road sign Verkehrszeichen nt 79
roast Braten m 45
roasted gebraten 47
rock Felsen m 85
roll *(bread)* Brötchen nt 38, 64
roller skate Rollschuh m 128
roll film Rollfilm m 124
roll-neck mit Rollkragen 117
romantic romantisch 84
room Zimmer nt 19, 23, 24, 25, 27, 28; *(space)* Platz m 32
room number Zimmernummer f 26
room service Zimmerbedienung f 23
rope Seil nt 107
rosary Rosenkranz m 122
rosé rosé 59
rosemary Rosmarin m 51
round rund 101, 117
roundtour Rundfahrt f 74
roundtrip *(ticket)* hin und zurück 69
rowing-boat Ruderboot nt 91
rubber *(material)* Gummi m 118; *(eraser)* Radiergummi m 105
rubber sole Gummisohle f 118
ruby Rubin m 122
rucksack Rucksack m 107
ruin Ruine f 81
ruler *(for measuring)* Lineal nt 105
rum Rum m 59
running water fließendes Wasser nt 23
rye Roggen m 38

s

safe *(not dangerous)* gefahrlos, ungefährlich 90
safe Safe m 26
safety pin Sicherheitsnadel f 111
saffron Safran m 51
sage Salbei m 51
sailing-boat Segelboot nt 91
salad Salat m 49, 50
sale Verkauf m 131; *(bargains)* Aus-verkauf m 101, 155
sales tax Mehrwertsteuer f 24, 40, 102
salmon Lachs m 41, 44; Salm m 44
salt Salz nt 37, 51, 64
salty salzig 62

same selbe 40; gleiche 118
sand Sand *m* 90
sandal Sandale *f* 118
sandwich Sandwich *nt* 64; *(open)* belegtes Brot *nt* 64
sanitary napkin Damenbinde *f* 109
sapphire Saphir *m* 122
sardine Sardine *f* 41
satin Satin *m* 114
Saturday Samstag *m*, Sonnabend *m* 150
sauce Soße *f* 48
saucepan Kochtopf *m* 107
saucer Untertasse *f* 107
sauerkraut Sauerkraut *nt* 50
sausage Wurst *f* 47, 64
scallop Jakobsmuschel *f* 44
scarf Halstuch *m* 117
scarlet scharlachrot 113
scenic route landschaftlich schöne Straße *f* 85
school Schule *f* 79
scissors Schere *f* 107, 110
scooter Motorroller *m* 74
Scotland Schottland *(nt)* 146
scrambled egg Rührei *nt* 38
screwdriver Schraubenzieher *m* 107
sculptor Bildhauer *m* 83
sculpture Bildhauerei *f* 83
sea Meer *nt* 85, 90
sea bass Seebarsch *m* 44
seafood Meeresfrüchte *f/pl* 43
season Jahreszeit *f* 149; Saison *f* 149
seasoning Würze *f* 37, 51
seat Platz *m* 69, 70, 87
seat belt Sicherheitsgurt *m* 75
second zweite 148
second Sekunde *f* 153
second class zweite Klasse *f* 69
second hand Sekundenzeiger *m* 122
second-hand *(books)* antiquarisch 104
second-hand shop Gebrauchtwarenladen *m* 99
secretary Sekretär(in) *m/f* 27, 131
see, to sehen 163; *(check)* nachschauen
sell, to verkaufen 100
send, to schicken 78, 132; senden 102, 103, 132
send up, to hinaufschicken 26
sentence Satz *m* 11
separately getrennt 63
September September *m* 150

service Bedienung *f* 24, 40, 63, 100; *(religion)* Gottesdienst *m* 84
serviette Serviette *f* 36
set, to *(hair)* legen 30
set menu Tagesgedeck *nt* 36, 40
setting lotion Haarfestiger *m* 30, 111
seven sieben 147
seventeen siebzehn 147
seventh siebte 148
seventy siebzig 147
sew, to nähen 29
shampoo Haarwaschmittel *nt* 30, 111
shape Form *f* 103
shape, to *(hair)* legen 30
share *(finance)* Aktie *f* 131
sharp scharf 52; *(pain)* stechend 140
shave, to rasieren 30
shaver Rasierapparat *m* 27, 119
shaving brush Rasierpinsel *m* 111
shaving cream Rasiercreme *f* 111
she sie 162
shelf Regal *nt* 120
ship Schiff *nt* 74
shirt Hemd *nt* 117
shoe Schuh *m* 118
shoelace Schnürsenkel *m* 118
shoemaker's Schuhmacher *m* 99
shoe polish Schuhcreme *f* 118
shoe shop Schuhgeschäft *nt* 99
shop Geschäft *nt*, Laden *m* 98
shopping Einkaufen *nt* 97
shopping area Geschäftsviertel *nt* 81, 100
shopping centre Einkaufszentrum *nt* 99
shop window Schaufenster *nt* 100, 112, 124
short kurz 30, 116, 117
shorts Shorts *pl* 117
short-sighted kurzsichtig 123
shoulder Schulter *f* 138
shovel Schaufel *f* 128
show *(theatre)* Vorstellung *f* 86, 87
show, to zeigen 11, 12, 76, 100, 101, 103, 119, 124
shower Dusche *f* 23, 32
shrimp Garnele *f* 44
shrink, to einlaufen 114
shut geschlossen 13
shutter *(window)* Fensterladen *m* 29; *(camera)* Verschluß *m* 125
sick *(ill)* krank 140, 156
sickness *(illness)* Krankheit *f* 140
side Seite *f* 30

sideboards/burns Koteletten *f/pl* 31
sightseeing Besichtigung *f* 80
sightseeing tour Stadtrundfahrt *f* 80
sign *(notice)* Schild *nt*, Aufschrift *f* 155
sign, to unterschreiben 26, 130
signature Unterschrift *f* 25
signet ring Siegelring *m* 122
silk Seide *f* 114
silver silbern 113
silver Silber *nt* 121, 122
silver plated versilbert 122
silverware Tafelsilber *nt* 122
simple einfach 124
since seit 14, 150
sing, to singen 88
single *(not married)* ledig 93; *(ticket)* einfach 69
single cabin Einzelkabine *f* 74
single room Einzelzimmer *nt* 19, 23
sinister unheimlich 84
sister Schwester *f* 93
six sechs 147
sixteen sechzehn 147
sixth sechste 148
sixty sechzig 147
size Format *nt* 124; *(clothes)* Größe *f* 114, 115; *(shoes)* Nummer *f* 118
skate Schlittschuh *m* 91
skating rink Eisbahn *f* 91
ski Ski *m* 91
ski, to skifahren 91
skiboot Skischuh *m* 91
skiing Skifahren *nt* 89, 91
ski lift Skilift *m* 91
skin Haut *f* 110, 138
skin-diving Tauchen *nt* 91
ski pole Skistock *m* 91
skirt Rock *m* 117
ski run Skipiste *f* 91
sky Himmel *m* 94
sleep, to schlafen 144
sleeping bag Schlafsack *m* 107
sleeping-car Schlafwagen *m* 66, 68, 69, 70
sleeping pill Schlaftablette *f* 109, 143
sleeve Ärmel *m* 117
slice Scheibe *f* 120
slide *(photo)* Dia *nt* 124
slip Unterrock *m* 117
slipper Hausschuh *m* 118
slow langsam 13
slow down, to langsam fahren 79
slowly langsam 11, 21, 135

small klein 13, 20, 24, 37, 62, 101, 118, 130
smoke, to rauchen 95
smoked geräuchert 44
smoker Raucher *m* 70
snack Imbiß *m* 63
snack bar Schnellimbiß *m* 34, 63, 67
snail Schnecke *f* 41
snap fastener Druckknopf *m* 117
sneakers Turnschuhe *m/pl* 118
snow Schnee *m* 94
snow, to schneien 94
soap Seife *f* 27, 111
soccer Fußball *m* 89
sock Socke *f* 117
socket *(outlet)* Steckdose *f* 27
soft weich 52, 123
soft-boiled *(egg)* weich(gekocht) 38
soft drink alkoholfreies Getränk *nt* 64
sold out ausverkauft 87
sole Sohle *f* 118; *(fish)* Seezunge *f* 44
soloist Solist *m* 88
some etwas, einige 14
someone jemand 95
something etwas 36, 54, 108, 112, 113, 125, 139
son Sohn *m* 93
song Lied *nt* 128
soon bald 15, 137
sore throat Halsschmerzen *m/pl* 141
sorry *(I'm)* Entschuldigung, Verzeihung 10; es tut mir leid 16
sort *(kind)* Sorte *f* 52, 120
soufflé Auflauf *m* 54
soup Suppe *f* 42
sour sauer 62
south Süd(en) *m* 77
South Africa Südafrika *(nt)* 146
South America Südamerika *(nt)* 146
souvenir Andenken *nt* 127
souvenir shop Andenkenladen *m* 99
Soviet Union Sowjetunion *f* 146
spade Schaufel *f* 128
spare tyre Ersatzreifen *m* 75
sparking plug Zündkerze *f* 75
sparkling *(wine)* Schaum- 59
spark plug Zündkerze *f* 75
speak, to sprechen 11, 135, 163
speaker *(loudspeaker)* Lautsprecher *m* 119
special Sonder- 20; Spezial- 37
special delivery per Expreß 132
specialist Spezialist(in) *m/f* 142
speciality Spezialität *f* 40, 60

specimen *(medical)* Probe f 142
spectacle case Brillenetui nt 123
spell, to buchstabieren 11
spend, to ausgeben 101
spice Gewürz nt 51
spinach Spinat m 50
spine Wirbelsäule f 138
spiny lobster Languste f 41, 44
sponge Schwamm m 111
spoon Löffel m 36, 62, 107
sport Sport m 89
sporting goods shop Sportgeschäft nt 99
sprain, to verstauchen 140
spring *(season)* Frühling m 149; *(water)* Quelle f 85
square viereckig 101
square Platz m 82
stadium Stadion nt 82
staff Personal nt 26
stain Fleck m 29
stainless steel rostfreier Stahl m 107, 122
stalls *(theatre)* Parkett nt 87
stamp *(postage)* Briefmarke f 28, 126, 132, 133
staple Heftklammer f 105
star Stern m 94
start, to beginnen 80, 87, 88; *(car)* anspringen 78
starter *(appetizer)* Vorspeise f 41
station *(railway)* Bahnhof m 19, 21, 67; *(underground, subway)* Station f 73
stationer's Schreibwarengeschäft nt 99
statue Statue f 82
stay Aufenthalt m 31
stay, to bleiben 16, 26; *(reside)* wohnen 93
steak Steak nt 46
steal, to stehlen 156
steamed gedämpft 44
stew Eintopfgericht nt 42
stewed gedämpft 47, 51
stew pot Schmortopf m 107
stiff neck steifer Nacken m 141
sting Stich m 139
sting, to stechen 139
stitch, to nähen 29, 118
stock *(supply)* Vorrat m 103
stock exchange Börse f 82
stocking Strumpf m 117
stomach Magen m 138

stomach ache Magenschmerzen m/pl 141
stools Stuhl(gang) m 142
stop *(bus)* Haltestelle f 72, 73
stop! Halt! 156
stop, to halten 21, 68, 70, 72
stop thief! Haltet den Dieb! 156
store *(shop)* Laden m, Geschäft nt 98
straight *(drink)* pur 59
straight ahead geradeaus 21, 77
strange seltsam 84
strawberry Erdbeere f 53
street Straße f 25, 82
streetcar Straßenbahn f 72
street map Stadtplan m 19, 105
string Bindfaden m, Schnur f 105
strong stark 126, 143
stuck *(to be)* klemmen 28
student Student(in) m/f 82, 93
study, to studieren 93
stuffed gefüllt 47
sturdy robust 101
subway *(railway)* U-Bahn f 73
suede Wildleder nt 114, 118
sugar Zucker m 37, 51, 64
suit *(man)* Anzug m 117; *(woman)* Kostüm nt 117
suitcase Koffer m 18
summer Sommer m 149
sun Sonne f 94
sunburn Sonnenbrand m 108
Sunday Sonntag m 150
sunglasses Sonnenbrille f 123
sunshade *(beach)* Sonnenschirm m 91
sun-tan cream Sonnencreme f 111
super *(petrol)* Super nt 75
superb prächtig 84
supermarket Supermarkt m 99
suppository Zäpfchen nt 109
surcharge Zuschlag m 68
surfboard Surfbrett nt 91
surgery *(consulting room)* Arztpraxis f 137
surname (Familien)name m 25
suspenders *(Am.)* Hosenträger m/pl 117
swallow, to schlucken 143
sweater Pullover m 117
sweatshirt Sweatshirt nt 117
Sweden Schweden *(nt)* 146
sweet süß 59, 62
sweet *(candy)* Bonbon nt 126
sweet corn Mais m 50

sweetener Süßstoff m 37, 51
swell, to schwellen 139
swelling Schwellung f 139
swim, to schwimmen, baden 90
swimming pool Schwimmbad nt 32, 90; *(open-air)* Freibad nt 9; *(indoor)* Hallenbad nt 90
swimsuit Badeanzug m 117
Swiss schweizerisch, Schweizer
Swiss army knife Schweizer Armeemesser nt 127
switch Schalter m 29
switchboard operator Telefonist(in) m/f 26
Switzerland Schweiz f 146
swollen geschwollen 139
synagogue Synagoge f 84
synthetic synthetisch 114
system System nt 138

T

table Tisch m 36, 107; *(list)* Tabelle f 157
tablet Tablette f 109
tailor's Schneider m 99
take, to nehmen 18, 24, 72, 77; *(time)* dauern 62, 72, 76, 102; *(bring)* bringen 18, 21, 96
take away, to *(carry)* mitnehmen 63, 102
talcum powder Körperpuder m 111
tampon Tampon m 109
tangerine Mandarine f 53
tap *(water)* Wasserhahn m 28
tape recorder Kassettenrecorder m 119
tax Taxe f 32; Steuer f 24, 40, 102
taxi Taxi nt 18, 19, 21, 31, 67
taxi rank Taxistand m 21
tea Tee m 38, 61, 64
team Mannschaft f 89
tear, to reißen 140
teaspoon Teelöffel m 107, 143
telegram Telegramm nt 133
telegraph office Telegrafenamt nt 99
telephone Telefon nt 28, 78, 79, 134
telephone, to telefonieren 133
telephone booth Telefonzelle f 134
telephone call (Telefon)gespräch nt 135, 136; Anruf m 136
telephone directory Telefonbuch nt 134
telephone number Telefonnummer f 96, 135, 136

telephoto lens Teleobjektiv nt 125
television *(set)* Fernseher m 23, 28, 119
television room Fernsehraum m 27
telex Telex nt 133
telex, to ein Telex schicken 130
tell, to sagen 12, 73, 76, 136, 153
temperature Temperatur f 90, 142; *(fever)* Fieber nt 140
temporary provisorisch 145
ten zehn 147
tendon Sehne f 138
tennis Tennis nt 89
tennis court Tennisplatz m 89
tennis racket Tennisschläger m 89
tent Zelt nt 32, 107
tenth zehnte 148
tent peg Hering m 107
tent pole Zeltstange f 107
term Ausdruck m 131
terminus Endstation f 72
terrace Terrasse f 36
terrible schrecklich 84
tetanus Wundstarrkrampf m 140
than als 14
thank you danke 9
that der, die das 10, 160
the der, die das 159
theatre Theater nt 82, 86
theft Diebstahl m 156
their ihr 161
then dann 15
there dort 13, 15
thermometer Thermometer nt 109, 144
these diese 160
they sie 162
thief Dieb m 156
thigh Schenkel m 138
thin dünn 113
think, to *(believe)* glauben 31, 63, 94
third dritte 148
third Drittel nt 148
thirsty, to be Durst haben 12, 35
thirteen dreizehn 147
thirty dreißig 147
this diese(r/s) 160
those die 160
thousand tausend 148
thread Faden m 27
three drei 147
throat Hals m 138, 141
throat lozenge Halspastille f 109
through durch 14

through train durchgehender Zug *m* 68, 69
thumb Daumen *m* 138
thumbtack Reißzwecke *f* 105
thunder Donner *m* 94
thunderstorm Gewitter *nt* 94
Thursday Donnerstag *m* 150
thyme Thymian *m* 51
ticket Karte *f* 87, 89; *(plane)* Flugticket *nt* 65; *(train)* Fahrkarte *f* 69; *(bus)* Fahrschein *m* 72
ticket office Fahrkartenschalter *m* 67
tide *(high)* Flut *f* 90; *(low)* Ebbe *f* 90
tie Krawatte *f* 117
tie pin Krawattennadel *f* 122
tight *(clothes)* eng 116
tights Strumpfhose *f* 117
time Zeit *f* 80, 153; *(occasion)* -mal 148
timetable Fahrplan *m* 68
tin *(can)* Büchse *f* 120
tinfoil Aluminiumfolie *f* 107
tin opener Büchsenöffner *m* 107
tint Tönungsmittel *nt* 111
tinted getönt 123
tire Reifen *m* 75, 76
tired müde 12
tissue *(handkerchief)* Papiertuch *nt* 111
tissue paper Seidenpapier *nt* 105
to zu 14
toast Toast *m* 38
tobacco Tabak *m* 126
tobacconist's Tabakladen *m* 99, 126
today heute 29, 150, 151
toe Zehe *f* 138
toilet paper Toilettenpapier *nt* 111
toiletry Toilettenartikel *m/pl* 110
toilets Toilette *f* 27, 32, 37, 67
toilet water Toilettenwasser *nt* 111
tomato Tomate *f* 50
tomato juice Tomatensaft *m* 61
tomb Grab *nt* 82
tomorrow morgen 29, 151
tongs Zange *f* 107
tongue Zunge *f* 46, 138
tonic water Tonic *nt* 61
tonight heute abend 29, 86, 87, 88, 96
tonsil Mandel *f* 138
too zu 14; *(also)* auch 15
tooth Zahn *m* 145
toothache Zahnschmerzen *m/pl* 145
toothbrush Zahnbürste *f* 111, 119

toothpaste Zahnpasta *f* 111
torch *(flashlight)* Taschenlampe *f* 107
touch, to berühren 155
tough *(meat)* zäh 62
tour Rundfahrt *f* 80
tourist office Fremdenverkehrsbüro *nt* 22, 80
tourist tax Kurtaxe *f* 32
towards gegen 14
towel Handtuch *nt* 111
tower Turm *m* 82
town Stadt *f* 19, 76, 105
town hall Rathaus *nt* 82
tow truck Abschleppwagen *m* 78
toy Spielzeug *nt* 128
toy shop Spielwarengeschäft *nt* 99
track *(station)* Gleis *nt* 67, 68, 69
tracksuit Trainingsanzug *m* 117
traffic *(cars)* Verkehr *m* 79
traffic jam Stau *m* 79
traffic light Ampel *f* 77
trailer Wohnwagen *m* 32
train Zug *m* 66, 68, 69, 70, 73, 159
tram Straßenbahn *f* 72
tranquillizer Beruhigungsmittel *nt* 109
transfer *(bank)* Überweisung *f* 131
transformer Transformator *m* 119
translate, to übersetzen 11
transport Transport *m* 74
travel, to reisen
travel agency Reisebüro *nt* 99
traveller's cheque Reisescheck *m* 18, 63, 102, 130
travelling bag Reisetasche *f* 18
travel sickness Reisekrankheit *f* 108
treatment Behandlung *f* 143
tree Baum *m* 85
tremendous außerordentlich 84
trim, to *(beard)* stutzen 31
trip Reise *f* 93, 152, 159; Fahrt *f* 72
trousers Hose *f* 117
trout Forelle *f* 44
try, to versuchen 135; *(sample)* probieren 60; *(clothes)* anprobieren 115
T-shirt T-Shirt *nt* 117
tube Tube *f* 120
Tuesday Dienstag *m* 150
tumbler Wasserglas *nt* 107
tunny *(tuna)* Thunfisch *m* 41
turbot Steinbutt *m* 44
turkey Truthahn *m* 48
turn, to *(change direction)* abbiegen 21, 77

turnip Kohlrabi m 50
turquoise türkisfarben 113
turquoise Türkis m 122
turtleneck mit Rollkragen 117
tweezers Pinzette f 111
twelve zwölf 147
twenty zwanzig 147
twice zweimal 148
twin beds zwei Einzelbetten nt/pl 23
two zwei 147
typewriter Schreibmaschine f 27, 105
typewriter ribbon Farbband nt 105
typing paper Schreibmaschinenpapier nt 105
tyre Reifen m 75, 76

U

ugly häßlich 13, 84
umbrella Regenschirm m 117; (beach) Sonnenschirm m 91
uncle Onkel m 93
unconscious bewußtlos 139
under unter 14
underdone (meat) blutig 47; zu roh 62
underground (railway) U-Bahn f 73
underpants Unterhose f 117
undershirt Unterhemd nt 117
understand, to verstehen 11, 16
United States Vereinigte Staaten m/pl 146
university Universität f 82
until bis 14
up hinauf 15
upper obere 69
upset stomach Magenverstimmung f 108
urgent dringend 12, 145
urine Urin m 142
use Gebrauch m 17
use, to benutzen 78, 134
useful nützlich 14
usual gewöhnlich 143

V

vacancy freies Zimmer nt 23, 155
vacant frei 13, 22, 155
vacation Ferien pl, Urlaub m 151
vaccinate, to impfen 140
vacuum flask Thermosflasche f 107
vaginal infection Scheidenentzündung f 141
valley Tal nt 85
value Wert m 131

value-added tax (VAT) Mehrwertsteuer f 24, 40, 102, 154
vanilla Vanille f 54
veal Kalbfleisch nt 45
vegetable Gemüse nt 49, 50
vegetable store Gemüsehandlung f 99
vegetarian vegetarisch 37
vein Vene f 138
velvet Samt m 114
velveteen Manchester m 114
venereal disease Geschlechtskrankheit f 142
venison Reh nt, Hirsch m 48
vermouth Wermut m 60
very sehr 15
vest Unterhemd nt 117; (Am.) Weste f 117
veterinarian Tierarzt m 99
video cassette Videokassette f 119, 128
video-recorder Videorecorder m 119
view Aussicht f 23, 25
village Dorf nt 76, 85
vinegar Essig m 51
vineyard Weinberg m 85
visit Besuch m 92
visit, to besuchen 94, 144; (look around) besichtigen 84
visiting hours Besuchszeit f 144
vitamin pills Vitamintabletten f/pl 109
V-neck mit V-Ausschnitt 117
volleyball Volleyball m 89
voltage (Strom)spannung f 27, 119
vomit, to sich übergeben 140

W

waistcoat Weste f 117
wait, to warten 21, 95, 108
waiter Kellner m 26; Herr Ober m 36, 56
waiting-room Wartesaal m 67
waitress Kellnerin f 26; Fräulein nt 36
wake, to wecken 27, 71
Wales Wales (nt) 146
walk, to (zu Fuß) gehen 74, 85
wall Mauer f 82
wallet Brieftasche f 156
walnut Walnuß f 53
want, to (wish) wünschen 12
warm warm 94
wash, to waschen 29, 114

wash and wear bügelfrei 114
wash-basin Waschbecken *nt* 28
washing powder Waschpulver *nt* 107
washing-up liquid Spülmittel *nt* 107
watch Uhr *f* 121, 122, 127
watchmaker's Uhrmacher *m* 99, 121
watchstrap Uhrarmband *nt* 122
water Wasser *nt* 23, 28, 32, 38, 75, 90
water carrier Wasserkanister *m* 107
waterfall Wasserfall *m* 85
water flask Feldflasche *f* 107
watermelon Wassermelone *f* 53
waterproof wasserdicht 122
water-ski Wasserski *m* 91
wave Welle *f* 90
way Weg *m* 76
we wir 162
weather Wetter *nt* 94
weather forecast Wetterbericht *m* 94
wedding ring Ehering *m* 122
Wednesday Mittwoch *m* 150
week Woche *f* 20, 26, 80, 151
weekend Wochenende *nt* 20, 151
well gut 9, 115; *(healthy)* wohl 140
well Brunnen *m* 85
well-done *(meat)* gut durchgebraten 47
west West(en) *m* 77
West Germany Bundesrepublik *f* 146
what was 10
wheel Rad *nt* 78
when wann 10
where wo 10
which welche(r/s) 10
whipped cream Schlagsahne *f* 54
whisky Whisky *m* 59
white weiß 49, 59, 113
Whit Monday Pfingstmontag *m* 152
who wer 10
why warum 10
wide weit 118
wide-angle lens Weitwinkelobjektiv *nt* 125
wife Frau *f* 93
wig Perücke *f* 111
wild boar Wildschwein *nt* 48
wind Wind *m* 94
window Fenster *nt* 28, 36, 69; *(shop)* Schaufenster *nt* 100, 112, 124
windscreen/shield Windschutzscheibe *f* 76
wine Wein *m* 57, 58, 59, 62

wine list Weinkarte *f* 59
wine merchant's Weinhandlung *f* 99
winter Winter *m* 149
winter sports Wintersport *m* 91
wiper Scheibenwischer *m* 76
wish Wunsch *m* 151
with mit 14
withdraw, to *(bank)* abheben 130
without ohne 14
woman Dame *f* 115; Frau *f* 159
wonderful wunderbar 96
wood *(material)* Holz *nt* 127; *(forest)* Wald *m* 85
wood alcohol Brennspiritus *m* 107
wood carving Holzschnitzarbeit *f* 127
woodcock Schnepfe *f* 48
wool Wolle *f* 114
word Wort *nt* 10, 14, 133
work, to *(function)* funktionieren 28, 119
working day Werktag *m* 151
worse schlechter 13
wound Wunde *f* 139
wrinkle resistant knitterfrei 114
wristwatch Armbanduhr *f* 122
write, to schreiben 11, 101
writing pad Schreibblock *m* 105
writing-paper Schreibpapier *nt* 27
wrong falsch 13, 77, 135

X
X-ray, to röntgen 140

Y
year Jahr *nt* 149
yellow gelb 113
yes ja 9
yesterday gestern 151
yet noch 15
yield, to *(traffic)* Vorfahrt gewähren 79
yoghurt Joghurt *m* 64
you du, Sie 162
young jung 13
your dein; Ihr 161
youth hostel Jugendherberge *f* 22, 32

Z
zero null 147
zip(per) Reißverschluß *m* 117
zoo Zoo *m* 82
zoology Zoologie *f* 83

Inhaltsverzeichnis

Say BERLITZ®

... and most people think of outstanding language schools.
But Berlitz has also become the world's leading publisher
of books for travellers – Travel Guides, Phrase Books,
Dictionaries – plus Cassettes and
Self-teaching courses.

Informative, accurate, up-to-date,
Books from Berlitz are written
with freshness and style. They
also slip easily into pocket or
purse – no need for bulky,
old-fashioned volumes.

Join the millions who know
how to travel. Whether for
fun or business, put Berlitz
in your pocket.

BERLITZ®

Leader in
Books and Cassettes
for Travellers

A Macmillan Company

♔ BERLITZ® Books for travellers

TRAVEL GUIDES

They fit your pocket in both size and price. Modern, up-to-date, Berlitz gets all the information you need into 128 lively pages with colour maps and photos throughout. What to see and do, where to shop, what to eat and drink, how to save.

AFRICA	Kenya
	Morocco
	South Africa
	Tunisia

ASIA, MIDDLE EAST	China (256 pages)
	Hong Kong
	India (256 pages)*
	Japan (256 pages)*
	Singapore
	Sri Lanka
	Thailand
	Egypt
	Jerusalem and the Holy Land
	Saudi Arabia

| AUSTRAL-ASIA | New Zealand |

BRITISH ISLES	Channel Islands
	London
	Ireland
	Oxford and Stratford
	Scotland

*in preparation

| BELGIUM | Brussels |

PHRASE BOOKS

World's bestselling phrase books feature all the expressions and vocabulary you'll need, and pronunciation throughout. 192 pages, 2 colours.

Arabic	Norwegian
Chinese	Polish
Danish	Portuguese
Dutch	Russian
Finnish	Serbo-Croatian
French	Spanish (Castilian)
German	Spanish (Lat. Am.)
Greek	Swahili
Hebrew	Swedish
Hungarian	Turkish
Italian	European Phrase Book
Japanese	European Menu Reader

FRANCE	Brittany French Riviera Loire Valley Paris	**SPAIN**	Barcelona and Costa Dorada Canary Islands Costa Blanca Costa Brava Costa del Sol and Andalusia Ibiza and Formentera Madrid Majorca and Minorca
GERMANY	Berlin Munich The Rhine Valley		
AUSTRIA and SWITZER- LAND	Tyrol Vienna Geneva/French-speaking areas Zurich/German-speaking areas Switzerland (192 pages)	**EASTERN EUROPE**	Budapest Dubrovnik and Southern Dalmatia Hungary (192 pages) Istria and Croatian Coast Moscow & Leningrad Split and Dalmatia
GREECE, CYPRUS & TURKEY	Athens Corfu Crete Rhodes Greek Islands of the Aegean Peloponnese Salonica and Northern Greece Cyprus Istanbul	**NORTH AMERICA**	U.S.A. (256 pages) California Florida Hawaii New York Toronto Montreal
ITALY and MALTA	Florence Italian Adriatic Italian Riviera Rome Sicily Venice Malta	**CARIBBEAN, LATIN AMERICA**	Puerto Rico Virgin Islands Bahamas Bermuda French West Indies Jamaica Southern Caribbean Mexico City Rio de Janeiro Caribbean Cruise Guide (368 pages)
NETHER- LANDS and SCANDI- NAVIA	Amsterdam Copenhagen Helsinki Oslo and Bergen Stockholm	**EUROPE**	Business Travel Guide – Europe (368 pages) Pocket Guide to Europe Cities of Europe
PORTUGAL	Algarve Lisbon Madeira		

Most titles with British and U.S. destinations are available
in French, German, Spanish and as many as 7 other languages.

BERLITZ

german
english
englisch
deutsch

DICTIONARY
WÖRTERBUCH

DICTIONARIES

Bilingual with 12,500 concepts each way.
Highly practical for travellers, with
pronunciation shown plus menu reader, basic
expressions and useful information.
Over 330 pages.

Danish	Italian
Dutch	Norwegian
Finnish	Portuguese
French	Spanish
German	Swedish

**Berlitz Books, a world of information in your pocket!
At all leading bookshops and airport newsstands.**

With a few foreign words, your trip (and you) can be more interesting. Enjoy the satisfaction of knowing a new language, meeting people, getting involved?

Now you can learn – easily, painlessly – without leaving your home. Berlitz, the company whose name is synonymous with language instruction has a basic Cassette Course for you in French, German, Italian or Spanish.

Here's what your Berlitz Cassette Course brings you...

1. 90-minute "zero" or beginner's cassette with 10 basic lessons.

2. Two 60-minute cassettes – 20 more lessons in all, on what to say when abroad.

3. Two illustrated books featuring the text of all cassettes with explanatory notes, instructions for easy reference.

4. Unique rotating verb finder showing tenses of all key verbs.

5. As an extra bonus, a Berlitz phrase book plus a pocket dictionary for any emergency.

There are thirty lively lessons in all – three and one-half hours of playing (and replaying) time. No grammar – not until you're ready. Just listen and repeat at your own pace – in the privacy of your own home.

Dial (no charge, USA)
24 hours, 7 days a week.

In the U.S.A.
1-800-431-9003

In Great Britain
0323-638221

Refer to Dept. No.11603. Why not give us a ring – right now!

Treat yourself to an hour with BERLITZ®

Just listen and repeat

It's fun, not work. And you'll surprise your friends and yourself: it's so easy to pick up some basic expressions in the foreign language of your choice. These cassettes are recorded in hi-fi with four voices. Bringing native speakers into your home, they permit you to improve your accent and learn the basic phrases before you depart.

With each cassette is a helpful 32-page script, containing pronunciation tips, plus complete text of the dual-language recording.

An ideal companion for your Berlitz phrase book, pocket dictionary or travel guide. Order now!

$9.95/£5.95 (incl. VAT)
use convenient envelope attached.

From:

To:

Affix First
Class or
Air Mail
Stamp

11603.

ORDER FORM

1. Name _____

Address _____

_____

2. Complete the address on the adjoining envelope for either:

Berlitz Publications, Inc.
P.O. Box 506
Delran, N.J. 08370-0506
U.S.A.

Cassell Ltd.
1 St. Anne's Road
Eastbourne
East Sussex, BN21 3UN
U.K.

3. Calculate:

In the U.S.A.

_____ European
$14.95 set = $_____
_____ Singles at
$9.95 each = $_____
_____ Courses at
$59.95 each = $_____
TOTAL $_____
(NJ residents add sales tax)

In the U.K.

_____ European
£10.95 set = £_____
_____ Singles at
£5.95 each = £_____
_____ Courses at
£35.00 each = £_____
TOTAL £_____
(VAT is included)

4. Indicate method of payment, please:

☐ Check or money order enclosed made payable to Berlitz

☐ American Express ☐ Master Charge

☐ Diners Club ☐ Visa

Credit Card No. _____

Expiration Date _____

Interbank No. _____
(Master Charge Only. Located above your name.)

Signature _____

Note: Credit card holders – it's faster ordering by phone. See numbers on reverse side.

5. Detach this order form. Insert check or money order in envelope. Please allow up to 4 weeks for delivery. (We pay postage.) Order Berlitz travel guides, phrase books and dictionaries through your bookseller. 11603.